THE BUSINESS
OF CHOICE

THE BUSINESS OF CHOICE

Marketing to Consumers' Instincts

Matthew Willcox

Publisher: Paul Boger
Editor-in-Chief: Amy Neidlinger
Acquisitions Editor: Charlotte Maiorana
Operations Specialist: Jodi Kemper
Cover Designer: Chuti Prasertsith
Managing Editor: Kristy Hart
Project Editor: Elaine Wiley
Copy Editor: Paula Lowell
Proofreader: Kathy Ruiz
Indexer: Tim Wright
Compositor: Nonie Ratcliff
Manufacturing Buyer: Dan Uhrig

Upper Saddle River, New Jersey 07458

For information about buying this title in bulk quantities, or for special sales opportunities (which may include electronic versions; custom cover designs; and content particular to your business, training goals, marketing focus, or branding interests), please contact our corporate sales department at corpsales@pearsoned.com or (800) 382-3419.

For government sales inquiries, please contact governmentsales@pearsoned.com.

For questions about sales outside the U.S., please contact international@pearsoned.com.

Company and product names mentioned herein are the trademarks or registered trademarks of their respective owners.

Printed in the United States of America

First Printing March 2015

ISBN-10: 0-13-405345-1
ISBN-13: 978-0-13-405345-5

Pearson Education LTD.
Pearson Education Australia PTY, Limited.
Pearson Education Singapore, Pte. Ltd.
Pearson Education Asia, Ltd.
Pearson Education Canada, Ltd.
Pearson Educación de Mexico, S.A. de C.V.
Pearson Education—Japan
Pearson Education Malaysia, Pte. Ltd.

Library of Congress Control Number: 2014959161

To the two women in my life: my mother Charlotte who raised me to be curious, and my wife and accomplice Patrizia who, using a cognitive process yet to be revealed by science, chose me

Contents

Acknowledgments

First I would like to thank Kimberlee D'Ardenne, without whom this book wouldn't have been written. Kim is a neuroscientist who just happens to be a fine writer and editor. She made sure that I didn't misrepresent the science and helped me write about complex matters with something that I hope approaches clarity. Really her name should be on the cover as well. I'd also like to thank the team at Pearson and FT Press, particularly Charlotte Maiorana who suggested that a book like this one might be interesting. Thank you Charlotte, for your confidence!

The book would have also not been possible were it not for the thousands of people who investigate behavior and delve into the whys and hows of human decision making, so my thanks to all of you. I have had many enlightening conversations with this community, be they with *éminences grises* or students presenting a poster of their research. In particular, I'd like to thank those in academia who have kindly given me time, advice, and encouragement and shown great patience explaining their work to an outsider. So, personal thanks to Sam McClure, Baba Shiv, Ming Hsu, Adam Alter, Vlad Griskevicius, Robert Cialdini, Dan Ariely, Richard Nisbett, David Gal, Carrie Armel, Barry Schwartz, Jonathan Baron, Andrea Weihrauch, Simona Botti, David Faro, Jonathan Zinman, Ben Hilbig, Sam Bond, Ishani Banerji, Christopher Hydock, Maya Shankar, Angela Leung, and Chris Chabris. Some of you may not remember helping me, but you did.

Friends and colleagues have also been a source of encouragement and content. Mark Barden, James Hallatt, Ralph Kugler, and Yumi Prentice pushed me to think about how this book could be really relevant to marketers. Tom Theys came up with some great ideas for material. Colleagues past and present who have inspired or supported me include David Thomason, John Kenny, Simon White, Kofi Amoo-Gottfried, Simon Bird, Rita Doherty, Ambi MG Parameswaran, Neil Adler, and Sara Bamber, all of whom seek to bring Behavioral Science to play in their work every day. Thanks to Michael Fassnacht, who named and sanctioned the Institute of Decision Making, and to Carly Kouba and Stephen Harries who were the original team. I'd like to thank Dominic Whittles for his support and patience on the West Coast, and Ricki Schweizer for her advice. Debra Coughlin, Jonathan Harries, Elyssa Phillips, Cindy Augustine, Vita Harris, Athena Manikas, Nigel Jones, and Carter Murray have all supported the Institute of Decision Making and deserve thanks. Wally Petersen, Stephen Martincic, Jen Comiteau, and Joan Lufrano have been brilliant at seeing its potential in terms of press coverage and speaking events. Many people already mentioned provided the quotes that conclude each chapter. Others who helped in this or other respects include Ryan Riley, Desi O'Brien, Dirk Herbert, Kim Lundgren, Leo Nagata, Ximena Vega, Heather Segal, Anirban Chaudhuri, Raphael Barreto, Adam Nowack, Arnie Jacobson, Vicky Johns, Harlan Kennedy, Ken Muench, Barb Murrer, Marci Reichbach, Laurel Beeler, Lori Sacco, Ana Suarez, John Graetz, Ken Kingsbury, Sarah Dey Burton, Leigh Caldwell, Brooks Day, Chris Shumaker, Ken Beatty, Niclas Wagner, Curt Munk, and Rona Saadeh. There are many others, including all the planners and clients I have worked with in San Francisco and around our network, who have invited me into their worlds and the problems they are trying to solve; Terry Peigh at IPG for involving me in New Realities; and ex-colleagues in Thailand, particularly Punnee Chaiyakul and Sunandha Tulayadhan. Thank you all for allowing me to explore a passion in the name of work.

About the Author

Matthew Willcox is Founder and Executive Director of the Institute of Decision Making, which is part of FCB, a global and fully integrated marketing communications company within the Interpublic Group of Companies, IPG. The Institute of Decision Making is a unique offering, charged with bringing the findings from scientists who study human behavior and how people make choices into the practice of marketing for our clients. Matthew is also Chief Strategy Officer of FCB West. He has more than 25 years of brand strategy experience throughout Europe, Asia, and North America. Over that time he has helped organizations such as Levi Strauss and Co., Electronic Arts, Hilton Worldwide, Unilever, Nestle, Shell, GlaxoSmith-Kline, and American Express get their products chosen. In the process, he has helped his clients win eight Effie awards for effective communication. He has acted as a subject matter expert on behavior change for the Food and Drug Administration and is a frequent speaker at business schools and at marketing and communication events, including the Cannes Lions in 2010, 2011, and 2013.

Matthew brings a global perspective to observing behavior. He is based in San Francisco, has worked in both London and Bangkok with Ogilvy & Mather, grew up in Ireland, and is married to an Italian.

Preface

In my first proper job as a trainee at an advertising agency in London, one of my tasks was to spend hours looking at video of toothpaste advertising from around the world. I studied and analyzed every copy claim, diagram, and tagline. Decades later, I still find myself involuntarily whistling a couple of bars from a jingle for Pepsodent or Aquafresh.

One consistent technique in the toothpaste ads was the use of spokespeople, normally men with gray-flecked hair and steel-rimmed spectacles, wearing a white lab coat, who, while reeking of apparent authority would say, "I am not a dentist, but...."[1]

In my current job, I often feel compelled to give a similar disclaimer. I'm certainly not a dentist, but I am also not a behavioral scientist—or any other sort of scientist—either.

But...over the last decade, I have had the opportunity to immerse myself in the work of people studying human behavior and how people make choices. What started as a professional interest has become a personal passion. I've met, talked to, interviewed, worked with, and taught alongside some of the brightest minds in the field of judgment and decision making. I've given talks at marketing and academic conferences alike, and I have even participated as a subject in the sorts of behavioral and neuroscience experiments I write about in this book. But my training and experience remains that of a marketing practitioner, and that is the perspective from which I write this book.

The Business of Choice isn't a science book. It's not even a business or marketing book in the conventional sense; it's not about brand management or how to put together a marketing plan. It is a book about how behavioral science and related fields cast light on human nature and how human nature

---

[1] This approach reached either a zenith or a nadir in 1986 in an advertisement for Vicks Formula 44 cough syrup that used Peter Bergman, the actor who played Dr. Cliff Warner in the long-running soap opera *All My Children,* as a spokesman. He started the commercial with the immortal line "I'm not a doctor, but I play one on TV."

affects our choices. It is a book about how and why people make choices and what that means for brands and businesses.

Another disclaimer: This isn't a book with silver bullets that will enable you to unlock the secrets of human behavior and change it at your behest. Dr. Robert Cialdini, author of the excellent and justifiably best-selling book *Influence—The Psychology of Persuasion,* told me about a colleague who had spent 16 years trying to identify the single most effective persuasive appeal, the golden rule of persuasion, if you will. His conclusion? The golden rule is that there isn't one. You have to size up every situation from a behavioral perspective and ascertain which tendencies are most active in those circumstances.

Every situation is different, and context has a profound effect on how we make choices. A behavioral principle that works in one scenario may fall flat in another scenario that seems, on the surface, to be very similar (as we will see in Chapter 6, "Thanks for Sharing [Whether You Meant to or Not]"). So, it's best to think of *The Business of Choice* as a selection of useful starting points to consider, experiment with, and adapt to the unique circumstances of the behavior you are trying to change and the choices you are trying to influence.

Finally, as a non-scientist immersing myself in decision science, I learned two lessons about the intersection of science and marketing. The first lesson is that rather than providing certainty, science is about advancing ideas. It is tempting for marketers, from the legendary Claude Hopkins[2] onward, to see the potential of science as proof that one approach will work better than another. This way of thinking misses the point of science—rather than thinking about it as validation, think of science as inspiration. Most of the revelations about human choice I refer to in this book come from scientists devising and conducting highly creative experiments that dig deep into human nature. Scientists' ingenuity in looking at things in different ways, and in creating decision experiments that reveal effects of non-conscious cognitive mechanisms, has led to breakthroughs in understanding how people arrive at their decisions. Science, it turns out, is surprisingly creative,

---

[2] Claude Hopkins was a creative director at the agency Lord & Thomas; his reputation was such that he commanded a salary of $185,000 in 1907 (which is equivalent to approximately $5 million in 2014). He published *Scientific Advertising* in 1923, a book that influenced industry giants such as David Ogilvy. In 1942, Lord & Thomas became Foote, Cone and Belding, the agency that also had the foresight to set up the Institute of Decision Making five years ago.

and if anyone can appreciate the effect of creativity to change the game, it should be those of us in marketing and advertising.

The second lesson I learned after immersing myself in the science of choice is that science is much more fluid than I had thought. Ideas that seemed immutable 10 or 20 years ago are now up for debate.

For example, what scientists know about the function of the amygdala—an important brain area for marketing—has changed greatly in the past two decades. The amygdala is involved in translating what we sense and perceive into emotions, and it plays an important role in recognizing emotions in social interactions and facial expressions. Just over 10 years ago, the amygdala was still considered to be absolutely essential for recognizing and experiencing fear. Today, its exact role is much less defined, but it is not essential for fear. The hypothesis of the amygdala being essential for recognizing and experiencing fear was based on studying a rare brain lesion patient called S.M., who has damage specific only to the amygdala. S.M. has abnormal behavioral responses to fear and also abnormal social interactions; additionally, lots of experiments with S.M. showed that she could not identify fearful-looking human faces.[3] But the same researchers who first uncovered S.M.'s inability to recognize fearful faces realized something fascinating 10 years after the first experiments: When S.M. viewed faces, she did not look at the eyes. Viewing the eyes is necessary to discriminate emotions from facial expressions, and when specifically instructed to look at the eyes, it turns out that S.M. could indeed recognize fear just like people with intact amygdala regions.[4] The function of the amygdala has since been refined to include being an important influence on the visual system. Recognizing fear involves more brain areas than just the amygdala, but one specific role the amygdala may play is in directing our eyes to where we will see signs of fear—such as people's eyes.

I want to make two points here. The first is that we are still learning, especially when it comes to understanding the human brain. To use a cliché, science is not a destination, but a journey. Marketers might do well to remember this cliché when being presented with research (I elaborate on

---

[3] Adolphs, R., Tranel, D., Damasio, H., Damasio, A. (1994) "Impaired recognition of emotion in facial expressions following bilateral damage to the human amygdala." *Nature* 372: 669–672.

[4] Adolphs, R., Gosselin, F., Buchanan, T.W., Tranel, D., Schyns, P., Damasio, A. (2005) "A mechanism for impaired fear recognition after amygdala damage." *Nature* 433: 68–72.

this caution in Chapter 15, "Think Differently About Market Research"). Research based on the "latest from science" probably won't remain the latest for very long. And, as the amygdala story demonstrates, science self-corrects, so research might not even be considered science for very long. Or, as Christian Jarrett says in his book *Great Myths of the Brain,*

> Anyone who spends time researching brain myths soon discovers today's myths were yesterday's facts.

Science does self-correct, but being a healthy skeptic is also a good idea.

In experimental psychology and other disciplines, this self-correcting is increasingly helped along by other scientists attempting to replicate the original research. But experiments don't always replicate and the reasons why are numerous. The most common reason is simple statistics; the world is noisy. For example, if you sample a group of 20 males and 20 females, sometimes the group of females will be taller than the men, but this result will not hold up with repetition. Another reason why an experiment might not replicate is context (something I cover extensively in Chapter 12, "If Content Is King, Context Is Queen"). Sometimes the effects shown in a particular study are exquisitely sensitive to the specific context of the experiment.[5]

Another, much less common, reason why experiments might not replicate is scientific fraud. Uri Simonsohn, from the Wharton School of the University of Pennsylvania, has a reputation as a "data vigilante,"[6] which he acquired by identifying practices that generate results that seem too good to be true. Simonsohn showed that continuing to collect data until a sought-after result is confirmed is not good practice. In science, this is called "p-hacking" (for collecting data until the desired statistic, or p-value, is reached), but it happens outside of the laboratory, too. It's human nature and something I discuss in Chapter 14, "The Power of Affirmation," under the scaffold of the confirmation bias.

---

[5] The exact number of experiments that do not replicate is unknown, in large part because it requires publishing a null result. There is a journal dedicated to null results, though: the *Journal of Articles in Support of the Null Hypothesis.* (www.jasnh.com)

[6] Simonsohn's investigations have led to two scientists resigning from their posts and to a number of papers being retracted. An article by Christopher Shea in the December 2012 edition of *The Atlantic* covers Simonsohn's efforts in more detail.

One of the themes of this book is that marketers don't embrace the findings of behavioral science and neuroscience as much as they could and should. At the same time, I also urge that marketers be cautious against basing a strategy or an idea on the latest scientific study to be written up yesterday in the popular press—be it a blog or a respected newspaper.

The second point I want to make about the fluidity of decision science is somewhat of an understatement: The brain is complex. Neuroscience experiments might single out individual brain areas—and elegantly relate regional responses to a specific behavior—but brain areas work together. Two decades ago, neuroscience was convinced that the amygdala specially processed fear. Today, the amygdala is just one part, albeit an important one, of a fear-processing network.

Neuroscience has also provided the evidence to demolish some popular myths about the brain.[7] One is the belief that "we only use 10% of our brains," the premise of the 2014 movie *Lucy,* starring Scarlett Johansson and Morgan Freeman. Neuroimaging shows that this clearly isn't the case. Another myth is that there are "left brain" people and "right brain" people. Certain functions are reliant on one side of the brain—speech is generally centered in the left hemisphere for right-handed people. But creative or (their supposed opposite) analytical tasks, nor the people who excel in either of these areas are more dependent on one side of the brain than the other.

In an interview with LiveScience,[8] Dr. Jeff Anderson, director of the fMRI Neurosurgical Mapping Service at the University of Utah said

> It is not the case that the left hemisphere is associated with logic or reasoning more than the right. Also, creativity is no more processed in the right hemisphere than the left.

So we will just have to find some other language to describe our colleagues who seem either more creative, or more analytical.

I also want to address some of the language and terms that you will come across in this book. The broad academic field from which I have drawn

---

[7] Christian Jarrett covers these two examples and more in *Great Myths of the Brain.* Jarrett is also author of *The Rough Guide to Psychology,* an excellent introduction to the subject.

[8] "Left Brain vs. Right: It's a Myth, Research Finds" by Christopher Wanjek, September 3, 2013. http://www.livescience.com/39373-left-brain-right-brain-myth.html

most of the material included in the book is judgment and decision making (JDM). I am aware that the term *decision making* often leads people to think of planned decisions, of the carefully considered steps that people may go through to make a choice. "To make a decision," does, after all, sound active and rather deliberative. One of the pioneers in JDM, the late Hillel Einhorn, was described as someone who specialized in studying how people *reach* decisions. Although a subtle distinction, the difference between *making* and *reaching* is, to me, a significant one. It suggests the importance of non-conscious factors of which the decision maker (or reacher) is unaware. Unfortunately, the "Institute of Decision Reaching" didn't roll off the tongue quite as easily as the "Institute of Decision Making." But when you read the term *decision making*, think of people reaching or arriving at their decisions as much as, or more than, deliberatively making them.

Research on how humans reach decisions shows that many of the processes leading to decisions are outside the realm of conscious awareness. Sometimes people (including myself until a few years ago) refer to these processes as being in the "subconscious." With all respect to Freud and Jung, that word now connotes a mysterious and vaguely sinister approach to studying cognition, like a black box that needs to be "unlocked." Psychology and neuroscience abandoned the term *subconscious* in favor of the terms *unconscious*, *non-conscious*, and *preconscious*.[9] Although these three terms can mean different things in spite of often being used interchangeably, I use the last two in this book. The term *unconscious* makes me think of people who are not just unaware of their cognitive processes, but pretty much unaware of anything. When it comes to how people reach decisions, *non-conscious* and *preconscious* seem to describe better what actually happens, and those are the words I use in this book.

I would also like to suggest that we in marketing are more careful with our own language, particularly with words that describe people to whom we market. In a March 2013 interview,[10] Keith Weed, Unilever's Global Chief Marketing Officer, described how prevalent terminology is problematic:

---

[9] Although the people who advise me on such matters tell me that the new favored word among psychologists and neuroscientists for reactions that are not conscious is *reflexive*. This creates a nice pairing with *reflective*, a term that can be used for conscious thinking.

[10] "Unilever Logic. Keith Weed wants Unilever to be the trust mark of sustainable living." *Hub Magazine*, March/April 2013.

Marketers need to...engage with consumers as people, not as consumers. I think the term "consumers" doesn't help. Once you start looking at people's lives, they are not a pair of armpits in search of deodorant or a head of hair in search of hair benefits. They are people with full lives and a lot of challenges in a rapidly changing world.

Weed's concern is the practice of defining people through the lens of consumption in an age when all of us (from governments, companies, to individuals) need to focus on sustainability. I agree. But, for this book, my beef with the word *consumer* is more about how we marketers label the people we want to choose our products. For example, we talk about them as "targets." In most aspects of life beyond marketing, things don't turn out so well for actual targets. As my colleague, Rebecca Pollock says, the word target is more properly used by hunters and hitmen.

Another example. I've often heard marketers say that a marketing tactic "should drive the consumer to retail."

Unfortunately, the meaning here isn't literally that the brand will drive the consumer to retail by laying on a car service to pick the consumer up at 10 a.m. on a Saturday to drop them off at the mall (which would be nice), but somehow that the marketing will herd them in droves, like cattle to the abattoir. Not only is this a ridiculous exaggeration of the likely effect of any marketing, but it also disrespects the people whose decisions to buy our products pay our salaries and finance our lifestyles.

I will try to use the word *target* as little as possible in this book, but I have not yet come up with an alternative I am happy with. Any suggestions are very welcome.

Instead of *consumer*, I suggest another option. In her excellent book *The Art of Choosing* Sheena Iyengar, a professor at Columbia Business School, frequently refers to people who are making, or have made a choice, as *choosers*. I like this word for two reasons. First, it reflects and respects the importance of the "consumer" in that purchasing/buying/consuming is their choice. Second, the word *chooser* aligns with something I believe in deeply and that is also a major theme of this book. Marketing should be about making it intuitive and easy for people to choose your brand, your product, your service, or your cause. To buy a product in the first place is a choice, to use a product is a choice, to continue buying a product and keep using it are further choices, and recommending a product (should we be so lucky) is yet another choice.

Marketing is more about choice than consumption.

While I may sometimes use *consumer* in this book (in fact, it is on the cover of the book), I aim to use *chooser* or *potential chooser* whenever it makes sense. And, of course, eschewing jargon, and just using the word *people* works pretty well, too.

Two things about the book format: First, at the end of every chapter, you'll see a number of comments from people saying what they found interesting about that chapter. I asked 40 people from around the world to give me their thoughts—many are marketers or come from advertising agencies, but I have also included the opinions of people from other businesses and professions, including realtors, management consultants, executive recruiters, lawyers, and judges.

Second, like most similar books, this one has many footnotes. Sometimes they are part of the story, other times they are references to research. We have collected a list of links to further information at the addresses in this footnote.[11]

I'll end this preface by telling you about the experience that led me to see the science described in this book in a whole new light. I think many people who have become proponents for the practical application of behavioral sciences have had an "aha" moment in which they understand how some principle or insight could improve something they are passionate about. This is how that moment happened for me.

One Tuesday in November 2009, I was in an Irish bar in Washington D.C., and things were getting ugly. I was watching my team, Ireland, play France in a playoff game to qualify for the 2010 FIFA World Cup finals in South Africa.

As the game went into extra time, Ireland was well on top and looked the most likely to score the goal that would take them to the finals. Until, in the 103rd minute, the French striker Thierry Henry blatantly handled the ball (not once, but twice) to set up a French goal that was against the run of play, giving them the victory that meant the French went to South Africa,

---

[11] Perhaps for the first time ever, a footnote about footnotes. You can find links to many of the studies and articles mentioned in this book at www.instituteof-decisionmaking.com/businessofchoice/references and www.thebusinessofchoice.com/references.

while the Irish stayed at home.[12] The goal should have been disallowed, but unsighted, the referee and his team of officials allowed the non-goal to stand, and a nation's hopes were dashed by an act of cheating that was captured on TV for all the world to see. The joshing between the some of the Irish fans in the bar and a small handful of French fans started to lose its good humor, which was unusual as the French and the Irish, united by a common sporting enemy, normally get on famously. I slunk out of the bar to catch my train to Boston, as I was due to attend a conference there for the Society for Judgment and Decision Making.[13]

The fallout from the incident went beyond the heated words exchanged between the patrons of that bar; it became a full-blown international crisis. Irish bookmaker firm Paddy Power ran ads in the arrivals area of Dublin Airport that said, "Welcome to Ireland, unless you are called Thierry." The Irish Prime Minister and the French President discussed it at a European Union meeting. FIFA[14] promised to set up an inquiry to study using extra officials and technology to reduce the chance of transgressions like Henry's going unnoticed. It was generally felt that more officials or increased technology might also help stamp out the practice of "diving" where a player pretends they have been fouled in order to gain a penalty kick.

All discussion was about detection rather than prevention.

A couple of days later, at the Society for Judgment and Decision Making conference in Boston, I listened to the inspirational Dan Ariely, a professor of Psychology and Behavioral Economics at Duke University and author of *Predictably Irrational*, present research he and his colleagues conducted on honesty. Ariely and colleagues showed that simple "nudges" could make people more ethical. (Nudges are anything that influences choices you

---

[12] The French team would have been better off staying at home. Their performance at the 2010 FIFA World Cup Finals was abysmal, with the team rent apart by infighting. They failed to reach the last 16, finished bottom of their group, and only scored one goal in the process. However, Ireland may not have done much better. Although the national team did qualify for the 2012 European Championship two years later, they lost all three games they played in that tournament, conceding nine goals while scoring just one, resulting in Ireland's worst ever performance at a major championship.

[13] Yes, this society really does exist and holds an excellent conference every year in North America.

[14] FIFA is the abbreviation for Fédération Internationale de Football Association, the global governing body of football (or soccer) and organizer of the World Cup, which is held every four years.

make, without limiting options and without force; I discuss them many times in this book.) In one of Ariely's experiments, having people sign their name on tax return forms *before* they filled in the form led to more honest claims than if people signed the form last.[15] A signature is, of course, a representation of our names, and we'll talk more about the effect that names have on people later in the book.

During Ariely's talk, it struck me that FIFA was looking at measures of enforcement, which would come at considerable cost and could only be used for the most prestigious tournaments and leagues. But something similar to Ariely's experiment could be applied to soccer[16] at any level and at relatively little expense.

Ariely agreed to let me use his name and research to approach a number of the leading soccer organizations (FIFA, UEFA, and the FAI—the global, European, and Irish bodies, respectively) with a proposal. My proposal was that they test the idea of having every player sign an agreement to an ethics code with specific do's and don'ts immediately before coming on to the field of play.

None of the federations or associations took us up on the offer, so we haven't yet changed the game of soccer yet. But if you are reading this and you have influence with a sports governing body with an interest in testing low cost ways of reducing cheating, we would be delighted to help with some experiments!

In a way, the purpose of this book is to encourage the kind of thinking that led to my idea for decreasing cheating in soccer. Ariely's original experiments had nothing to do with sports. Would the same mechanism that led to greater compliance in the relatively uncharged environment of filling out insurance forms affect soccer players' decisions in the physical tussle and adrenaline rush of a game? I don't know the answer, but the glimpse into human nature revealed by Ariely and his colleagues made me feel that it's worth trying.

---

[15] Shu, L., Mazar, N., Gino, F., Ariely, D., Bazerman, M. (2012) "Signing at the Beginning Makes Ethics Salient and Decreases Dishonest Self-reports in Comparison to Signing at the End." *Proceedings of the National Academy of Sciences of the United States of America* September, 109(38): 15197–15200.

[16] Before any readers get on my case for using the word "soccer," in Ireland (where I grew up), the beautiful game has been historically known as soccer in order to distinguish it from Gaelic Football. A map can be found at http://i.imgur.com/2GHdRDg.jpg that shows how football/soccer is named around the world. "Soccer" is not just an American thing...

In the world of commercial market research, most studies are designed to answer a specific brand question. In contrast, very few of the science experiments discussed in this book were designed to cast light on a specific brand or business issue. But all of them reveal something about human nature that could be relevant to helping get your brand chosen, or creating the behavior change you need for your organization to succeed (which is, of course, why they are in the book). If this book does nothing more than spark some thoughts as to how you can engineer behavioral change, I'll be very happy.

PART I

The Business, Science, and Nature of Choice

1

The Business of Choice

For a brand or business to be successful, it needs people to choose it, so it is important to understand how people choose.

> *We are all faced throughout our lives with agonizing decisions. Moral choices. Some are on a grand scale. Most of these choices are on lesser points. But! We define ourselves by the choices we have made. We are in fact the sum total of our choices.*
>
> *—Professor Louis Levy*

Before you go looking for the "Collected Works of Professor Louis Levy," I should explain that Levy is a character in Woody Allen's film *Crime and Misdemeanors*, and this quote is part of a monologue about human destiny, love, and our choices that draws the movie to a close.

It might seem almost insultingly obvious that *we are in fact the sum total of our choices*, as Levy says. If I hadn't chosen to accept a job with an advertising agency nearly 30 years ago, I wouldn't have been in San Francisco 20 years later working on a new business pitch for a client that offered its customers a dizzying array of choices. If I hadn't been working on that pitch, I wouldn't have decided to contact Barry Schwartz, Professor of Social Theory and Social Action at Swarthmore College and author of the excellent book, *The Paradox of Choice*. He wouldn't have suggested I attend the Society of Judgment and Decision Making Conference, and I wouldn't have had the experience outlined in the preface that led to my writing this book.

Yet, if our choices define us, as Woody Allen via his mouthpiece Professor Levy suggests, if they determine to a large extent whether we will be happy, how comfortable our retirement will turn out, and even how healthy we will be, then it is amazing that while we spend huge amounts of time pondering the outcomes of our choices, we spend so little time thinking about *how* we make the choices we make. (Now don't feel bad about that—there are very good reasons why we think so little about how we make our choices that we'll explore in Chapter 4, "Shortcuts Versus Analysis—Ignoring is Decisional Bliss.")

Perhaps more surprising is how little time and money marketers, whose paycheck, bonuses, job security, and promotion prospects are dependent on influencing the choices of others, spend seeking to understand how humans choose. The success of businesses depends on ensuring people choose the "right" way: be it the procurement team at an airline wrestling with the decision to spend billions on Airbus or Boeing; a shopper in a supermarket choosing between Crest, Colgate, Aquafresh, or store brand toothpaste; a middle-aged man opting to try on a pair of slightly more fitted jeans for the first time; or a homeowner deciding to install energy-efficient light bulbs. The outcomes of these choices, and hundreds of billions like them every day, can edge marketing teams closer to or further away from their goals and lead companies to post a bullish or a bearish outlook for the next quarter. Every business is dependent on how people choose, and marketing is simply how businesses influence choices to contribute to their objectives.

Businesses fail or succeed based on products or services being chosen; marketing is at the sharp end of this—it is the business of choice. And marketers spend a lot of time, effort, and money learning about things that may affect that choice—understanding purchase paths and decision journeys, where their brand sits in culture, how their brand is perceived or how likely people say they are to purchase it. But, for how important choice is, businesses spend little time thinking about how our choices are actually made, and how they are guided by the instinctual aspects of human behavior.

When I interviewed Robert Cialdini, one of the world's authorities on what actually influences people to act, at the 2010 Behavior, Energy and Climate Change conference, he noted this discrepancy:

> I think marketers study things that are related to behavior. They study attitudes, they study beliefs, they study perceptions, they'll study memories of brands and the relationships people have with them. But it seems to me that these are all under investigation in the service of predicting behavior. Why don't we just cut to the chase? Why do we examine those things that are bridges and links of an imperfect sort to behavior when we can study behavior itself?

Funding isn't an excuse for this oversight. We are in an era where marketers spend more on research every year. We are awash with data: dashboards with real-time sales data; brand equity studies tracking changes on how brands are perceived; web metrics revealing what potential choosers are researching, liking, recommending, buying, and even what they are discarding from their shopping baskets at the last moment; and face-to-face discussions to understand at a deeper level how people seem to feel about brands and how marketing approaches might resonate with them.

Not surprisingly, the market research industry is doing pretty well. According to business intelligence publisher, IBISWorld, the industry has achieved annual growth rates over the last five years of more than three percent and global revenues of $21 billion last year.

However, a huge gap exists in this research, as Cialdini suggested.

You might disagree, and argue that you and your team are very familiar with the decision-making process when it comes to buying cars, insurance, pet food, or whatever line of business you are in.

You also might argue that you understand how people use different channels and can even give a very accurate estimate for return on marketing investment for activity in these channels. The point I want to make is not so much about how marketers understand decision-making in their specific category, but more about how little attention we pay to understanding how humans generally make decisions. The car buyer, the insurance buyer, and the pet food buyer are not different species (even if the end consumer in the latter example is). Although the choices may differ, they are made by the same overall decision-making system, which has been evolving in its current form for around six million years. It is, of course, the human brain. Although most successful marketers are pretty good at understanding the proximate nature of choices, we don't consider the importance of the decision-making system that drives them, the overall anatomy of how we make choices.

If we were doctors, we would be very good at understanding the personal and specific nature of our patients' ailments, but not how the body operates as a whole. Let's say our patient Mrs. Smith suffers from coccyx pain, for example. Our understanding of Mrs. Smith's problem would be based on that small piece of bone, rather than how it fits overall in the body, how it moves with the body in different environments, how it might be affected when the weather turns colder, or even how our evolutionary history might be relevant in understanding tailbone function and problems. (The bone's common name, *tailbone*, is a bit of a giveaway here—the coccyx is the remnant of a vestigial tail in humans and other tailless primates.)

Understanding the broader picture is vital to understanding how people arrive at their decisions. If marketing is about influencing choice, then it seems critical to learn about not just product or category insights but also about the more universal aspects of human decision-making. We should understand how humans are naturally effective decision-makers and where we fall short; how different circumstances affect our choices; and the nature of choice, rather than just its consequences.

For a business preoccupied with insights, not seeking to understand *everything* about how decisions are made is a pretty massive oversight. Marketing is obsessed with being consumer-centric. I think the opportunity is for it to become more *decision*-centric.

By decision-centric, I mean using an understanding of how humans choose as the starting point for developing marketing. It seems to be common sense that this will lead to more efficient and effective marketing. Perhaps this is what Cialdini meant when he said, "just cut to the chase." If your starting point for developing marketing comes from understanding how humans choose, then it seems a reasonable bet that your marketing will be more efficient and effective.

Starting from an understanding of how people choose, and taking a decision-centric approach could be important for another reason. Choice has become a bigger and more time-consuming aspect of people's lives. An excellent 2010 article in *The Economist* titled "You Choose" quantified just how consuming choice has become:

> ...the average American supermarket now carries 48,750 items, according to the Food Marketing Institute, more than five times the number in 1975. Britain's Tesco stocks 91 different shampoos, 93 varieties of toothpaste and 115 of household cleaner.

In this environment, spending some time understanding how people choose—not, as Keith Weed says, as "a pair of armpits in search of deodorant or a head of hair in search of hair benefits," but as humans making thousands of choices everyday—could be one of the best investments a marketer can make.

Choice isn't just tough for those trying to choose what brands to buy. Deciding what approach to take has become really difficult for marketers as well. A few years ago, an infographic made the rounds in marketing and advertising circles. It illustrated the frightening complexity that technology has brought to the landscape of choices marketers need to make. The revised version for 2014, by Scott Brinker,[1] is even scarier, showing 947 different companies (he acknowledges this is a conservative number) classified into 42 different groups. When I started in advertising, there were six different groups: TV, radio, print, outdoor, direct mail, and point-of-sale.

Marketing is increasingly complex, and even in this age of advanced data analytics where a sea of data comes in waves across your desk, it is still really hard for most companies—particularly those that don't do most of their business direct to the public—to pin down what is working and what is not. The old adage "half of my advertising is working, I just don't know which half"[2] still rings true. While speaking at an Advertising Research Foundation conference on Big Data in 2014, I made an off-the-cuff comment that the modern version of this quip may be "half my data analytics is wasted, I just don't know which half." I was surprised that many of the attendees, who knew far more about data and analytics than me, agreed.

Beyond the sheer number of choices, another thing has made it more difficult for marketers to get their brands chosen. Brands—with a few glorious exceptions—are becoming less powerful. In his 2008 book *The Brand Bubble*,[3] John Gerzema analyzes data from his company's BrandAsset Valuator, a very robust dataset that covers many hundreds of brands. It shows that consumers feel that brands in general have become significantly less trusted, liked, and respected, as well as less salient over the 14-year period from 1996–2008. While I wouldn't discourage any marketers from taking measures to increase their brand strength in these areas, I think we should all be concerned that the issue may not be about making brands stronger, but might be about choosers using "brand" less as a no-questions-asked shortcut in their decision-making. For years, focusing on just checking the boxes about how a brand delivered emotional and functional benefits, and managing it for consistency, was a guarantee of a reasonable level of success. Blind brand belief may have made us complacent as marketers and

---

[1] You can find the full infographic with very insightful thoughts on the different categories at http://chiefmartec.com/2014/01/marketing-technology-landscape-supergraphic-2014/.

[2] Attributed to both U.S. retailer John Wanamaker and British industrialist Lord Leverhulme, depending on which side of the Atlantic you reside. There is some doubt that either of them actually said it.

[3] BrandAsset Valuator is a formidable study, covering 50,000 brands and 51 countries since its initiation by Young & Rubicam in the 1990s.

overly reliant on the gravitational pull of our brands to attract people to choose them.

But that, clearly, is no longer enough. I think the remedy to the decline that Gerzema notes should not be just to strengthen your brand in the traditional way, but to think of it from a different perspective.

Everything I have learned about how people make decisions points to how powerful brands can be. When brands work best they dovetail beautifully with how we make choices. They are in tune with how we store memories and trigger us to create vivid and lasting ones. They are active at the right times and places to recall those memories as compelling feelings and emotions. They work beautifully with how the mind filters information to enable it to make fast and efficient choices. Brands are the ultimate man-made decision short cuts. At their best, they enable us to make quick, easy choices that feel right. In doing so, brands are perfectly aligned with how our brain's decision-making systems have evolved; this, I believe is the real power of brands. To make the most of the relationship between brands and our decision-making systems, brands need to become more "brain centric." In an episode of a recent TV series called "Thinking Money," produced in conjunction with Maryland Public Television, noted Stanford neuroeconomist Baba Shiv (who I think makes the science of decision-making and how it relates to marketing more approachable than almost anyone else) was asked why saving money is so difficult, when it clearly makes sense at a rational level. Shiv's reply was

> The rational brain simply *rationalizes* what the emotional brain has already decided to do. The only long-term solution for this is to make saving more sexy...for the brain.

Asking how to make your brand and approach to marketing more "sexy" for the brain is a great idea. We all know the saying, "sex sells" (and it does). But making your brand and marketing sexy for the brain may take this concept to a whole new level.

This approach requires a different way of thinking. Very often with marketing we think about our user or chooser's needs from the category, we think about what is compelling about our brand equity and create a cocktail of persuasion, and point it at our (I know I said I wouldn't use this word) target. I call this a "brand in" approach. To be "sexy for the brain" means you need to form an understanding of what the brain wants. What are the things the brain just can't ignore? What works with how the brain guides the choices we make? How can the stimulus you provide align with the speed and efficiency of the brain? Instead of starting from your brand, this means starting from the brain. I call this a "brain out" approach.

In all of the research I've read, brilliant people I have spoken with, and practical experience I have accumulated, I have seen plenty of complexity. Complexity is inevitable. Humans are complex beings whose behavior is driven by a brain, that even though inside our heads, contains as much scientific mystery as the universe does outside. Despite this complexity, I have reached one simple conclusion. From a cognitive and behavioral perspective, marketing has an impact in only three ways:

- It can create, through emotional associations, long-lasting memories of a brand. These memories are implicit, in that we attribute them to the brand at a non-conscious level. The real power of a brand is the amount of people with whom it has created strong, positive, and implicit memories.

- It can act as a trigger to recall those memories. The Apple logo or the Nike swoosh are nothing without our memories of the feelings we have had about those brands—either through experience or the suggestion of marketing and advertising. After those associations are made, they are constantly hovering in the background, ready to color any decision that may involve that brand.

- It can make choices intuitive, or instinctive, in effect making them "no-brainers." The first two points relate to memories and come from what we have experienced and thus learned as individuals. This third impact has a different source—it is baked into how our brain works. It is our cognitive inheritance or the hand that human nature has in our choices.

In this book I touch on all three of these potential roles for marketing, but the emphasis is on the third. From what I have observed, understanding how human nature and the workings of our brain affect our choices hardly figures in the daily workings of most marketers.

The takeaways from this chapter are

- Think about your "consumer" not just as someone choosing products within your category, or as "a pair of armpits in search of deodorant or a head of hair in search of hair benefits." Think about how the choices they make, whether buying a car, a pair of jeans, or shampoo, emanate from the same decision-making system.

- Don't just rely on the magnetic pull of your brand. Understand how to make your brand "sexy for the brain." Think "brain out" rather than "brand in." Keep this in mind as you read the remaining chapters of this book.

- Consider allocating a percentage of your insights/research budget to understanding the innate behaviors that may be relevant to getting your brand chosen.

What stood out for other people in this chapter:

- "Marketers beginning not with what their brand wants, but with what the brain wants is a potent new approach to reaching today's decision-fatigued consumer."

- "It's clear we need to move beyond marketing insights that look at surface behavior to cognitive insights that drive choice deep within us. This is where the real advantage lies."

2

The Ever-Advancing Science of Choice

We're getting a lot better at understanding how people make decisions, thanks to advances in behavioral science and neuroscience.

We are learning more about how people choose and learning it faster than we have ever done before. I am very fortunate to be writing this book at a time when we are in the middle of a golden age of decision sciences.

In spite of the wealth of knowledge about human behavior and the future potential of the decision sciences to tell us even more about how humans decide, it is important to understand that, like life on earth, science is in flux and continually evolving.

Decades ago, the study of the brain was just "neuroscience." These days we see the emergence of specialized fields like "decision neuroscience," "cognitive neuroscience," and "social neuroscience." The science of decision-making is more precise today than it was decades ago because of the natural progression of science (refining your questions and experiments based on previous results) and because of advances in technology—researchers today have access to non-invasive technologies that allow the human brain to be studied in real-time as choices are made. But, even though we have many answers about how humans behave and make choices, there remain many outstanding questions. This fragmentation of expertise is an indicator of the complexity that science has found in our minds. Neuroscience is doing for our understanding of the brain what the Hubble Telescope and its successors are doing for our understanding of the universe. We are learning more than we have ever known, but at the same time revealing how much we have still to learn. Be wary of anyone telling you they have figured out how the brain works or that they have located the "buy button."

Three big trends are driving the golden age of decision science, leading to an explosion of learning from behavioral and social sciences. The first is an intellectual revolution which prompted the acceptance that intuitive processes, rather than rational ones, drive human choices. Theories based on the importance of intuition in decision-making started to gain traction about two decades ago and inspired entire new research fields, such as behavioral economics and more recently, neuroeconomics.

Many of you will have heard of behavioral economics. It is a wonderfully fascinating area, and I say without exaggeration, it should lead to one of the biggest changes to marketing thinking in the history of marketing. But, from a practitioner perspective, I don't think it is particularly well named. *Behavioral economics*, as a name, comes from the origin of the field, which was when experimental psychologists studying behavior started investigating economic choices (and indeed, collaborating with enlightened economists). Hence *behavioral economics*.[1] But I think this makes it sound much more about economics and fiscal policy than about human behavior.

My lay-person's description of behavioral economics is this:

> Behavioral economics is an area of psychology that explores how humans behave and make choices by studying the differences between how we should act from a rational, economic perspective and how we really behave. In so doing, it reveals many of the nonconscious processes that drive human decision-making.

I'll use the term behavioral economics in this book, but I will also use related terms like "judgment and decision making" or simply "behavioral science."

By dissing its name, I hope I am not diminishing the importance of behavioral economics. It should be considered game-changing thinking for marketers. Its gift to marketing, though, has much less to do with economics and much more to do with revealing deep insights into human behavior and, in the process, providing the evidence to displace conscious, rational, or deliberative thinking as the lynchpin for how people make choices.

---

[1] Readers familiar with advertising agency structures may see a comparison with the origin of the term *behavioral economics* and origin of the term *account planning*, the creative strategy discipline which was named from the merging of some skills from *account* management and some from media *planning*. Although this reflects the discipline's origins, it doesn't intuitively describe it. I feel the same about the term behavioral economics.

The second trend is one of resource and capacity—a sort of human brain-power version of "Moore's Law." Gordon Moore's observation suggests that the number of transistors on an integrated circuit doubles every two years, which enables a step change increase in computer processing power. We have seen a dramatic increase in the number of minds, and thus brain-power, focused on understanding human behavior and decision-making. Behavioral and social sciences have become the hot ticket in leading academic institutions across the world, and an estimate based on the sizes of the leading faculties and academic societies suggests that more than 5,000 professors and graduate students[2] are today involved in conceiving, carrying out, and analyzing experiments relating to behavior and decision-making. The popularity of behavioral and social science research has led to large, interconnected communities of discussion and collaboration, the output of which is peer-reviewed papers (I estimate that the leading five journals[3] and conferences that cover human decision-making have yielded 1,500 papers over the last two years that are of at least some interest to marketers) and, of course, books like this one, jostling for space in the non-fiction section of airport bookshelves. Countless blogs on the subjects exist, and scientists like Dan Ariely have amassed Twitter followings that approach rock star proportions.[4]

The third trend is more like the real Moore's Law, because it is one facilitated by technology. Behavioral and social scientists benefit from the decreasing cost and increasing availability of technology to perform experiments that were inaccessible to decision science greats when they made their landmark contributions—scientists like Kahneman, Amos Tversky, George Lowenstein, Paul Slovic, Richard Thaler, Paul Glimcher, and Bill Newsome, to name just a few. The field of neuroeconomics, for example, relies on functional magnetic resonance imaging (fMRI) scanners that were not available outside of medical schools until the first decade of this century.

---

[2] Estimate based on combined membership of relevant societies.

[3] Some examples are *Nature*, the *Journal of Consumer Psychology*, the *Journal of Consumer Research*, *Cognition*, the *Journal of Judgment and Decision Making*, and the *Journal of Advertising Research*. There are many, many more—the SCImago Journal Rank Indicator counts 5,000 active journals in the broad field of social sciences. A list of conferences I have found useful is in the appendix.

[4] Well, maybe not rock star proportions, but @danariely seems to lead the pack of behavioral scientists with 72,900 followers as of September 2014, and he had significantly more followers at that time than institutions and brands like Carnegie Hall (52,000), the Nissan Leaf (41,000), Samuel Adams (51,000), and 7Up (54,000).

Now most leading business schools have MRI scanners in their basements (you will learn more on what these machines have revealed so far and their future potential in Parts II and III). Also, we can see the application of crowdsourcing to behavioral science experiments: Amazon's Mechanical Turk,[5] a service that distributes Human Intelligence Tasks (HITs) to online workers, enabling inexpensive and fast fieldwork for experiments; the use of everyday technology like smartphones and webcams records behavior and choices in natural environments; and the data trail from the Internet and mobile web reveals actual behavior rather than stated preferences and intentions.

This third movement also presents the opportunity for huge learning in the social sciences but especially in marketing. The organizers of the Conference on Digital Experimentation (CODE), a conference at MIT that brings the worlds of social science and computer science together, introduced their inaugural event with the statement: "The ability to rapidly deploy micro-level randomized experiments at population scale is, in our view, one of the most significant innovations in modern social science." Enabled by the ability to track real behavior in real-life digital environments, this approach allows *randomized controlled tests* (RCTs) to be conducted with a robustness of scale that would have been prohibitively expensive to previous generations of researchers. These massive RCTs can also be implemented with a speed that makes them significantly more useful for marketers than most research conducted to academic standards.

Studies that take this approach have the potential to help us understand human nature at a macro level, in a way that avoids something that bedevils nearly all research—whether academic or commercial. Whether study participants are lying in an fMRI scanner; are taking part in a behavioral test and being rewarded with coffee mugs, pens, or course credits; or are in a focus group room answering questions about whether packaging design may lead them to buy a particular brand of yogurt on their next trip to the supermarket, virtually all research has to make methodological compromises that remove it from the real world, and therefore from the real behavior and outcomes it seeks to predict. Behavioral researchers refer to this phenomenon as concerns about *ecological validity*.

While real-world RCTs of the type advocated by CODE hold great promise, marketers need to tread a little warily, as potential exists for ethical criticism

---

[5] Amazon Mechanical Turk was originally set up as an internal service for Amazon to find duplicates and repeated information among its web pages.

and negative associations from the public for brands that participate in this kind of research.

In June 2014, there was significant backlash when it emerged that two years earlier, data scientists had slanted the newsfeeds to several hundred thousand Facebook users to give them a more negative or more positive bias. The experiment lasted a week, and the aggregate posts of targeted users were analyzed to see whether the emotional balance of a newsfeed affected what they subsequently posted.

Because participants were not explicitly told that they were part of this study, and because it appeared that half the sample were being fed information that might have made them less happy, a number of critical articles appeared including one in *Slate*[6] with the headline "Facebook's Unethical Experiment." The subhead continues, "It intentionally manipulated users' emotions without their knowledge."

If experiments such as these can be designed and conducted in such a way as to avoid creating ethical concerns about privacy or unwilling participation, they hold great potential to reveal more about human nature. We will see in Chapter 6, "Thanks for Sharing (Whether You Meant to or Not)," how such an RCT with tens of thousands of participants has been key in helping increase consent for organ donation.

It is a wonderful time for the academics who are and will be the pioneers of discovery and learning about how people make choices. Equally, it should be a wonderful time to be a marketer and to be a pioneer of putting this decision-making knowledge into practice.

A couple of years ago, I suggested in an interview with *InDecision—Inside Decision-Making Sciences* (a blog run by researchers and practitioners in judgment and decision making)[7] that the decision sciences revolution was as important to marketers, in terms of how it should change thinking about

---

6 Katy Waldman, June 28, 2014. http://www.slate.com/articles/health_and_science/science/2014/06/facebook_unethical_experiment_it_made_news_feeds_happier_or_sadder_to_manipulate.html

7 Indecision Blog; March 2013. http://indecisionblog.com/2013/03/04/in-the-wild-matthew-willcox-draftfcb/. In a subsequent interview on the Indecision Blog, Ogilvy & Mather's Rory Sutherland, one of the leaders in bringing behavioral science into marketing practice, took this one step further when he said, "I truly believe that 'The Next Big Thing' is not a technology at all. Most progress in the developed world in this coming century—economic, social, hedonic—could in fact come from improvements in the social sciences. This is bigger than the Internet."

marketing and brand strategy, as the emergence of the Internet has been in terms of how it has changed the output of marketing. With a few exceptions, marketers have yet to embrace this new take on a fundamental aspect of what it is to be a human, not just a consumer, by considering the what, why, and how of choice.

The Business of Choice is about how marketers can embrace what science has revealed about how people choose. It is not a science book, and I don't believe that marketers need to become scientists. (I'm not sure that scientists becoming business people is a good idea either, but that might be simply a result of seeing too many villains following that course in movies like *Spider-Man*.) *The Business of Choice* includes practical examples of where good work has already started. I write about some intentional uses of decision science and other areas where marketers and their agencies have intuitively landed on ideas that leverage the science of human intuition. The book also highlights research that might make you think differently about how to change behavior, and I would be delighted to hear whether it inspires any ideas that actually do.

More than anything else, my aim is to demystify decision science. I want to enable marketers to see this wonderful and fascinating area as compatible with a practical and ethical approach to marketing. It is possible to leverage knowledge from decision science in a way that doesn't just help brands get chosen but can also create positive brand equity by helping the people who choose them.

I have already discussed how the growing understanding about the role of non-conscious aspects of choice has led to a wholesale reappraisal of how people make decisions. In his book *The Social Animal, The Hidden Sources of Love, Character and Achievement* David Brooks tells us how John Bargh, the James Rowland Angell Professor of Psychology at Yale, sees the deepening understanding about the influence of non-conscious processes on our behavior as being on a par with some of the greatest paradigm-busting moments in human history:

> (Bargh) argues that just as Galileo "removed the earth from its privileged position at the center of the universe," so this intellectual revolution removes the conscious mind from its privileged place at the center of human behavior.

Whether history will agree that the demotion of the conscious mind is on a par with Galileo's discoveries (it's rather difficult to really know how far-reaching a revolution is going to be when you are living through it), there can be little doubt that science has revealed enough to give marketers pause for thought about how the people they are trying to influence make the choices they do.

This role of non-conscious processes on our judgments and choices has been popularized and made accessible to the broad public with the publication of Nobel Memorial Prize for Economic Sciences winner Daniel Kahneman's *Thinking, Fast and Slow*. To say the book has been successful would be an understatement—in 2011, it was recognized as one of the best books of 2011 by the *New York Times Book Review;* as one of *The Economist's* 2011 Books of the Year; and as one of *The Wall Street Journal's* Best Nonfiction Books of the Year 2011. The book threads together the story of how people make choices through Kahneman's own pioneering work with his research partner Amos Tversky and that of other notable experimental psychologists. He, Tversky, and a handful of other psychologists and economists (most of whose work you will encounter in some way or another in this book) are the founders of the field known as *Behavioral Economics,* which we discussed earlier. In his book, Kahneman uses the metaphor of *System 1 and System 2* to illustrate the roles, power, and limitations of conscious and unconscious thinking in guiding our decisions. His book is an important reference for *The Business of Choice*.

But surprisingly, the sea change this growing understanding about the influence of non-conscious processes on behavior has led to in academia has barely rippled the waters of marketing practice (if you are one of the few practitioners who is embracing these new ideas, let me confer on you the title of *exceptional visionary*). By and large, processes and research methods remain largely unchanged in the more than two decades I have worked in the field. Although it is true that many aspects of marketing have transformed, this is mainly because of the impact of digital technology and not because of any new understanding about how people make choices.

This reluctance of marketing practice to embrace these new ideas is all the more extraordinary when you think about the implications of Bargh's point beyond its application to science. What he and a legion of credible experts have shown over the last few decades is that our choices and actions are, in the majority of situations, driven more by non-conscious processes than conscious ones. The role of non-conscious brain processes in choice matters to marketers for the very simple reason that the simplest (and best) definition of marketing I have been able to come up with is, "Marketing is the creation, management, and measurement of programs designed to influence the choices you need people to make to meet your objectives." It seems a statement of the obvious, but marketers need to know as much as they can about how choices are made in order to influence them.

When I interviewed Dan Ariely at the 2010 Society of Judgment and Decision Making Conference in St. Louis, Missouri, he was puzzled by marketers' lack of attention to what was being learned about behavior and choice:

> ...for academics, it's a little frustrating. We've been working for a long time, generating a lot of data, and nobody's using it.... The idea that there will start to be more systematic use of this base of data is actually quite exciting.

Marketing has started to change how it approaches findings from academics studying decision science in the last five years, and a lot of the credit for that must go to Ariely. He has been an evangelist for Behavioral Economics—his books make the area accessible, and he was the impetus behind a free online study program with Coursera that was popular in advertising agencies (our entire strategic planning department in London and many of our planners around the world took the course).

I think a number of very good reasons exist for why decision science isn't having more than a surface effect on marketing practices. Some of these reasons are rooted deep in human nature. (We marketers, lest we forget, are as human as anyone else, and a cognitive mechanism called *status quo bias* that we will talk about in Chapter 8, "Loss and Ownership," is very likely to have a lot to do with this.)

One reason is that the science is big, complex, often vague, and frequently contradictory, and is lacking a framework that helps translate basic science findings to marketing applications. It also doesn't help itself with impenetrable terms and jargon. Decision science appears to hide the keys to consumer decision-making out of the reach of marketing practitioners in the mysterious black box of the brain's "subconscious," and it's kind of scary in there. We may have Freud to blame for this. Most of us marketers who aren't versed in modern psychology may still use Freud's (and Jung's) ideas and accompanying language when thinking and discussing the mysteries of the non-conscious mind. Freud's explanations suggested the "subconscious" as the seat of emotions and irrationality, almost as a separate persona to the conscious, rational self. Today, psychologists see conscious and non-conscious processes as working hand in hand—even if, as Kahneman says, the (unconscious system) "is the secret author of many of our choices."

A second reason decision science has not had more of an impact on marketing is that translating decision science into marketing practice requires time. Some of what has been learned and leaned on in marketing needs to be unlearned. New approaches need to be experimented with, and this involves risk in addition to time. Shorter tenures of Chief Marketing Officers[8] and marketing teams combined with a demand for short term results mean that the success of a marketing program is these days often measured by proxies that are not necessarily indicators of the actual behavioral shifts required. In most companies, fixing longer-term problems or developing fundamentally new approaches isn't going to help anyone keep their job or get their bonus. But just as the organizations that use digital marketing best are ones that started experimenting with small digital budgets when the Internet was in its infancy (and did similarly with mobile in its early days) progressive marketers might be wise to try out behaviorally based approaches on small projects to introduce new thinking and ideas that science has revealed.

In some cases marketers doggedly hold on to the view shared by rational economists that people make decisions based on expected utility. To some extent, this feeling that choice is rational is almost inevitable, as we as marketers try to rationally untangle how people choose. As Duncan Watts says in *Everything is Obvious: *Once You Know the Answer,*

> When we think about how we (humans) think, we reflexively adopt a framework of rational behavior

Also, research that asks people what they want, and what messages will persuade them to buy may lead them to report being more swayed by rational information than they in fact are. This, in turn, can lead marketers to believe their assumptions about their potential choosers being persuaded by rationality are correct (we'll cover some solid reasons why such research may be misleading in Chapter 15, "Think Differently About Market Research"). In a world where hard and precise data are promising to bring an unsurpassed level of exactitude to marketing decisions, the thinking and language of social and behavioral sciences can seem squirrely, although that is to ignore that most experiments from these fields are backed by robust and peer-reviewed data before publication.

At the opposite end of the spectrum some marketers (especially in categories that are felt to be more creative, more emotional, or more intuitive) may be concerned that application of knowledge from decision science

---

[8] The average tenure of a CMO is just 45 months, according to a 2014 study by executive recruiting firm Spencer Stuart.

may lead to an impersonal formula, or "marketing by numbers," making it a less creative discipline. I believe this is not only avoidable, but that, by and large, what we are learning from science suggests that we put a greater premium on creative thinking in marketing. For an amusing look at what creativity by numbers may look like, try to get hold of a copy of *Painting by Numbers: Komar & Melamid's Scientific Guide to Art.*[9] These two Russian artists polled thousands of people worldwide on what they wanted or didn't want in paintings, and then used the data from that quantitative research as the basis for a series of paintings that represented *The People's Choice.* The ironically intentional bad art (or is it, because of the irony, good art?) is a visual demonstration of taking research literally.

Ethics are also a concern. The advertising business incurred the wrath of consumer advocates and regulators in the 1950s in the wake of subliminal advertising experiments (which subsequently turned out to be bogus[10]). As a result of the furor and an enduring superstition, advertising and marketing practitioners are concerned about being seen as "hidden persuaders" and manipulators of the unconscious.

Ethics should always be front of mind in marketing (and particularly in the much-maligned business of advertising[11]), and practitioners need to think carefully about whether they are erring from persuasion to deception, or from leading the chooser's cognitive mechanisms to misleading them. As always, just as in the cases of product claims and responsible marketing, the integrity of the individuals and the companies who employ them, be they marketing companies or agencies, will be critical in this. But I think it is highly likely that regulatory bodies in a number of countries will develop a

---

[9] From *Library Journal* "the Russian emigre art collaborators Komar and Melamid began a statistical market research poll to determine America's 'most wanted' and 'most unwanted' paintings. Since then, the whimsical project has spread around the world. Polls in the United States, Ukraine, France, Iceland, Turkey, Denmark, Finland, Kenya, and China revealed that people wanted portraits of their families and always 'blue landscapes.' After conducting research, the pair painted made-to-order works that meet the wanted (landscape) and unwanted (abstract) criteria."

[10] The story of James Vicary's fraudulent experiments from the 1950s is covered in Douglas Van Praet's excellent book *Unconscious Branding.*

[11] Advertising has often been seen as an untrustworthy profession populated by unscrupulous scam artists. One apocryphal story tells of a British adman, who, when asked the question, "What is your view on ethics in advertising" replied, "Ethics? I thought that was a county east of London" (the county to the east of London, is of course, Essex).

code of conduct that covers approaches to marketing inspired by behavioral science.[12]

A related view is that accepting non-conscious processes drive so much of our decision-making demeans the human spirit and flies in the face of free will and self-determination.

The preceding concerns are all valid in different ways, but I think that they come, by and large, from a misconception of decision-making science and what it reveals. Rather than thinking of non-conscious processes as a capricious driver of irrational behavior or as something that allows us to get suckered into bad decisions, these processes—refined over years of evolution—allow us to make intuitive, quick, effective, and in the majority of cases, successful decisions. Marketers should use this knowledge for the latter, rather than for the former.

Marketing that uses a scientific understanding of human nature to either guide people toward a choice that is beneficial for the marketer and the chooser or that makes a trivial choice quick and intuitive, thus saving the chooser time and stress, is to my mind not just ethical marketing, but desirable marketing.

The takeaways from this chapter are

- It is now accepted by most experts that most of our choices are non-conscious, or intuitive. Remember that the role of rational thinking is largely for post-rationalization. Focus less how you want people to *think* and more how you want them to *feel*.

- Become a student again. At the back of this book you will find a list of books, blogs, and conferences that will help you keep abreast of how science is informing what we know about how people choose. Our blogs at thebusinessofchoice.com and instituteofdecison making.com are sources of the things that we find interesting.

- Find ways to experiment. Set aside a small percentage of your marketing budget to try behavioral approaches.

---

[12] This has already happened to some extent. The 1906 Kellogg ad that I mention in the next chapter used the principle of scarcity, but suggested an artificial shortage, which is now considered illegal in a number of countries. Also, there is an active debate about the uses of nudges, their legality, and to what extent they should be used and disclosed in public policy. See "Nudging legally: On the checks and balances of behavioral regulation," by Alberto Alemanno and Alessandro Spina, *International Journal of Constitutional Law* (2014).

What this chapter made other people think:

- "I think marketers have over-indexed on strategies and techniques based on what is visible and more easily measurable, and now we're starting to grasp how much these invisible, preconscious, and implicit human behavior traits determine every decision we make."

- "The application of science to marketing is more art than science. Determining what will work how and when (i.e., what message will elicit which cognitive mechanism) cannot be reduced to a formula and will always require talent and creativity."

3

The Natural History of Choice

The choices humans make today are driven by our evolutionary history, or human nature.

There's an opening line I've used at a number of technology conferences where I've been a speaker; it has never really had the effect I'm going for, but for some reason I persist in using it—a bit like an uncle who always tells the same joke even though no one ever laughs at it. The line is this: "Most of the people talking at this conference are here to tell you about what will happen in the next six months. I'm here to remind you what has happened in the last six million years."

While I may need to find a better way of saying it, there is a truth in it. We can only really hope to get close to guessing what will happen in the next six months when we truly understand human nature, which is the product of what has happened in the last six million years.

Five to six million years ago is when, according to a range of experts, a hominid brain emerged that can be seen as a direct ancestor to today's human brain. The hominid brain was when the foundations of today's decision-making system were laid. Five to six million years ago is when the decision-making systems started to develop that we use now to select one toothpaste over another, to choose to order fries with our burger, and whether to put a financial windfall into our savings account or to buy an iPhone 6.

So just how similar are these foundations to our brain today? A couple of years ago as part of background research for a talk I was to give at Adtech London, an interactive marketing and technology conference, I spoke with Dean Falk about the evolution of the human brain. She is a biological anthropologist who specializes in paleoanthropology and is famous for providing evidence that a small human-like fossil, found in 2003 on the Indonesian island of Flores (dubbed "Hobbit" by the popular press and *homo floresiensis* by scientists) was not from a deformed modern human but an entirely new species.[1]

One of the questions I asked Falk was how our brains and decision-making systems have changed, since, say, sometime as long ago as five or ten thousand years? The time of the ancient Egyptians or even the birth of civilization? Her answer was, "In terms of human brain evolution, that is essentially today."

This ancient nature of the brain was absorbed into popular culture in the 1970s through Carl Sagan's book *The Dragons of Eden* that made Paul Maclean's *triune brain theory* famous. Triune means "three in one," and the theory proposes that we have three separate brain structures that developed during different stages of animal evolution. The oldest, the so-called reptilian brain, captured the popular imagination as the "lizard brain." The triune brain theory[2] is now largely discredited, but there is certainly some truth in the idea that the most highly conserved parts of our brain—the brain structures whose lineage dates to before the existence of humans—have an evolutionary history of as much as 500 million years.

For my purposes in this book, the five or six million-year mark is more relevant. The very primitive parts of the brain are associated with controlling *autonomic* functions, such as heart rate, breathing, and body temperature. The parts of the brain that regulate how people make the choices that marketers battle to influence evolved much later, with the emergence of our genus, the hominids.

When I run workshops, I use the information in Table 3.1, which puts brain history in a modern day context.

---

[1] Dean Falk is the Hale G. Smith Professor of Anthropology at Florida State University and author of *The Fossil Chronicles: How Two Controversial Discoveries Changed Our View of Human Evolution*, a book about the discovery and debate around the *homo floresiensis* fossils and the Taung Child fossils (discovered nearly a century earlier).

[2] MacLean, P.D. *The Triune Brain in Evolution: Role in Paleocerebral Functions.* Springer, 1990.

Table 3.1 Hominid Brains Have Been Evolving for 5–6 Million Years

The % of that time	Before...
97%	Homo Sapiens emerges
99.9%	Ancient Egypt founded
99.99%	Columbus sets sail
99.999%	WW2 starts
99.9999%	Launch of first iPhone

Now, this is not to say that our brains are concrete cast replicas of our Stone Age ancestors. Your brain and my brain have a remarkable ability to change in many ways, through a process called *plasticity*. Brain plasticity is also known as cortical remapping and is the biological mechanism underlying learning and the formation of memories. The brain is especially plastic in youth but plasticity is not limited to that period of development. Sometimes after traumatic brain injuries, people recover cognitive functions. After injury, the brain can sometimes rewire itself, and other brain areas can step in and perform the functions previously carried out by damaged areas.

Plasticity is often studied in animals, but in 2000, researchers at University College London demonstrated plasticity in the adult human brain, using licensed London taxi drivers—the ones who drive the famous black cabs.[3] The researchers, led by Eleanor Maguire, focused on changes in the size of the hippocampus in taxi drivers. The hippocampus is an area of the brain that is crucial for memory formation and in particular for spatial memory. (It's not just London taxi drivers who rely on spatial memory. Animals rely heavily on spatial memory, and birds that cache food, like chickadees and their Eurasian counterparts tits, or migratory birds have larger hippocampal regions than birds that don't exhibit these behaviors.[4]) Maguire and her collaborators studied licensed London taxi drivers because of the arduous training, known as "The Knowledge," where drivers have to learn 320 routes, 25,000 streets, and 20,000 landmarks in and around central London.

---

[3] Maguire, E.A., Gadian, D.G., Johnsrude, I.S., Good, C.D., Ashburner, J., Frackowiak, R.S.J., Frith, C.D. (2000) "Navigation-related structural change in the hippocampi of taxi drivers." *PNAS* April.

[4] Pravosudov, V.V., Kitaysky, A.S., and Omanska, A. (2006) "The relationship between migratory behaviour, memory and the hippocampus: an intraspecific comparison." *Proc. Biol. Sci.* 273(1601): 2641–2649.

Using functional magnetic resonance imaging (fMRI), a technique that measures brain activity by mapping changes in blood flow and something we will talk much more about later in the book, the researchers measured the size of the hippocampus in taxi drivers. Drivers were classified into two groups: those with substantial experience driving around London and a control group of drivers who had not spent as much time navigating the city. The size of the hippocampus varied linearly according to the drivers' experience; drivers with more experience had larger hippocampal regions.

In an interview with the BBC just after the research was published, Maguire said, "There seems to be a definite relationship between the navigating they do as a taxi driver and the brain changes. The hippocampus has changed its structure to accommodate their huge amount of navigating experience."

Our brains can rewire themselves and increase or decrease the size of certain structures depending on our life experiences, as the taxi driver study illustrates.

You don't have to recover from injury or be a taxi driver in London to experience brain plasticity. Everyday life (even playing video games) can rewire our brains.

Separate studies conducted over a five-year period at the University of Rochester and the University of Toronto shows that playing video games can lead to improved visual acuity and attention. Participants in these studies played first-person shooter (FPS) games, which are a visually demanding genre of video games where you have to seek out and shoot your opponents before they shoot you, and puzzle games like *Tetris*.[5, 6] People who played FPS games showed more improvement at visual tasks than those who played *Tetris*. Further, measures of the brain's electrical activity suggested that playing FPS games modified the neural computations underlying how visual attention is allocated, or where and when you decide to look.

Brain changes at an individual level shouldn't be confused with an evolutionary re-engineering of our innate decision-making systems. A good analogy for what happens when our brains undergo plastic changes as a result of certain experiences is our physique—we can develop brawn by

[5] Green, C.S., Bavelier, D. (2007) "Action-video-game experience alters the spatial resolution of vision." *Psychol Sci* 18: 88–94.

[6] Wu, S., Cheng, C.K., Feng, J., D'Angelo, L., Alain, C., Spence, I. (2012) "Playing a first-person shooter video game induces neuroplastic change." *J Cogn Neurosci* 24: 1286–93.

lifting heavy weights. Athletes can make quite remarkable changes to their body and their performance by shifting mass from one area to another through reducing fat levels and building muscle or the sharpening of their reflexes, respectively. (However, my inability to shift mass from my midriff might be a strike against any theory of body plasticity....) In spite of these changes to the athlete's body, the critical life-supporting functions of the body (like circulation, respiration, and digestion, for example) work in pretty much the same way since Falk's "essentially today" of ancient Egypt and even for many tens of thousands of years before that. So do the cognitive systems that drive our decision-making.

These decision-making systems really are like the life-supporting functions our body carries out. Fully opposable thumbs evolved because they gave us the capability to successfully perform tasks that emerged as critical to our survival and success as a species, such as making and using tools; thumbs still determine how we hold and use things today. There is little difference between how I gripped the handle of a hammer that I used to beat down some loose nails on our shingled siding last weekend and how my ancestor *Homo Erectus* might have grasped a tool a million or so years ago. Likewise, our cognitive systems evolved to help us make choices that were equally critical to our survival. These cognitive functions comprise the mental toolbox that determines how we make choices today. I give these cognitive functions a thumbs up; they've served us pretty well.

While we are on the subject of thumbs and plasticity, there is some evidence that, at an individual level, frequent (and recent) use of touch screen smart phones enhances the brain's response to our fingertips touching something. A recent study[7] measured cortical potential (the electrical activity between parts of the cerebral cortex) associated with stimulation of the tactile receptors on fingertips amongst touch screen smartphone users and non-users (people who owned older technology phones). When the thumb, index, and middle finger were touched mechanically, the researchers saw enhanced cortical potential among the touch screen smartphone users versus those using flip phones and the like.

There are a couple of important points to be made here. What the touch screen study, the video game studies, and the taxi-driver research I've referenced in this chapter show is that our individual brains adapt to handle

---

[7] Gindrat, A-D., Chytiris, M., Balerna, M., Rouiller, E.M., Ghosh, A. (2014) "Use-Dependent Cortical Processing from Fingertips in Touchscreen Phone Users." *Current Biology* Dec.

different or new tasks and activities. First, there is not much evidence of the lasting effects of these adaptations if the activity they accommodate is neglected. As many of us will know, muscle mass and strength can be built by frequent weight training. But if you are too busy to get to the gym for a couple of weeks, you may find yourself struggling on your third set of repetitions in a way that you didn't when you were working out frequently. The second is that these individual adaptations should in no way be confused with brain evolution. The children of the taxi drivers who have developed bigger hippocampi, the video gamers who have enhanced their visual acuity, and the smartphone users whose fingertip use has led to greater cortical activity will not biologically inherit their parents' adaptations. Giraffes don't have long necks because their forebears stretched their necks reaching for leaves on trees.[8] Giraffes have long necks because those in the population that had slightly longer necks could reach an additional source of leaves, survived, and reproduced in disproportionate numbers to those without this characteristic.

If at this point you are thinking, "I didn't buy this book to read about why giraffes have long necks," first I want to reassure you that we are nearly done with giraffes, and second, I want to thank you for your patience. Just as a giraffe's neck defines how a giraffe lives day to day, so do the decision-making systems we have inherited from a long line of successful ancestors define how we go about our lives everyday. Although understanding how our brains and behaviors change through technology or what is happening in culture is helpful to marketers, it overlooks the elephant in the room (I won't get into the story of the evolution of the elephant's elongated proboscis, though it is, of course, similar to that of the giraffe's neck): It is as important—or, I would say, more important—to understand the underlying aspects of behavior that allow for these individual adaptions. Understanding human nature is critical to influencing and guiding people's choices.

Congratulations for Being Part of Our Successful Team!

You know those new employee orientation manuals that tell you how great the company you have just joined is? Well, if there were one for the human race, it might remind you that you are part of the most successful animal

---

[8] This is how an early evolutionary theorist, Jean Baptiste Lamarck, explained giraffes' long necks through the *Theory of Inheritance of Acquired Characteristics*.

species in the history of life on this planet. That this success isn't just a flash in the pan, and has been sustained since we became the dominant hominid around 60,000 years ago, which is, even in the slow pulse of natural history, a significant amount of time. That competitively we are atop a pile of tens of thousands of vertebrate species that we share the planet with today. And that this is just a fraction of the total number of species we have shared the planet with—but that are no longer with us—that either fell victim to our dominance, or to hostile conditions that we, somehow, survived. Humans succeeded where beasts that were bigger, faster, or stronger failed. We reign over creatures that can fly thousands of miles in migration, can create millions of offspring versus our handful, that can see us, smell us, or hear us hundreds, and in some cases thousands of yards, before we are aware of them.

If species survival were a competitive sport, we humans would be celebrating as if we had won the World Cup, the World Series, the Super Bowl, and swept every gold medal at the summer and winter Olympics. If we had a management off-site, after the mutual back-slapping and individually contemplating what we are going to do with our bonuses, then we might start to think about the best practices that got us so far to work out how to continue our success and face the challenges that are inevitably ahead of any winners.

Over the long journey that has brought us to where we humans are now, I sometimes wonder what we might identify as our success factors. Opposable thumbs come up a lot, as do large brains and the very human trait of curiosity. But the most significant, in my view, is the array of intuitions or instincts that drive our choices.

Understanding the ingrained tendencies that have allowed us to survive and thrive isn't only important to us as individuals and as a species. It is also important for businesses and in particular, brands. Brands succeed when they are aligned to human nature and innate behaviors. The factors that have made humans successful are mirrored in all successful brands, and the more successful, and more sustained that success, the more evident these factors are.

Some brands do it unwittingly. Some do it wittingly. Later in the book I'll discuss how Apple doesn't just provide an intuitive user experience, but makes its brand and products intuitively easy to choose. I'll also discuss how one of Coke's most significant marketing programs used innate behaviors to make the beverage universally appealing and how another approach used innate behaviors to make each can of Coke feel deeply personal.

So, what factors have driven human success? Ultimately, it comes down to one brutally simple concept.

Over the long haul as a species, our ancestors made more good decisions than bad decisions. This idea applies in most cases to individuals as well; in general, we each make more good choices than bad during our lives. Thanks to my ancestors' smart choices I was able to write this book, and thanks to your ancestors' smart choices, you are now reading it. (And hopefully you are not still considering whether that is a smart decision.)

The "long haul" is very long. As I've already discussed, the evolutionary roots of the most primitive parts of our brain go back eons.

Survival, and thus success, is about making the right instinctive choices. Understanding the unconscious motivations that drive decisions, what Douglas Kenrick and Vladas Griskevicius outline in their book *The Rational Animal* as our seven evolutionary goals, is critical for any brand's success.

Evolutionary psychologists like Kenrick and Griskevicius describe natural selection as a gradual process by which biological traits—just like the giraffe's neck—become more or less common in a population depending on their contribution to a species' survival. You could argue that one of the most significant contributors to humans surviving, and thriving, has been the cognitive mechanisms underlying our choices.

For humans, these mechanisms are often shortcuts. Decision-making is computationally taxing in terms of cognitive load. So the brain has developed ways to reach choices in an efficient manner and in a very short time. These cognitive shortcuts are the basis of human intuition (your and my gut reactions) and include special rules called heuristics, which I discuss in the next chapter. These biases developed to help us make choices that gave us an advantage during our life on the savannah. They may not always do the same in the quantifiable, immediately gratifying, distance-collapsed digital world of present day.

The human brain is very good at filtering information and only processes a portion of incoming sensory information. As I discuss in Part II of this book, an apt description of the human brain is an "ignoring machine." Cognitive mechanisms underlying our choices are no different than sensory processes; the brain sifts through information, only using a fraction of what is seen, heard, felt, or smelled to reach a decision. Some mechanisms underlying choice are labeled *cognitive biases* because, in the modern world, they often lead to seemingly irrational decisions. Although construing cognitive biases as human shortcomings or design flaws is possible, Kenrick and Griskevicius choose to see them in a positive light, as design features. Over the course of our natural history, these design features have served humans well, leading us to intuitively filter, or, as German psychologist and champion of heuristics, Gerd Gigerenzer says, ignore most incoming information and be most affected by information that is important to human success.

As well as making these shortcuts drive our decisions so quickly that they are difficult—and often impossible—to override, evolution has another way of enforcing its sway. We feel pain, anxiety, and discomfort when decisions don't feel right. We feel pleasure and excitement or peace when they do feel right. Understanding how to construct your marketing so that it can allow people to reach effortless decisions that leave them feeling good can provide a significant competitive edge to businesses. It will improve the chances of your brand being favored by the processes we have inherited through natural selection and therefore increase the likelihood of its being naturally selected by the people you want to choose it.

Human Nature (Sometimes) Comes Naturally to Marketers

It's very clear that many marketers, creatives, and planners in advertising agencies have an intuitive feel for how instinctual, non-conscious processes affect decision-making. Many good examples from the archives of advertising exist that use behavioral principles and would make you think that the practitioners' intuitive grasp of human nature has been ahead of the scientists' understanding at times.

In 1906, W.K. Kellogg ran one of his first ads, for Sanitas corn flakes. The ad informed readers of the *Ladies Home Journal* that an adequate quantity of Sanitas corn flakes could not be produced and they should ask their grocers to act now to ensure an adequate supply. This ad relies on *scarcity,* a principle that Robert Cialdini believes to be one of the most instinctual levers of influence.

British Airway's 1989 blockbuster ad "Faces," created by Saatchi & Saatchi and directed by Hugh Hudson, used the *bandwagon effect* exquisitely, by artfully giving a sense of the hundreds of thousands of people who flew British Airways, making it, at the time as their tagline reinforced, *The World's Favorite Airline.* More recently, the "Mac vs. PC" commercials (where a cool and hip Justin Long as a Mac converses with a dweeby-looking John

Hodgman as a PC) used our innate reliance on using points of reference to make decisions, in a very cultured way.

If you look closely enough at any great piece of advertising or marketing, you can probably find a behavioral principle from decision science lurking inside it. The best creative directors—though they may deny it—have more than a touch of the behavioral scientist about them.

The most innovative marketing ideas are celebrated every year at the Cannes Lions International Festival of Creativity, and the very best are awarded a coveted Cannes Lion. Perhaps there should be an award category for those that best use the insights into instinctual human behavior that have been revealed by science.[9]

The takeaways from this chapter are

- The brain that guides our decisions today has its roots in the brains of hominids that lived five or six million years ago. Human nature has a very long history, and isn't changing anytime soon!

- Our decision-making systems have helped humans make the choices that have let us survive and thrive as a species. When thinking about how to get your brand chosen, remember to align it to human nature, and how humans have evolved to choose.

- The best marketing and advertising have hooks that appeal to human nature. Think about this and try to identify them when you see ads you like. How are you incorporating an understanding of human nature in your own marketing?

How this chapter made other people feel:

- "As marketers we are so wrapped up in the minutiae of the day-to-day competitive bustle that we rarely get our heads up enough to think about the deep human truths that have driven behavior not just over years and generations, but for millions of years. Get that right for your brand and the chances are you will be tapping into something truly fundamental."

- "Now I can say, despite what many might think, I am the result of a long line of good decisions!"

---

[9] The Instinctual Lion?

PART II
Getting Practical Today

4

Shortcuts Versus Analysis—
Ignoring Is Decisional Bliss

Heuristics and cognitive biases affect people's choices.

In his book, *Gut Feelings: The Intelligence of the Unconscious*, Gerd Gigerenzer, who is the director of Berlin's Max Planck Institute for Human Development, writes about how ignoring information has been a highly efficient and quick decision-making strategy for humans, be it conscious or non-conscious. It seems as if the human brain is as much an efficient "ignoring machine" as it is a noticing one. What the brain does is less about deciding where to allocate our attention, but instead is more about working out what won't be ignored.

Let me give you a personal example showing how the brain can help by ignoring information. I am an atrociously bad golfer—possibly because I only play about once every five years, though I suspect it is something more than just playing frequency. Normally when I play, I'm in a foursome with three people who play more frequently than I do and are much better golfers than me. After the first couple of holes (following slices from the tee, shots from the fairway that have less desire to become airborne than an aviophobe, and putts that go further beyond the hole than the entire distance of many of the shots that preceded them), the advice starts coming in.

There is an illustration that appears on many golfing sites that captures this scene perfectly. It shows a golfer addressing a ball on a tee. He is poised to swing and is completely surrounded by a hundred or more pieces of advice as to how he should execute his shot. (I think I've heard all of them.) The advice includes gems like the following:

- Grip the club as though it were a baby bird.
- Count to three at the top of your swing.

- ☒ Left heel down for control.
- ☒ Flex your knees.
- ☒ Shift your weight from right foot to left foot.
- ☒ One-piece takeaway.
- ☒ Cock your wrists.
- ☒ Breathe out as you swing down.
- ☒ Finish with your chest facing the target.

With just a touch of irony, the last piece of advice says, "Have fun!" The real point, made in a caption at the bottom of the illustration is that the golfer has to factor all of this advice in "1.5 seconds of thought," or the amount of time it takes for the brain to plan the movement and for the body to actually swing the golf club.

All this wealth of advice does is make me shank, slice, or hook the ball, or whiff and miss it completely. Trying to deliberately execute my golf swing (which is a very complex movement[1]) while factoring in the new information about how to improve my technique is at odds with how humans go about their daily business. Yet, if I focus on just one thing (that one thing that seems to work best for me is to keep my gaze rooted on where the ball is on the ground, and to resist the temptation to look up at where I think the ball may be heading as I swing through it) and ignore everything else, I play something that at least starts to resemble golf.

Although we often like to think of our brains as super computers,[2] calculating and recalculating the trigonometry of angles or the calculus of velocity (or even simple probabilities), human brains don't actually work like that. Much to our second grade teacher's chagrin, rather than doing long division, the brain takes short cuts, by zeroing in on one piece of information and ignoring pretty much everything else.

In his book *On Second Thought: Outsmarting your Mind's Hard-Wired Habits*, Wray Herbert writes about the brain's shortcuts:

---

[1] It's a complex movement for humans, using at least six muscle groups. My awkward efforts are particularly complex in terms of biomechanics.

[2] Christian Jarrett's *Great Myths of the Brain* goes into the pros and cons of this frequently used analogy. Although there are some similarities (both receive information, process it, respond with outputs; both store information in two ways—as short term/quick retrieval and long-term/slower retrieval memory), brains and computers work in quite different ways.

Our lives are composed of millions of choices, ranging from trivial to life changing and momentous. Luckily, our brains have evolved a number of mental shortcuts, biases, and tricks that allow us to quickly negotiate this endless array of decisions. We don't *want* to rationally deliberate every choice we make, and thanks to these cognitive rules of thumb, we don't need to.

Behavioral psychologists call these shortcuts *heuristics*. This term can be a little confusing to people involved in website and other digital design as it is also used by user experience (UX) designers to mean the broad rules of thumb that interface design should follow.[3]

A great example of a heuristic, and one that Gigerenzer uses frequently, is how we intercept an object that is flying through the air (such as a fly ball in baseball). It was long thought that the brain calculated all the variables (spin, air resistance, wind, and velocity, to name a few) and then iteratively and rapidly solved complex equations in the manner of a supercomputer.

Gigerenzer writes in *Gut Feelings* about how what we actually do couldn't be further away from solving complex calculations. Research that tracked athletes' gazes when they attempted to catch fly balls showed that they followed a very simple process,[4] which Gigerenzer calls the "gaze heuristic":

> When a ball comes in high, the player fixates the ball and starts running. The heuristic is to adjust the running speed so that the angle of gaze remains constant—that is, the angle between the eye and the ball. The player can ignore all the information necessary to compute the trajectory, such as the ball's initial velocity, distance, and angle, and just focus on one piece of information, the angle of gaze.

> By paying attention to only one variable, the player will end up where the ball comes down without computing the exact spot.

---

[3] "10 Usability Heuristics for User Interface Design" were developed by Jakob Nielsen and Rolf Molich in the 1990s. Nielsen (often called "the guru of web page usability") describes them as follows: "The 10 most general principles for interaction design...they are called 'heuristics' because they are more in the nature of rules of thumb than specific usability guidelines."

[4] McBeath, M.K., Shaffer, D.M., Kaiser, M.K. (1995) "How baseball outfielders determine where to run to catch fly balls." *Science*, April, 268 (5210): 569–573.

The gaze heuristic is a good example of how people's behavior[5] and decisions aren't driven by a rational analysis of facts. There's a very good reason for this, which is that for most of human history, by the time we had reached a decision based on rational analysis the opportunity would have eluded us or the threat would have killed us. The shortcuts we use are not just quick, they are also very efficient in terms of cognitive load. And efficiency is important, because while our brain is only just 2% of our body mass, it requires about 20% of our calorie and oxygen intake. A brain that used less efficient processes (such as detailed analysis) and that could still guide our decisions as quickly would both increase our requirements for oxygen and calories, and would require a bigger housing. The latter point would be particularly problematic, because of the difficulty babies with larger skulls would have passing through their mother's narrow bi-pedal pelvis. That human babies are *altricial*, or born relatively helpless, is likely an evolutionary solution to the tradeoff between the evolutionary value of our already big brains and of walking upright.[6]

Humans survived and evolved by making quick decisions, which worked out well for us more often than they didn't. By making good and efficient choices, our ancestors lived long enough to reproduce, and we inherited their innate decision-making capacities.

In order to make these quick decisions, we developed efficient cognitive processes, like the gaze heuristic, and these processes operate at the speed of neurons firing. Just as we jump when startled, these neural processes kick in before we can consciously consider action. It is not that these processes are sinisterly "subconscious," but more that they are "preconscious," because their job is to operate at a speed quicker than conscious thought.

We seldom realize we are using them, and when asked directly we often post-rationalize our decisions. If you ever feel indecisive (and who doesn't?) it is probably because these shortcuts are being subverted in some way.

---

[5] It's also used by predatory birds such as falcons to zero in on their prey, and according to research by McBeath and Shaffer, by dogs to catch Frisbees.

[6] Another trade-off is the evolution of "soft spots" and sutures in the skulls of baby hominids, allowing for the skull to expand after passing through the constraint of the birth canal and thus accommodating the rapid growth of the infant's brain after birth. This feature—which comes at the cost of some vulnerability—is found in humans and was found in other hominids, but it is not found in our relatives the apes. Expandable and delicate has worked for our evolutionary development; fixed and robust has worked for theirs.

When a decision feels good, it is because these shortcuts are giving it their instant approval, making the decision as smooth as a gear change on a well-tuned and lubricated bicycle. When this happens, the decision seems "intuitively right" and we make it more quickly and feel better about it.

In addition to heuristics, there are around 100 processes and shortcuts known as *cognitive biases*, which we touched on in the last chapter. Most of these have been discovered by behavioral scientists during the last 50 years. The difference between a heuristic and cognitive bias is subtle. Heuristics are rules of thumb we instinctively follow; heuristics require us to ignore many factors and base our decision on one key factor. Cognitive biases happen when focusing on one factor leads to seemingly irrational decisions.

My personal (and non-scientific) way of thinking about cognitive biases is that they are basically heuristics that lead us to sometimes fall short of what, from a rational perspective, appears to be the optimal choice in the modern world.

Some cognitive biases sound like they were named in the throes of a drinking game—*the Texas sharpshooter fallacy* is one of my favorites. It describes the human tendency to focus on a small subset of a larger pool of data and see patterns that wouldn't appear if you considered the larger set as a whole. *The Texas sharpshooter fallacy* gets its name from a joke about a rifleman in Texas who has been firing shot after shot at his barn, and then circles the area where the most holes are, declaring that the target.

Jodi Beggs, a lecturer in economics at Northeastern University, runs the economics section on the website about.com and also hosts a blog called *Economists Do It With Models.* She recently authored an amusing paper on how the bad decisions the characters in *The Simpsons* make week after week can be attributed to cognitive biases.[7] Not surprisingly, Homer Simpson is the star in this respect, but we see Marge, Bart, Lisa, Millhouse, and even Mr. Burns falling foul of their instincts.

While the names of many cognitive biases are very modern (for example, the *IKEA effect* is a bias that leads us to put a disproportionately high value on things we have invested effort in making), all of these brain mechanisms have their basis in evolution. Like anything that evolution has bestowed on

---

[7] Beggs, Jodi N. "Homer Economicus or Homer Sapiens? Behavioral Economics in *The Simpsons*." Economists Do It With Models website, http://www.economists-doitwithmodels.com/files/Simpsons.pdf. May 2011.

us, some biases remain critical whereas others seem to have less relevance to modern life.

If you were designing "human 2.0" for the 21st century and beyond, you might choose to drop features like toenails, wisdom teeth, or male nipples. And you might want to do some housekeeping on our inventory of cognitive mechanisms while you were at it.

However, artifacts or not, these brain processes drive our choices, big and small. A number of scientists estimate that 90%–95% of our decision-making is pre-conscious, or intuitive.

As marketers we should think of heuristics and cognitive biases not as some profound philosophy or complex psychology, but simply as *insights into human nature*. They are the bedrock upon which humans intuitively make choices.

Of the near hundred heuristics and biases, some are highly relevant to marketers, others less so. Some seem to overlap and blur. Others seem very specific to very specialized areas. Part II of this book addresses what I think are the most important heuristics and biases for business. I package them in ways that relate less to their scientific descriptions and relationships and more to how they can be applied to the practical business of marketing: the business of how people choose.

The takeaways from this chapter are

- Think less about being noticed and more about not being ignored. What might you be able to communicate that from an instinctual perspective is difficult to ignore?

- The bedrock of human decision making is cognitive shortcuts called heuristics and cognitive biases. The more you understand these, the more you will understand how people reach the choices they make.

- Our brain has developed these cognitive shortcuts to help us make very quick decisions that don't use much energy. That's why we love "no brainers." If you can make choosing your brand a "no brainer," you are ahead of the game.

What other people thought when they read this chapter:

- "In the consumer packaged goods world, we often spend years crafting the most compelling, logical reasons our product is tastier, healthier, better than the three other brands on the shelf, assuming our consumer carefully considers all twenty items in their cart. In this chapter, we're reminded of the real task—make the decision to choose us easy, instinctual."

- "Reading this made me remember that in marketing (and perhaps in most cases where humans are involved), 'feeling right' trumps 'being right.'"

5

Getting Familiar

Familiarity is so important for brands—learn how you can make it work for yours.

F ew marketers would argue that a brand being familiar wasn't a good thing. And they'd be right. While it is not the only requirement for a brand to be chosen, feeling familiar—being recognized, being top of mind, or being salient—is critical for success.

Being top of mind correlates directly with brand share; we know this from years of tracking studies. Generally, the brands that people know best are the ones that people feel perform better in all the attributes important in their category—they are more trusted and are felt to be more reliable, to work better, and to be a better value.

While it's accepted that familiarity is a good thing, it's worth asking why.

Robert Zajonc, a giant in the field of social psychology, would explain this from the perspective of human evolution by saying, "If it is familiar, it has not eaten you...yet."

As our prehistoric ancestors navigated the hazardous savannah, the animals that they were lucky enough to encounter more than once were less dangerous. The ones they encountered over and over, by definition, were those most unlikely to cause them harm. Familiarity was a proxy for safety, and today, this proxy remains with us as an intuition.

Zajonc's research shows that familiarity communicates safety and other generally good things. His most famous work is a series of experiments that demonstrated what became known as "The Mere-Exposure Effect." In one of his best-known studies, Zajonc exposed individuals who were unfamiliar with Mandarin to written Chinese characters.[1] People were shown some characters 5 times, some 10 times, and some 25 times. Participants were told all the Chinese characters were adjectives and at the conclusion of the experiment were asked to guess whether a character had a positive or negative meaning. Even though the characters were meaningless to the participants, people consistently felt that the characters seen most represented good things.

The key finding of Zajonc's landmark 1968 research and similar studies (hundreds of papers report research showing this effect) is that the more frequently people are exposed to something, the more positive their associations of it are.

When something feels familiar, we feel good about it.

Another study by Zajonc some decades later reveals a further and interesting layer to the mere exposure effect.[2] In this experiment, one group of participants was given one exposure to 25 different written Mandarin characters. A second group was only shown five characters, but each character appeared five times. The group who had multiple exposures to the symbols reported experiencing better moods than those who had limited exposures to each character.

This finding about mood is interesting for brands and marketers. Familiarity with something doesn't just make us feel more positive about that particular thing in comparison to something else; it makes us also feel better about ourselves. This may provide some explanation about why brands are so powerful—they are familiar, and familiar things make us feel good. We spend a lot of time being concerned about how people feel about our brands, whereas the real power of a brand may be in how it makes people feel.

And there's more. Familiarity and recognition don't just create positive perceptions and warm and fuzzy feelings. They are the foundation for two of our most powerful and frequently used heuristics, which have a profound influence on our choices. (Remember that heuristics are the cognitive shortcuts I wrote about in the previous chapter.)

---

[1] Zajonc, R. B. (1968) "Attitudinal Effects of Mere Exposure." *Journal of Personality and Social Psychology* 9: 1–27.

[2] Monahan, J.L., Murphy, S.T., and Zajonc, R.B. (2000) "Subliminal mere exposure: specific, general, and diffuse effects." *Psychological Science* 11: 462–466.

The two heuristics are the *availability heuristic*[3] and the *recognition heuristic*,[4] and the scientists behind them (Kahneman and Gigerenzer, respectively) are also the faces of a debate about how heuristics manifest in the brain. As a marketer, I am in a wonderful position of not needing to take a side in the debate, and it is an active debate.[5] I am not looking to prove a point either way, but just to shine a spotlight on how the heuristics relate to human nature, how they influence choice, and how they can be most useful to marketers.

The availability heuristic is driven by what comes to mind most easily and is thought to be an unconscious process, unable to be controlled. The recognition heuristic is a deliberatively applied rule; you choose the familiar, what you recognize. By focusing our cognitive effort on these criteria and ignoring other information, the pre-conscious aspects of our brain processes are able to make remarkably accurate assessments of quite complex choices before our deliberative brain systems even get out of bed. Whatever comes to mind most quickly and with the least effort drives a lot of our decision making. Another way of thinking about the recognition heuristic is as a shortcut our brain takes by focusing only on information that is most *easily available* from our memories; everything else is filtered. This convenient focus on the already familiar is one of the reasons why brand leaders are so difficult to topple. The recognition heuristic is a powerful force that makes us plump for what is most familiar and enables us to ignore other options—most of the time. Using the recognition heuristic allows us to make incredibly quick and intuitive choices that are often as accurate as those arrived at after detailed and rational analyses.

Recognition is a good way of quickly working out the "best" option in many cases. It is certainly a good rule of thumb to use to predict success in sporting competitions. In *Gut Feelings: The Intelligence of the Unconscious,* Gigerenzer references a study from Germany where both amateur tennis players (people who played tennis at a local club) and non-experts (people whose interest in tennis was similar to that of the general population) were asked which names they recognized of the 112 of the players who started

3 Tversky, A., and Kahneman, D. (1974) "Judgment under Uncertainty: Heuristics and Biases." *Science* 185: 1124–1131.

4 Goldstein, D.G., and Gigerenzer, G. (2002) "Models of Ecological Rationality: The Recognition Heuristic." *Psychological Review* 109: 75–90.

5 See Leigh Caldwell's piece here: http://rwconnect.esomar.org/kahneman-bingo-and-gigerenzer-golf/; also see Tim Adam's piece "Nudge economics: has push come to shove for a fashionable theory?" in *The Guardian,* 31 May, 2014.

the Wimbledon Men's single tournament in 2003.[6] This turned out to be a remarkably accurate measure for who would win—players whose names were more recognized by the amateurs beat those less recognized in 72% of the matches; players more recognized by the non-experts beat less recognized names 66% of the time. The recognition scores of these two groups turned out to be as good a predictor of who would win as using the formula that the individual ranked most highly by the Association of Tennis Professionals (ATP) would win. Using two relevant rankings, this approach predicted the winner 66% (ATP Entry Ranking) and 68% (ATP Champions Race) of the time.

Recognition may also have an interesting effect in the selection of luxury goods. In his bestselling book *Spent: Sex, Evolution, and Consumer Behavior,* evolutionary psychologist Geoffrey Miller writes, "...all ads effectively have two audiences: potential product buyers, and potential product viewers who will credit the product owners with various desirable traits. The more expensive and exclusive the product, the more the latter will outnumber the former."

Miller's insightful point is that those who buy luxury goods are buying them more because other people recognize and understand these goods as valuable, than because of any innate qualities of the product.

A number of evolutionary psychologists, including Miller, suggest that luxury goods are markers of sexual selection. The beautiful and rare objects that we prize are really signs to others that they should prize us. But that relies on those others being familiar with these "markers."

Thus, luxury brands will often be visible not just to potential purchasers, but to the wider public, as a large part of their *raison d'être* is to infer status on their aficionados and advocates. Rolex has a level of broad prominence via its celebrity ads and significant presence at golf and tennis tournaments, such as the U.S. Open and Wimbledon, which exceeds its potential user base. Aston Martin's long-term relationship with the James Bond franchise is all about making the brand recognized by people who will never own one, clearly establishing that those who do buy one know they will be sending a strong impression to other people.

---

[6] Serwe, S., Frings, C. (2006) "Who will win Wimbledon? The recognition heuristic in predicting sports events." *Journal of Behavioral Decision Making*, 19: 321–332.

But there is a twist...

Human behavior is full of what seem like contradictions and paradoxes. Behavioral economists often talk about humans, and even individuals, as being inconsistent. It's not just that what we say is different from what we do but that some of our cognitive mechanisms seem to be at odds with each other. I'm often reminded of a comic strip called *The Numskulls*[7] that I enjoyed as a kid. The strip featured a team of "large-headed, thin-limbed homunculi who lived in the head of a central human character known (to them, and us) as 'Our Man.' Each 'section' of the head—Ears, Nose, Mouth, Eyes, Brain—was controlled and maintained by an individual numskull, with the various 'departments' communicating through an intercom system."[8]

The "Brain" was the numskull-in-chief and he managed the differing goals and personalities of the individual numskulls to ensure "Our Man" could navigate his way around the challenges of day-to-day life. It was a full-time job. Our cognitive mechanisms and innate behaviors seem a little like these numskulls. They are all trying to help their man or woman (us) get to the same place (efficient and effective decisions that feel good), but their methods sometimes seem to clash. One good example is the contradictory force of the *primacy effect* (the tendency to weigh initial events more than subsequent events) and that of the *recency effect* (the tendency to weigh recent events more than earlier events).

To me, these apparent contradictions are nothing more than reinforcement of a point I made earlier, which is there are no golden rules for applying decision science to marketing and business. Everything depends on context, and while we don't understand the whole story of how context prompts one cognitive mechanism or another, a key to applying behavioral principles to marketing is to accept that these apparent contradictions exist.

I sometimes explain the apparent contradictions in the following way. Think of how, if you are searching for a small object such as a screw in a dark garage, you might use a flashlight as you peer around, eyes as wide open as they can be. Suddenly, the door opens, and the garage is now flooded with sunlight, making you shield your eyes and squint to continue

---

[7] The great thing about writing a book is what you learn while writing it. I had completely forgotten *The Numskulls* and was delighted to discover that they still exist, published in the comic book *The Beano*.

[8] "Of Free Will and Suggestion Boxes" by John George Byrne, http://www.fustar. info/2006/12/02/193/.

your search. In the first case you are trying to maximize the effect of the light source; in the second you are trying to minimize it. These opposite "strategies" are in service of the same objective—finding the screw—but they kick in depending on the context. Cognitive mechanisms likely work in the same way.

We'll come across a number of these paradoxes as we go through the instinctual aspects of human behavior. One such paradox is that while we are intuitively drawn to familiarity, we are also intuitively drawn to surprise and novelty.

This human trait is why creativity has always been, and will always be, a critical component of marketing. If marketing success could be achieved by simply making your brand familiar, the only strategy we need follow would be to pile our money into the most prominent media vehicles and let the power of familiarity do the rest.

Early last year, I was part of a team reviewing the best of Levi's television advertising over the last 30 years, with Levi's Chief Marketing Officer, Jen Sey. It is a great body of work, created by some of the world's most awarded agencies, when each was at the height of their creative powers. As we paused to take a break from the brilliance (watching a reel of the best of Levi's advertising is probably the closest someone in my profession can get to experiencing the Stendhal syndrome[9]), Sey said, "You know, the funny thing is that when these commercials really work, the stories are almost clichés. Almost clichés... but they're not!"

There's something deeply true about what Sey said. The power of successful advertising is in using familiarity to draw us in, yet the ad somehow gives us a new perspective. Jonathan Harries, who as FCB's Global Chief Creative Officer sees more advertising than virtually anyone else on the planet, calls this principle "familiar with a twist," and believes that it is a common feature of the best work created by the industry.

The validity of Harries' idea of "familiar with a twist" is supported by research detailed in a paper published by Stewart Shapiro and Jesper Nielsen

---

[9] "Stendhal syndrome, hyperkulturemia, or Florence syndrome is a psychosomatic illness that causes rapid heartbeat, dizziness, fainting, confusion, and even hallucinations when an individual is exposed to art, usually when the art is particularly beautiful or a large amount of art is in a single place." (Wikipedia). These symptoms were frequently reported by tourists visiting Florence in the mid-19th century, but today there is some skepticism as to whether this phenomenon really exists.

in the *Journal of Consumer Research* in 2013.[10] The paper opens with a terse statement—or understatement—of a fact that I have battled against my entire career: "Consumers often lack the motivation to process advertisements." Having got that one out of the way, Shapiro and Nielsen develop an interesting line of thought that flies in the face of normal marketing practice. A typical approach of marketers and the agencies that advise them is to run advertisements that are as near identical as possible. Ads should only be replaced with new executions when the original ads are deemed to have reached a level of "wear out" (a phrase coined by copy testing companies) or when there is something newer to say. From what I have been telling you (and you have been good enough to read) in this chapter, this would seem to make sense. The more someone sees something, the better, right? And if that is the case, surely seeing it in exactly the same way each time will be better still... but Shapiro and Nielsen's experiments showed the exact opposite. Participants were shown a range of ads, with small changes made to each ad during repeated exposures. The changes were simple, inconsequential adjustments such as moving the logo or product description in a print ad from one corner to the opposite corner. They were also shown other ads where nothing changed position over repeated viewings. In one experiment, for ads where the logo had moved around, participants responded more quickly in an implicit test of how easy the logos were to process and reported that they found those logos more eye-catching and attractive than the ones that had remained in the same positions. In another experiment, ads where the logos and other components moved around led to a greater preference for the products in those ads versus the products featured in ads where everything stayed in the same location. Respondents were not consciously aware of the change of position of logos or descriptions in either experiment.

Conventional marketing wisdom says that disruption is a good thing. It is tempting to think that effective disruption comes from something unusual, something unfamiliar, and that it is the insertion of the unfamiliar that attracts people's attention. But something intimately familiar, like your name, can attract your attention just as well as the unexpected.

A famous phenomenon from cognitive neuroscience called the "cocktail party effect" shows that the deeply familiar and relevant can be a great way

---

[10] Shapiro, S.A,. Nielsen, J.H. (2013) "What the Blind Eye Sees: Incidental Change Detection as a Source of Perceptual Fluency." *Journal of Consumer Research* 39: 1202–1218.

of getting people's attention. When we hear multiple streams of sound, such as many conversations at a crowded and noisy party, we are nonetheless easily able to carry on a coherent conversation. We do so by selectively attending to the auditory stream (in this case, spoken words) relevant to the conversation we're having and seemingly ignoring all other auditory information. Even though we are not actively paying attention to the other auditory information, we are not truly ignoring it, either. Experiments testing the cocktail party effect (or "dichotic listening" in technical terms) show amazing findings. For example, the same word could be repeated over and over (like 50 times!) in the ignored ear, and we would not notice it. Maybe we could report whether the voice were male or female. But if our name were said just *once* in the unattended ear, we immediately hear it. Just like if, in the middle of our cocktail party conversation, we hear our name said across the room, we immediately stop talking and look for who called us.

Though the tendency in marketing is to think, "let's be disruptive to get people's attention, and then maintain their attention with what is familiar and relevant," it may actually be that the reverse is what really works. Familiarity gets our attention, but the disruption of what is unexpected maintains our attention. Imagine in our cocktail party experiment that if in one scenario my unattended ear heard the words "Your pants are on fire!" followed by "Matthew Willcox," but in another scenario my unattended ear heard "Matthew Willcox" and then "Your pants are on fire!" The second case would lead me to pay more attention to my burning britches.

Over the last 15 years I've had the opportunity to work with a number of video game companies, with SEGA at the time when its DreamCast platform was at the height of its powers; on the Lara Croft *Tomb Raider* franchise (in one interesting exercise, we got a psychoanalyst to delve deep in to Lara's personality); and more recently with Electronic Arts. Video game designers understand the idea of familiarity drawing people in but needing something more challenging and surprising keeping them engaged. They often describe the best video games as "easy to play; difficult to master."

There is some evidence that the power of surprise may go beyond capturing our undivided attention. Many of us have felt the delight of the unexpected upgrade when checking in for a flight or a hotel. That delight, it seems, doesn't just come from feeling special and privileged.

It turns out that our brain views surprises as valuable information that is useful for making good decisions. I've talked about how to get to where we are today: Our ancestors made more good decisions than they made bad ones. But what is a "good" decision? It can be defined many ways, of course: Economists would say a good decision is a rational one, while neuroscientists and psychologists would say it maximizes reward—in all its forms. The brain treats novelty, or surprising information, like a special kind of reward.[11] Something new entices us to investigate it; we feel an urge to explore a new environment. While we all have our "go to" brands or products—be they beer, deodorant, or even varieties of fruit—we will still, from time to time, slip the shackles of habit from time to time and try something different. For our evolutionary brain, exploring novelty helped us avoid bad outcomes, and sometimes led us to better ones, and we continue that behavior today.

We love the familiar and its consistent rewards; we *exploit* what we know. But, we are intuitively drawn to *explore* other options that are potentially rewarding. Experiments looking at how pigeons and rodents balance exploiting and exploring resulted in the development of the *matching law*.[12]

If an animal is navigating a maze, and turning right at the corner results in a reward 80% of the time whereas turning left results in a reward 20% of the time, you might expect the animal to favor the 80% option 100% of the time. After all, turning right will be the fruitful option four times as often as turning left, so why not turn right every time? But what actually happens is animals turn right roughly 80% of the time and left 20% of the time. Choices are made in proportion to how often each pays out a reward. Matching behavior has been observed in many kinds of animals—including humans.[13]

An evolutionary explanation for the matching law might be that we seek out variety, even when there is no immediate need to do so, because dependency on one source of anything is a bad survival strategy in general. For

[11] Kakade, S., Dayan, P. (2002) "Dopamine: generalization and bonuses." *Neural Networks* 15: 549–559.

[12] Herrnstein, R.J. (1974) "Formal Properties of the Matching Law." *Journal of the Experimental Analysis of Behavior* 21: 159–164.

[13] Matching Law is evident in shot selection amongst basketball players. Vollmer, T.R., and Bourret J. (2000). "An Application of the Matching Law to Evaluate the Allocation of Two- and Three-Point Shots by College Basketball Players." *Journal of Applied Behavior Analysis* 33.2: 137–150.

marketers, this explanation supports Byron Sharp's point of view in *How Brands Grow: What Marketers Don't Know*[14] that loyalty is more of a marketer's dream than a consumer's reality. Sharp discusses data from the UK that shows that 72% of Coke drinkers also on occasion buy Pepsi, and he suggests that loyalty is a function of market share. As one commentator on Sharp's perspective concluded that if marketers want loyalty, "they should get a dog."[15]

Complete loyalty to a resource amounts to dependence. Eschewing of dependence has motivated humans to persistently explore the unfamiliar, despite the strong pull of the familiar that I wrote about earlier in this chapter. We see this today at a geopolitical level with energy policy, and it was true of our ancestors in their day-to-day existence. We may have inherited their mental shortcuts that prompt us to sample variety because to be dependent on one source is another kind of shortcut, but one that leads to extinction.

Variety is a factor in many of our choices, but it is a particularly marked feature of our food choices. In one of the best books to bring the perspective of evolutionary psychology to consumer behavior, *The Consuming Instinct: What Juicy Burgers, Ferraris, Pornography, and Gift Giving Reveal about Human Nature*, Gad Saad[16] points to a number of studies that show that when offered variety in foods, we consume more (including a study where the variety had nothing to do with the taste or nutritional value of the food—researchers found that increasing the variety of colors in different batches of M&Ms increased the amount that people consumed[17]).

---

[14] Published in 2010, *How Brands Grow* by Professor Byron Sharp, director of the Ehrenberg-Bass Institute for Marketing Science at the University of South Australia, became one of the most talked about marketing books of recent years. In the book Sharp debunks many conventional wisdoms of marketing. One that he dismantles is the belief that a brand's strength and growth can come from the fraction of its purchasers that are the most loyal. He demonstrates that for brands to grow, they must focus on attracting new users.

[15] A great summary of *How Brands Grow* appears at http://brandgenetics.com/how-brands-grow-speed-summary/, but you should still buy the book! It's a good, provocative read.

[16] Saad is Concordia University Research Chair in Evolutionary Behavioral Sciences and Darwinian Consumption.

[17] Kahn, B. E., Wansink, B. (2004) "The Influence of Assortment Structure on Perceived Variety and Consumption Quantities." *Journal of Consumer Research* March, 30(4): 519–533.

Saad adds two further suggestions as to why we have such a desire for variety when it comes to food choices:

> ...the evolution of variety seeking in food foraging is linked to two distinct mechanisms: (1) maximizing the likelihood of obtaining the necessary amount of varied nutrients and (2) minimizing the likelihood of ingesting too great an amount of toxin from a singular food source.

Just as gravitating toward the comfort of the familiar is instinctual, so at times, is seeking variety and new experiences.

Brands that successfully pull off this paradox of "familiar with a twist" can build deep connections with the public. Google's "Doodles" operate within the constraints of spelling the word *Google* and fitting on the top of a browser page—a familiar name and placement—yet because they are fresh and unexpected, delight us. In 2012, FCB and 360i developed the "Oreo Daily Twist,"[18] a campaign to celebrate Oreo's 100th birthday for our client Mondelez. Rather than going down the route of nostalgia, the advertising—initially appearing on Oreo's Facebook page and then very widely shared—showed Oreo, one of America's most familiar and loved products, giving a whimsical commentary on the news story of the day. The idea itself was a twist on a familiar and long-running TV campaign that centered on the bonding moments around the "Twist, Lick, and Dunk" ritual of eating an Oreo.

Every day for a hundred days, the iconic Oreo was used as a canvas to capture a different news story or event relevant to that day. One day the Oreo had a rainbow of fillings to celebrate gay pride; another day it was an open Oreo showing track marks across a red cream filling in recognition of the Mars Rover's landing on the red planet; and on another, the Oreo had the jagged bite marks of a shark to mark Discovery Channel's Shark Week.

---

[18] You can find a good description of the campaign and how it was put together at http://www.nytimes.com/2012/09/25/business/media/oreos-daily-twist-campaign-finale-enlists-consumers.html?_r=0.

The takeaways from this chapter are

- We feel more positive about things simply because they are familiar. Keeping your brands in the public eye isn't just about awareness—it also drives liking.

- Familiarity also drives our choices: Through simply recognizing something, or having it come to mind quickly makes us more likely to choose that option.

- We have an instinct for exploration and surprise. Surprises are like a special kind of reward—our brain treats them as if they are the keys to future good decisions. Balancing the familiar with surprises is the perfect blend for good marketing. Be relevant and unexpected, or familiar with a twist.

Some thoughts from other people as they read this chapter:

- "I was left with this thought... It's the twist that reminds you of why the familiar matters so much."

- "Too often behavioral economics is seen as a tactical tool for marketers, but this chapter lays out how it is fundamental to understanding how and why great brand campaigns work."

6

Thanks for Sharing (Whether You Mean to or Not)

People's best indicator of what to do comes from the signals they receive from others.

Over the years, I have sat on the viewing side of two way mirrors watching hundreds of focus groups in Europe, Asia, North America, and South America, and seen thousands of people explaining their choices for pet food or credit cards, video games or business computing systems, or jeans or cars.

In all of that time, I think I've only heard a handful of people say that they have made a choice because it appeared to be what others were doing. This concurs with the experience of Vicky Johns, co-founder of the particularly enlightened qualitative research agency QRC (which predictably stands for Qualitative Research Centre). She has moderated and observed more focus groups than I have had hot dinners (this is almost certainly not an exaggeration), so I asked her how often people attributed their purchase decisions to mirroring other people's choices. "Almost never," Johns said. "And even when it is pretty obvious that is why they made the choice, they'll find other reasons to explain their decision."

The signals we receive from others have a profound effect on our choices, even if we prefer not to admit to it or are unaware of it. Basing our choices on what others have done is a good decision-making shortcut and has served humans well. This behavioral strategy is one that transcends the evolution of the human brain. It is one practiced up and down the animal kingdom. This shortcut goes beyond human nature to, well, nature.

If you have ever tried to approach a flock of wild birds, you will probably have the following experience. When you take the first couple of paces toward the birds, one or two wary individuals take flight while the rest stay put. As you get a bit closer, a few more take off. Seconds later, the whole flock bursts into flight. What has triggered the behavior of the majority of the birds isn't a direct reaction to you, the threat. It is a reaction to the behavior of the other birds, which has been processed as a signal of danger. With nearly all animals, including humans, the behavior of others is the best indication of whether something constitutes a threat or an opportunity. In a reverse of the bird-scaring scenario, I'm sure you have unwillingly attracted a large number of pigeons or gulls while having a sandwich on a park bench. It starts with one or two pigeons, but within minutes you are mobbed. The first birds were attracted directly by the food, and the presence of those few birds attracted many others.

The impulse of nature is to follow the market.

Like other animals, we humans are constantly tuned into the behavior of others. Of all the cues out there, the behavior of other humans is our most powerful guide as to how we should behave. These signals and cues often are much more subtle than a large and obvious physical movement, such as a bird taking flight. Fleeting and slight movements of facial muscles reveal to us what others are feeling and consequently how we should behave.

In a must-watch 1987 acting master class with Michael Caine on BBC Television, Caine talks about the importance of facial expressions in film acting. While stage acting is much more about physical gestures and using variations in the voice to convey what the character is feeling, film records every subtle facial movement and imparts this information to the viewer. A slightly raised eyebrow, a momentary tightening of the lips conveys emotion in ways that dialog just can't. Film makes extraordinary—even implausible—things seem real, from monsters stomping through Manhattan to asteroids careening toward the earth. But rather than these jaw-dropping illusions, I often wonder if film's enduring appeal is its ability to record and transmit subtle and simple movements of facial muscles in so faithful a way that the viewer can decode them instantly as a meaningful facial expression, saturated with emotional meaning.

The power of non-verbal cues is something we forget too easily in advertising and marketing. Albert Mehrabian, an expert in non-verbal communication, conducted experiments[1] from which he concluded that our liking of

---

[1] The "7%–38%–55%" rule is based on two studies reported in the 1967 papers "Decoding of Inconsistent Communications" and "Inference of Attitudes from Nonverbal Communication in Two Channels."

someone was driven 53% by face and body language, 38% by tone of voice, and 7% by the actual words they use. While the resulting "93% non-verbal" is often misquoted and disputed, it is likely that in many circumstances things other than the actual words uttered are really important to how the communication is received. In marketing and advertising we tend to focus on words, often leaving facial expression as an afterthought for the director on set, but for viewers, those expressions can mean much more than words. For the clients and the agencies the non-verbal aspects of film advertising can mean gold, in terms of sales and in terms of awards at shows like Cannes.

One of the most loved American commercials in recent years is "The Force" or "Mini Darth" spot for Volkswagen. This commercial was developed by our sister agency Deutsch LA and is discussed in detail in Doug van Praet's book *Unconscious Branding.* (van Praet is the strategic planning director on the VW account.) The commercial shows a young boy who, while dressed as Darth Vader, tries to exert "the force" on inanimate objects around the house. Each time his efforts fail, and he becomes more frustrated. Then, he uses his "powers" on his parents' VW Passat, which his father has just parked in the driveway. To his delight (and surprise) the engine suddenly roars to life. We cut back to the father in the kitchen with his wife and see that he has pressed the car's remote auto start function on the key fob. There is no dialog in the commercial, but we understand entirely what is going on from a fraction of a second sequence where the father raises his eyebrow conspiratorially to his wife. Every year since 2008, Sands Research, a neuromarketing company (with whom I did my first neuroscience project in 2007, which involved assessing people's reactions to different hotel lobbies) publishes an analysis of the neurophysiological response to every ad that appears in that year's Superbowl. VW and Deutsch's "The Force" that ran in the 2011 game has rated higher than any ad they have tested.[2] van Praet gives many valid reasons why the commercial was so engaging and emotionally appealing, but personally, I wouldn't underestimate the effect of that tiny, momentary but perfectly timed gesture of the raised eyebrow.

A study that looked at facial emotion expression in charity advertisements[3] adds some further depth to the how facial expressions of people in ads

---

[2] You can see a video that shows overall engagement measured via EEG and hot spots that show where viewers were looking measured via eye tracking here: http://www.sandsresearch.com/VW_Darth1.aspx.

[3] Small, D.A., Verrochi, N.M. (2009) "The Face of Need: Facial Emotion Expression on Charity Advertisements." *Journal of Marketing Research* December.

affect us. Beyond telegraphically communicating an unspoken narrative, the facial expressions we see can lead to a transference of feeling called *emotional contagion*. Sad faces made participants feel sadder, but they also led them to donate more—when shown an ad featuring a sad face, they donated an average of $2.49, while for one with a happy face they gave $1.37 and for one with a neutral face, $1.38.

Facial expressions have been well studied over the last 30 years, with research showing that the human brain is a specialized face detector and that face processing is closely linked to the generation of emotions. Neuroscience work identified an area of the brain, the fusiform face area (nicknamed the FFA), which responds selectively to faces in general[4] and also showed that the brain can identify a face very quickly, in less than 200 milliseconds.[5] Using fMRI, Paul Whalen's lab at Dartmouth College finds reproducible patterns of brain activity corresponding to different facial expressions.[6] Whalen and colleagues found that activity in the amygdala, a brain area intricately involved in emotional responses, reliably differentiated between many facial expressions (when, if you remember from the preface, you look at the eyes). Responses to fearful and angry expressions are particularly pronounced in the healthy amygdala. The amygdala can even tell an angry from fearful face when you're only presented with just the whites of the eyes![7]

Strong evidence also exists that facial expressions are innate, rather than learned. Neuroscientist David Matsumoto teaches in two diverse fields: He is a professor at San Francisco State University, where his research revolves around expertise in facial expressions, non-verbal behavior, and microexpressions, but he is also a seventh-degree black belt in judo and the owner and head instructor of the East Bay Judo Institute in El Cerrito, California.

---

[4] Kanwisher, N. (2010) "Functional specificity in the human brain: A window into the functional architecture of the mind." *Proc Natl Acad Sci* 107(25): 11163–11170.

[5] Ito, T.A., Thompson, E., Cacioppo, J.T. (2004) "Tracking the timecourse of Social Perception: The Effects of Racial Cues on Event-Related Brain Potentials." *Personality and Social Psychology Bulletin* 30(10): 1267–1280.

[6] Whalen lab research summary: http://whalenlab.info/research-projects-fearful_angry.html

[7] Whalen, P.J, Kagan, J., Cook, R.G., Davis, F.C., Kim, H., Polis, S., McLaren, D.G., Somerville, L.H., McLean, A.A., Maxwell, J.S., Johnstone, T. (2004) "Human Amygdala Responsivity of Masked Fearful Eye Whites." *Science* 306(5704): 2061.

Matsumoto combined both of his interests in a fascinating study[8] that compared sighted judo athletes at the 2004 Athens Olympic Games and blind judo athletes at the 2004 Athens Paralympic Games. Both competitions took place in the same venue, the latter being held a month later than the former, and in both cases the athletes (or judokas) were observed during medal matches.

Athletes in both tournaments were photographed at the same three points—immediately at the end of the bout, when receiving their medal, and when posing on the podium with the other medal winners. In this study, Matsumoto studied facial expressions of athletes with three different levels of sightedness: sighted, non-congenitally blind, and congenitally blind. (In the Paralympics unsighted athletes are identified as to whether they are congenitally or non-congenitally blind.)

Matsumoto and Willingham found negligible differences between the athlete's facial expressions whether they were sighted or not. Nor was there a difference between the expressions of those who were blind from birth from those who had become blind later in life, strongly suggesting that facial expressions are innate.

One of the most remarkable findings of this study was that the judokas who had been blind from birth didn't just spontaneously exhibit "Duchenne Smiles" (the almost unfakeable smile of true joy that uses not just muscles from around the mouth but around the eyes as well) when they won gold, but they also showed the socially polite "Pan Am" smile (named for the smile-flashing flight attendants of the now defunct airline) if they had fallen short and won silver. Not only are the facial expressions that convey raw emotion innate, it seems likely that the ones that act as more sophisticated social signals may be as well.

While a facial expression is a signal to us of how another person is feeling, which in turn is a signal of how we should act, what people are looking at is very direct indicator of what we should be looking at.

From a young age we are drawn to look at what others appear to be gazing at—research in *Joint Attention* shows that an adult can bring objects to an

---

[8] Matsumoto, D., Willingham, B. (2008) "Spontaneous Facial Expressions of Emotion of Congenitally and Noncongenitally Blind Individuals" *Journal of Personality and Social Psychology* 96(1).

infant's attention by looking at those objects.[9] Eye-tracking studies show that we keep this tendency in adulthood. One experiment used an advertisement that had an image of a model's face (and hair) with a shampoo bottle in the foreground. In one version the model looked straight ahead at the camera. In another, she looked out of the corner of her eyes at the shampoo bottle. For the first version, the "heat map" of where people viewing the ad had fixated their gaze showed the "hotspots" around the headline and the model's face. For the second version, where the model was looking at the bottle, the hotspots were on the headline, on the model's eyes, and on the shampoo bottle.

In a similar experiment, James Breeze, an Australian usability testing and user experience specialist, tested two ads, both with a baby next to a pile of diapers. In the first, the baby was facing the camera, while in the second we see the baby in profile, gazing upward and to the side, so it appears that he is looking at the headline of the ad. For the first ad, the only real eye-tracking hotspot was the baby's face. For the second, the eye-tracking hotspots were the headline the baby is gazing at, and quite remarkably, the body copy under the headline.

The Power of Other People—Be Social

Social norms, which are expectations of appropriate behavior, and social biases such as the *bandwagon effect*, which is the behavioral impact of what others are doing, can underpin existing behaviors and provide keys to unlocking behavioral change. A number of practical experiments examining energy behavior illustrate the bandwagon effect. One such experiment compared the effect of information about how your energy consumption compared to your neighbors' consumption (this kind of information is known as a *descriptive social norm*) with the effect of an indication that your energy consumption was considered acceptable or unacceptable (known as an *injunctive social norm*).[10] The study used simple, yet effective symbols to show what was acceptable or not: a smiling face ☺ for approval and a frowning face ☹ for disapproval. Descriptive social norms decreased energy consumption in those homes with above-average rates but increased

---

[9] Moore, C., Dunham, P. *Joint Attention: Its Origins and Role in Development.* Laurence Erlbaum Associates, 1995.

[10] Schultz, P.W., Nolan, J.M., Cialdini, R.B., Goldstein, N.J., Griskevicius, V. (2007) "The constructive, destructive, and reconstructive power of social norms." *Psychological Science* 18: 429.

consumption in those homes with below-average rates. However, when injunctive social norms (the smiling or frowning faces) were combined with descriptive norms, those homes with below-average energy consumption did not increase their energy usage. Another study examining how the bandwagon effect modulated water usage showed that the bandwagon effect is transient.[11] Behavioral changes wane as time passes, and the regression to previous behaviors is most pronounced in the outliers, corresponding to the homes using the most resources.

The scientists who developed the energy consumption study have also provided additional insights into human nature by examining what people staying in hotels do with their towels after using them. (It's a wonderful thing that mundane activities often reveal so much about what underlies our choices.)

Hotels, motels, and other lodgings use a lot of water in the U.S.—the Environmental Protection Agency estimates they account for around 15% of the total water used by commercial and institutional facilities.[12] That figure works out to about 2.5%[13] of the water withdrawals from the U.S. public water system—a heavy toll on the water system and also on the finances of hotel operators. Laundry, at 17%, is the second biggest source of hotel water usage.

Not surprisingly, hotels have focused on water usage as an area of potential savings, which is why, in nearly every hotel bathroom, you see some kind of sign displaying a message that asks you to use your towels more than once. Invariably, the focus of these messages is the impact that the water and fuel used in laundering hotel linens has on the planet. The messages that implore you to "do your part to help" rely on personal empowerment as the motivation to get guests to leave towels on the rack rather than the bathroom floor. By and large, personal empowerment is an effective approach, with the majority of people choosing to reuse their towels at least once during their stay.

[11] Ferraro, P.J., Price, M.K. (2013) "Using nonpecuniary strategies to influence behavior: evidence from a large-scale field experiment." *The Review of Economics and Statistics* 95: 64–73.

[12] Howard, B.C. "Hotels Save Energy with a Push to Save Water." *National Geographic Magazine,* December 24, 2014.

[13] According to the EPA, hotels use about 15% of the water used by commercial and institutional facilities in the U.S.

But decision science research suggests there may be a more effective message than personal empowerment. Instead of appealing to hotel guests in the name of them helping the environment and saving the planet (what could, rationally, be more worthy of action, especially given the suggested action of placing the towels back on the rail neither costs the guests money or very much effort), the researchers tested messages telling them what other guests had done, which is an example of a descriptive social norm.

In one experiment, a card that carried a standard appeal to environmental consciousness was randomly placed in half the hotel rooms used in the experiment. The standard environmental message served as the experimental control. Another message, placed in the remaining hotel rooms, told guests that the majority of guests in the hotel had reused towels at least once during their stay. One of the researchers leading the study, Noah Goldstein, reported on his *Psychology Today* blog: "guests who learned that the majority of their fellow guests had reused their towels were 26% more likely than those who saw the basic environmental protection message to recycle their towels."

In a second experiment, the researchers went one step further. This time the message informed guests that the majority of guests who had stayed in *this very same room* had chosen to reuse their towels at least once during their stay. This small change in wording led to a 33% increase in guests reusing their towels compared to the control message that focused on concern for the environment.

This hotel towel study is considered a classic in the social sciences and is relevant to marketers in many ways. Two things are worth noting. The first is how powerful social proof can be and that the effect of social proof increases the closer people feel to the targeted behavior. (This is true even if this closeness is pretty circumstantial.) The second is a personal observation and frustration. In all the hotel rooms that I have stayed in since I became aware of this study in 2009 (and the number of hotel rooms easily exceeds 100, from independent hotels to all the big chains, across Europe, North and South America, and Asia), I have not seen *one* message urging me to reuse my towels for any reason other than saving the environment. I've seen cards and hangers with pictures of polar bears in the Arctic, of parrots in the Amazonian rainforest, but never one that relates to the behavior of our own species.

There is a temptation to see social proof as a tool that has most application for mass marketers, but not as a something that will work, or even be desirable as an approach for luxury products or fashion.

Anyone watching TV in the U.S. in the late 1990s will probably be familiar with a series of GAP ads, all shot in a white studio that featured 30 or 40 attractive and diverse young people all dressed very similarly. "Khaki Swing" had a troupe, all wearing GAP khakis, doing a swing dance known as "The Lindy Hop" to a Louis Prima recording of "Jump, Jive, and Wail." In subsequent efforts in the series, GAP used social proof even more explicitly, with similar ads featuring people wearing similar clothes, ending with a title at the end that read "Everybody in Vests," "Everybody in Cords," or "Everybody in Leather." These campaigns are associated with a time when GAP enjoyed massive popularity, and the company's stock price more than doubled in the space of nine months.

Social proof can also work for luxury products, though it may be better to use it in the more discrete context of one-to-one digital marketing. The Wine Society, a prestigious, invitation-only wine club (founded in London in 1874, it is the world's oldest) does just that through a section on its website dedicated to its "best-selling" wines that provides helpful reassurance in a complex category where choices can be quite subjective. And social proof is also the mechanism that online retailers like Amazon are betting on when they serve you messages saying, "People who bought *The Business of Choice* also bought *Thinking, Fast and Slow*."[14]

Even "norming" a private social behavior, like parents talking to their children about sex,[15] can increase the frequency of that behavior. One recent study utilized public service announcements touting the message "Talk to your kids about sex. Everyone else is." The messages were displayed on billboards and also ran on television and radio. Exposure to the messages predicted whether parents had already talked with their children about sex and if they planned to in the future. This study used social norms to alter individual communication, specifically one-on-one conversations between a parent and child. To affect behavioral change, social norms need to be used in ways that can be related to the behavior of many. Social media provides ways of scaling up individualized communication, both in terms of customizing messages (remember how "in this room" worked better than "in this hotel"?) and in terms of people posting their behaviors to their social network.

---

[14] I am also cunningly using anchoring here, a bias we will describe in detail in Chapter 11, "Never Be Above Comparison."

[15] DuRant, R.H., Wolfson, M., LaFrance, B., Balkrishnan, R., Altman, D. (2006) "An evaluation of a mass media campaign to encourage parents of adolescents to talk to their children about sex." *Journal of Adolescent Health* 38: 298.e1-298.e9.

Popularity is important (in most cases). Most of us know this, whether we call it the *herd instinct* or the aforementioned bandwagon effect. Showing or inferring that many people are doing what you want them to do has been proven to alter a wide array of behaviors, like reusing hotel bathroom towels to selecting airlines. This shortcut, based on an intuitive response to what we observe others doing, worked as well for our ancestors as it does for us today. If many of our ancestors were drinking from a watering hole, then it was reasonable to conclude that it was a relatively safe option. Our ancestors' experience became our instinct. But caution needs to be used in applying the bandwagon effect—it generally works when the situation motivates people to seek safety and risk avoidance but not when they are motivated to stand out, as we will discuss in Chapter 12, "If Content Is King, Context Is Queen."

It's what people are doing! One of the most powerful forms of persuasion is telling people what other people, in particular those like them, are already doing. Even a simple statement like, "Most people of your age/in your area are doing this," or "More and more people are doing this" is effective.

Robert Cialdini explained the power of this type of persuasion like this to me:

> One fundamental way we can decide what to do when we are uncertain is to look around us, at what those like us are doing. I saw an article in a journal from China that showed that if a restaurant manager puts on the menu "These are our most popular items" those items immediately become 17%–20% more popular. You don't have to spend any money on it, you don't have to convince people—you just point to something that is inherently there in the situation, that usually drives people. And this can be enough to drive a 17%–20% uptick immediately.

This menu effect is driven by one of Cialdini's maxims, which is that our intuitions "tell us that a behavior is more correct to the degree that we see other people doing it."

As the examples show, you can use it for more than just increasing sales. Think about other behaviors you want to change that could help your business. The hotel towel study used social proof to increase the percentage of hotel guests who put their towels back on the rack, by leaving a card in the room telling them that this is what most guests did, and encouraging this behavior could help a hotel increase their margins and meet environmental goals. The e-commerce arm of a company we work with found that rates of returns, while still small, were increasing for no clear reason. Our hypothesis was that brands like Zappos had made returning a social norm, and recommended a test where a small thank-you slip would be placed in the box that told the customer that most of our customers are happy with the goods first time (but also making clear that they could return them unconditionally if they weren't happy).

Marketers can unwittingly fall foul of social proof. Sometimes we are tempted to try to shame people into doing what they are not doing. "Surely showing that they are not being rational will shake them from their irrationality or laziness" we seem to think. Unfortunately, this can do worse than having no effect—it can lead to people doing the exact opposite of what you would like them to do, normally by reinforcing what they are doing or what they aren't doing.[16] Some years ago I got a mailer sent to my home in San Francisco saying something like

> Only 12% of homes in California have earthquake insurance. But there is a 60% chance that your house will be affected by an earthquake in the next 20 years.

This message makes me feel that, in not having earthquake insurance, I am in the majority. And despite the clearly stated risk of an earthquake, if the norm is not to have insurance, that makes me feel it is OK—and even safe—for me not to have it. (There's another bias at work here as well—the *optimism bias*. We have an innate tendency to think bad things are less likely to happen to us than others...perhaps the houses on my block will get destroyed, but mine will miraculously remain unscathed.) One of our clients in the financial services sector realized their business could benefit from encouraging people to make financial plans, and wanted to make the point, through a marketing program, that only 17% of people in their market had financial plans. Consumers had even told them in qualitative research that this fact was a motivating kick in the pants. Our advice was that the last thing they should do was to make not having a plan a social norm as this would make not having a plan seem like a good plan for consumers. We recommended that instead they focused their messages on how easy it is to take the first step toward creating a plan.

---

[16] Cialdini, R.B. (2003) "Crafting Normative Messages to Protect the Environment." *Current Directions in Psychological Science* 12: 105–109.

But sometimes the wrong thing can be motivating. The flipside of popularity is unfairness. Unfairness drives us to action; when we feel that something is unfair, we have a gut reaction. In the lab, unfairness is studied using the ultimatum game, which typically consists of two players. The first player makes a monetary offer to the second player, such as splitting $10 into $3 for the second player and keeping $7. If the offer is accepted, both players get money; if it is rejected, neither player gets any money. The anterior insula is one of several brain areas that responds to unfairness.[17,18] The insula is a complex brain area, to say the least, and the anterior region of the insula is associated with arousal and with negative emotions like anger and disgust, pain, and distress. Knowing that something is unfair lingers with us until we resolve it.

This phenomenon is called *inequity aversion*, a term coined by Ernst Fehr (whose surname is unfortunately pronounced "fear" and not "fair") and Klaus Schmidt—and the term means pretty much what it says it is. A sense of inequity pushes us to action. That feeling of anger and disgust, often disproportionate to the infraction from a rational perspective, is so unsettling, and so nagging, that it does a very rare thing. It overcomes our procrastination and inertia and makes us do something. Just a few years ago, hundreds of thousands of people in the U.S. switched banks. Switching banks might not seem like a big deal, but it is something any marketer with a background in retail finance will tell you people only do a few times in their lives and only then because of a major life event like relocating or marriage. But in 2011, major banks, like Bank of America, introduced a $5 monthly debit card fee, and people felt the banks were gouging an unfair level of profit, so they switched in droves. A 2011 survey from research company Javelin suggests that people moving their account out of a large bank showed, "nearly a three-time increase over the amount of people who took their funds out of large banks for highly similar reasons during the previous 90-day period."[19]

Also in the third quarter of 2011, Netflix had a similar fate—600,000 subscribers canceled their subscriptions to this once much-loved brand over a

[17] Sanfey, A.G., Rilling, J.K., Aronson, J.A., Nystrom, L.E., Cohen, J.D. (2003) "The neural basis of economic decision-making in the ultimatum game." *Science* 300: 1755–1758.

[18] Corradi-Dell'Acqua, C., Civai, C., Rumiati, R.I., Fink, G.R. (2013) "Disentangling self- and fairness-related neural mechanisms involved in the ultimatum game: an fMRI study." *SCAN* 8: 424–431.

[19] "'Bank Transfer Day,' What Really Just Happened?" Javelin Strategy and Research Blog, January 26, 2012.

three-month period—because the company separated the streaming plan and doubled the monthly rate. Customers thought the change was unfair.

There is no doubt that social media amplified the response to unfairness in both the bank and Netflix examples. The powerful effect of what others are doing can be a double-edged sword, with the potential to cut your competitors off at the knees and to slice deeply into your own profits.

Social proof can be very powerful, but don't assume that it is the most powerful tool in every case. Robert Cialdini talks about how agents of influence need to be like detectives. Just as in most whodunits where the first suspect you encounter in the story is seldom the culprit, the first behavioral principle that comes to mind isn't necessarily the one that will yield greatest influence. Like a good detective, you need to keep investigating.

A good example of this comes from the work of a group that has done more to bring learnings from behavioral science out of the lab and into the real world than anyone else. In 2010 the Cabinet Office of the United Kingdom government set up a group called the *Behavioural Insights Team* (abbreviated to BIT, it also became known as the Nudge Unit), with the mandate of using behavioral economics in public policy, particularly to influence positive behavior in areas related to the environment, philanthropy, health, and well-being.

If you are a UK resident and you want to donate your organs, you should join the Organ Donation Register, as this quickly provides confirmation of your wish after your death, increasing the chances of your organs helping a living person in need. In the UK, you have to explicitly *opt-in* to give consent for organ donation (more on this in Chapter 10, "Make It Easy—For the Mind and the Body"), and while 9 out of 10 people in the UK support the idea of organ donation, fewer than 1 in 3 have joined the National Health Service (NHS) Organ Donation Register. One of the main routes to joining is a prompt on the Driver and Vehicle Licensing Agency (DVLA) website where people apply for driving licenses and renew their vehicle tax.

The BIT ran a Randomized Control Test[20] (as introduced in Chapter 2, "The Ever-Advancing Science of Choice") where tens of thousands of visitors to the DVLA website each saw one of eight variants of a prompt to

---

[20] The full report can be downloaded here: https://www.gov.uk/government/uploads/system/uploads/attachment_data/file/267100/Applying_Behavioural_Insights_to_Organ_Donation.pdf.

encourage them to register for organ donation as they went about their business of license applying or vehicle tax renewing.

The first variant was the control. It simply asked people to join the NHS Organ Donor Register. The second, third, and fourth variants used a classic social proof appeal: "Every day thousands of people who see this page decide to register." The second variant just had this as text, the third accompanied it with a photograph of 20 or so people to underscore the point, and the fourth variant placed the organ donation logo next to the message.

The fifth variant used loss: "Three people die every day because there are not enough organ donors." We will examine the power of messages that use loss as a frame in Chapter 8, "Loss and Ownership." The sixth used a positive frame: "You could save or transform up to 9 lives as an organ donor."

The seventh used the approach of reciprocity (one of Robert Cialdini's six rules of influence): "If you needed an organ transplant, would you have one? If so, please help others." The eighth highlighted the dissonance between intentions (most people support organ donation) and action (most people don't register as donors), an approach that has been successful in areas like exercise, sexual health, and smoking cessation.

An article in the UK newspaper *The Independent*[21] suggested that the BIT team had expected the social proof approach to pull best (I would have certainly bet on that outcome, given everything I've learned about social proof's power to change behavior, and I suspect there were three variants using that mechanism because the BIT researchers felt the same).

But the results pointed to another approach. Two variants fared significantly better than the control, and neither of them used social proof—in fact, the social proof variant with photograph performed worse than the control. The second most successful was the loss frame ("Three people die every day..."), but the clear winner was the reciprocity message ("If you needed an organ transplant..."). According to the Behavioural Insights Team,

> The most successful prompt (reciprocity frame) significantly increased sign up rates. The results show that it is likely to lead to around 100,000 additional registrations in a year.

---

[21] Wright, O. "How organ donation is getting nudge in the right direction: trial could pave way for 100,000 extra donors each year," *The Independent*, December 24, 2013.

Social proof and social norms are incredibly powerful; but just like any other behavioral lever, you can't assume that they are going to work in every situation. With human beings, nothing is a foregone conclusion.

The takeaways from this chapter are

- Social proof is extremely powerful and one of the most intuitive of cognitive mechanisms. One simple way to use it is to let people feel your popularity by showing the number of customers or subscribers you have.

- Beware of unintentionally creating messages that suggest that many people are doing the thing you don't want them to do, or aren't doing the thing you want them to. These can backfire!

- The signals that we get from others through facial expressions might be very subtle, but they score a direct hit in the gut and the heart. As discussed in this chapter, they are innate and are processed very quickly. They are also easy to get wrong. (The animated movie, *The Polar Express* is a good example of getting facial expressions wrong—a review on CNN.com noted how, despite the brilliant technology, the movie seemed "creepy" because they technology couldn't capture the emotions expressed by the mouth and the eyes.) If you are making a commercial or video where you need actors to convey emotions, make sure you are working with a director who can capture this. Unfortunately, the ones who really can aren't always the cheapest.

What others shared about this chapter:

- "I've always tended to think when I do what others are doing, it's a sign of weakness. It's good to know that, in fact, I'm following an efficient, effective, and smart strategy!"

- "I've just finished making some instructional videos. We spent ages in pre-production talking about casting, wardrobe and lighting—even where the actor was going to be moving. But we didn't talk about what we wanted his facial expressions to communicate once!"

7

Now, and the Future—Different Places with Different Rules

How the future, sequence, and the most recent thing that people have experienced drive how they choose and how they feel.

P ut yourself in the shoes of one of your forebears some 20,000 years ago (and there really is a pretty good chance they would have been wearing shoes, as anthropologists estimate footwear use started about 40,000 years ago[1]). Your ancestor is around 20 years old, but he and his mate have not yet managed to rear a child beyond infancy. He and other males from his clan are out hunting for life-sustaining protein; they are committed followers of the Paleo diet, of course. Hunting is a routine but risky activity, and he must have his wits about him. If he makes the right choices, he avoids danger and gets the food that will allow him and his mate to survive. If he makes the wrong choices, he either gets killed or injured, or he doesn't get food. His survival and your existence are on the line.

While following the still-fresh trail of a caribou, he hears a rustle ahead in the six-foot high grass. He freezes. He feels the tingle of blood rushing to his forehead. His longer-term objective of tracking down the caribou is interrupted. All his attention is focused on that noise in the grass. The most important thing for him at that moment is to work out if the source of the noise is a threat or not. Is it his next meal or something that wants to make him their next meal? Because you exist and are reading this book, we know he made the right choice—whether that was to chase with abandon, or abandon the chase. Being distracted from his task and intuitively letting an interruption grab his attention paid off, for him and for you.

---

[1] Trinkaus, E. (2005) "Anatomical evidence for the antiquity of human footwear use." *Journal of Archaeological Science* 32: 1515–1526.

Which is why, 20,000 years later, when you are having a heart-to-heart with your wife or husband, or a discussion with your boss about your career, or driving down the freeway, you respond the way you do when you feel your smartphone vibrate, or, out of the corner of your eye, see its LED flash to announce the arrival of a new e-mail. The message is more likely to be an e-mail from the HR department about the roll-out of a new expense reporting policy in two months' time, or one from the sandwich shop near your office letting you know their special of the week (you got an extra stamp on your loyalty card when you signed up for the e-mail alerts, and have kept meaning to unsubscribe for the last six months) than anything as important as what you are doing. Nonetheless, you feel a compulsion to momentarily divert your gaze from your spouse's eyes, from your boss's steely stare, or from the road ahead to your phone and find out that...it's not important. You really shouldn't have done that—especially if you were driving.

News, or the possibility of news, is irresistible to us. Especially if it is what copy testing companies rather redundantly refer to as "new news." In terms of how we process things, the latest very often is the greatest. Not only are we are distracted by and attracted to the latest piece of information, we are more likely to remember it, we will place undue importance on it, and the last part of an experience can not only transform our memories of the entire experience, but also change our future behavior as a result.

Let's consider memory. A wide range of psychology studies, going back as far as Hermann Ebbinghaus's work from 1885 to more recent studies[2,3] demonstrate the *serial position effect*. The serial position effect explains how, when asked to recall words from a list, people are most likely to remember words from the end of the list (the *recency bias*), pretty likely to remember words from the beginning (the *primacy bias*), and least likely to recall words from the middle of the list. One explanation for the serial position effect is that we pay more attention to the first few words and there is enough time for them to be filed in our long-term memory, and the last words go into our cognitively less-demanding short-term memory. The middle words straddle both memory systems and are not encoded well in either system. Getting caught in the middle isn't the best path to saliency or success.

---

[2] Brodie, D.A., Murdock, B.B. (1977) "Effect of presentation time on nominal and functional serial-position curves of free recall." *Journal of Verbal Learning and Verbal Behavior* 16: 185–200.

[3] Crano, W.D. (1977) "Primacy versus recency in retention of information and opinion change." *The Journal of Social Psychology* 101: 87–96.

The conventional wisdom of the benefits of being the first or last agency in a pitch, or a brand having the first or last slot in a commercial break makes sense. For cognitively demanding tasks, you may be better off going first; for things that require lower involvement, being last may be the way to come out on top. When I worked in Thailand, I had a client whose media strategy was always to buy—often at inflated costs—the billboard that would be seen immediately before his key competitor's billboards. Because passively viewing a billboard is cognitively easy and therefore the recency effect is at play, being the last billboard rather than the first may have been a better bet. If I had known then what I know now, I would have made the case for my client to do exactly the opposite of his favored approach, making his advertising work harder, and cost less in the bargain.

Beyond simply being favored in memory recall, the latest information has, like a young cuckoo in a songbird's nest, other tricks up its sleeve to supplant the previous inhabitants. One trick that is talked about a lot in the field of behavioral finance is the abovementioned *recency bias*. The recency bias leads both amateur and professional investors to place greater importance on more recent information than on potentially more significant, but older, information. This bias is a major reason investors and business decision makers will make knee-jerk reactions based on the latest developments rather than on what they have witnessed more consistently over a longer period.

As Jason Zweig writes in his book *Your Money and Your Brain*, "It is human tendency to estimate probabilities not on the basis of long-term experience but rather on a handful of the latest outcomes." What happens last can color an entire experience, whether that is the climax of the final movement of a symphony, the gripping ending of a movie, a sales presentation, or even an invasive medical procedure.

For example, today, thanks to the widespread use of the sedative Propofol, screening colonoscopies are no longer the painful and uncomfortable procedures that, in 1994, made them the perfect setting for a famous experiment[4] by Daniel Kahneman, Donald Redelmeier, and Joel Katz.

Kahneman and his two collaborators, both of whom are medical doctors with specific interests in health policy, screening procedures, and anesthesia,

---

[4] Redelmeier, D.A., Katz, J., Kahneman, D. (2003) "Memories of colonoscopy: a randomized trial." *Pain* 104(1-2): 187–94.

recruited 682 people who were scheduling a colonoscopy. During the actual procedure, every participant was asked to do three things:

- Rate the pain level every 60 seconds during the procedure on a scale of 1–10.

- Rate the level of overall discomfort for the colonoscopy after its completion.

- Compare it to one of eight unpleasant experiences, such as "an average visit to the dentist" or "two days in bed with the flu."

A colonoscopy requires a gastroenterologist to move a scope through the entire colon. These scope movements consist of a lot of wiggling, probing, and pulling, and the gastroenterologist tries to perform the operation with the least amount of discomfort possible to the patient. At the end of the procedure, the scope is removed immediately. Half of the participants in this study had a colonoscopy using standard procedures at the time. The procedure was modified ever so slightly for the remaining participants. After all the wiggling and movement of the scope had stopped, the scope was left in place just inside the entrance to the rectum for a couple of minutes. This colonoscopy change resulted—critically—*"in final moments that were less painful,"* according to the researchers. What difference did this small change make to the participants?

Both groups indicated nearly identical levels of pain during the colonoscopy using the 10-point scale. But when it came to rating how they felt about the overall procedure, the group who had experienced the gentler ending rated the overall experience as being 10% less painful. The gentler ending also affected future behavior. An analysis of the participants' patient information over subsequent years showed that those who had been administered the modified procedure were also about 10% more likely to have returned for their next checkup.

For marketers, there is a clear implication from this study: Whatever you do, finish strong. How you bid people farewell as they leave your plane or hotel will be more important than how you welcomed them. With e-commerce, the experience will often terminate abruptly with a confirmation page, rather than something that will stoke your anticipation for what you will be receiving in a couple days' time. In our struggle to win the transaction, to get the sale, we forget about engineering an experience that is emotionally satisfying for the customer. The legendary car salesman had it right when he said, "When I'm selling someone a new car, I'm already selling them the next car they are going to buy from me in five years' time."

If "now" is so powerful, what does this mean for the future? What do you do if you are a marketer, and your product isn't about doing something this moment, or getting an immediate reward?

Humans, along with a range of other species, have an instinctive eye to the future that goes beyond the creation and nurture of future generations. Mammals from the squirrel family are well known for hoarding nuts during times of plenty. This behavior has passed into the English language, as in to "squirrel" something away. Gray squirrels take this to a further level of future planning—they differentiate between acorns from white oaks and red oaks. The less bitter white acorns are more likely to decay during storage and so are eaten immediately. The tannin-rich red acorns will not sprout or decay during a few months underground and may also lose their bitter taste in the meantime. Many ant genera that inhabit the southern U.S., Mexico, and Central America are known as leafcutter ants because they collect and cut leaves, but not for immediate consumption. Leafcutter ants use the leaves to cultivate and feed the fungus that is the food of their larvae. Finally, acorn woodpeckers (on whom Woody Woodpecker's laugh was allegedly modeled) store acorns as a community effort, hiding and later extracting acorns from holes they drilled into utility poles and trees. (Acorn woodpeckers don't just cooperate on food storage; they help each other raise offspring as well.)

Some ability to plan for the future, such as having the foresight to store food for times when it may be in short supply, does provide an evolutionary advantage. But letting the future weigh too much on our decisions could have disastrous consequences for our ability to navigate the present. Tali Sharot, a neuroscientist at University College London and author of the book *The Optimism Bias*, suggests a compelling reason why humans may have developed the cognitive bias for which her book is named. The so-called optimism bias is much picked-over by those keen to point out human irrationality. It leads people, seemingly foolishly, to overestimate good outcomes or underestimate bad ones in terms of how those outcomes will affect them personally. Yet, people give more accurate predictions about how outcomes will affect others. The emergence of the optimism bias in human development may have a critical role in allowing us to conceive of the future without being paralyzed by contemplating its gloomy inevitability. Sharot writes in her book, "...an ability to imagine the future had to develop side by side with positive biases. The knowledge of death had to emerge at the same time as its irrational denial...It is this coupling—conscious prospection and optimism—that underlies the extraordinary achievements of the human species."

In short, planning for the future is fine as long we don't let its consequences weigh on us too much. Our cognitive mechanisms have evolved a few other tricks, beyond the optimism bias, to ensure contemplating the future and the decision uncertainty that might bring doesn't inhibit us from making the quick decisions we need to make now that will help us get beyond today.

Many of these cognitive mechanisms and biases are inconvenient for marketers whose products and services do not have an obvious or compelling payout in the present but that have value to people who might choose them at some stage in their future.

Future value is a tricky thing to sell, as demonstrated by one of the fundamental principles of behavioral economics: *temporal* or *hyperbolic discounting*. (The word *hyperbolic* refers to the shape of the curve showing how the subjective value of something decreases as you move away from the present into the future.) Classic research on hyperbolic discounting can be demonstrated through people's intuitive desire to opt for a smaller reward now instead of a bigger one in the future. I've tested this phenomenon numerous times at conferences. First, I wave a $50 bill in the air and then a $100 bill. I ask the audience to choose whether they would rather have the $50 bill now or $100 in a year. Unscientific though my experiment may be, the show of hands typically illustrates a preference for the immediate reward among about three-quarters of the audience. This result is broadly in line with behavioral experiments looking at people's propensity to choose a smaller reward immediately rather than a larger one in the future.

Things get interesting when the time frame is shifted. What if, instead of offering $50 now and $100 in a year, you offer $50 in a month's time and $100 in one year and one month's time? This change leads to an almost complete behavioral reversal, with the majority saying they would rather take the $100 than the $50, even though the length of time between the two offers remained an unchanged 12 months.

Another way that our judgments about the future are affected is by how we interpret, or construe, things differently depending on the time horizon. *Construal level theory* (CLT) explains the impact of time on choice. CLT classifies thinking into abstract or concrete based on "psychological distance" from a reference point, which is the present day self.

In research that looked at how time changes people's preferences, participants who were asked to describe themselves one week in the future preferred to open a new banking account at a bank superior on instrumental attributes (for example, "low transaction fees" and "good interest rates on credit cards") whereas participants who described themselves 10 years in the future preferred to open a new banking account at a bank superior on identity attributes (for example, "customers are treated with respect and dignity" and "customer complaints are considered very seriously").[5]

The further something is from the present-day self, the more abstract the accompanying thought processes are while immediate events are thought of in more concrete terms. Consider planning a wedding. When the happy couple selects the date a year or so in the future, their focus is pleasantly on the time of year that would offer the kind of ambience they want for their perfect day. (Perhaps an outdoor evening wedding, in late summer?) As the day approaches, their focus shifts to more concrete and detailed (and not so pleasant) aspects of thinking, like devising harmonious seating charts.

Dan Ariely suggests a "hack" for this tendency. If someone asks you to give a talk, write an article, or make some other commitment for a date that is a long way off, think about whether you would say yes if that commitment were in four weeks' time.

CLT also, unfortunately, applies to debt. When you borrow money you are in a very concrete level of construal, while the repayment date is so abstract and so far in the future as to seem like it will never come.

In an example from "Homer Economicus or Homer Sapiens? Behavioral Economics in The Simpsons" Jodi Beggs points to a situation where the future becoming today causes Homer pain. In the episode "No Loan Again, Naturally" Homer complains to his mortgage broker, Gil Gunderson:

> When you gave me that money, you said I wouldn't have to repay it until the future. This isn't the future, it's the lousy stinking now.

According to both CLT and hyperbolic discounting, it's not just Homer Simpson's thinking about the future that is opaque—it's true for all of us. What hope is there for marketers who are selling retirement savings, long-term health care, or any product that requires handing cash over now for a benefit in the future? Fortunately, ingenious neuroeconomics and behavioral economics experiments by Hal Hershfield, now an Assistant Professor of Marketing at UCLA's Anderson School of Management, suggest a very interesting way to fight human nature...by using human nature.

More than most experiments I have seen, Hershfield and his collaborators' studies hint at the potential power of neuroeconomics for marketing.

---

[5] Kivetz, Y., Tyler, T.R. (2007) "Tomorrow I'll be me: The effect of time perspective on the activation of idealistic versus pragmatic selves." *Organizational Behavior and Human Decision Processes* 102(2): 193–211.

While he was in graduate school at Stanford University, Hershfield examined how people's perception of self related to temporal discounting. In one landmark experiment, Hershfield and colleagues used fMRI to measure brain activity when people were thinking about themselves and other people in the present and the future.[6] Strikingly, when people were thinking about themselves in the future, their brain responses were indistinguishable from when they were thinking about other people. The difference in brain response between present and future self also correlated with measures of temporal discounting. In the example of receiving a $50 bill today or $100 in one year, people with brain responses to their future self that looked more like brain responses to other people were more likely to choose the $50 instead of the $100. The implication of this study is that our brain treats our future self like someone else, a stranger maybe, which can make activities with future benefits, like saving for retirement or dieting, quite challenging.

In a follow-up study, Hershfield and colleagues showed the brain could be effectively tricked into treating our future self like our present self. The researchers took each participant's headshot and, using computer software, age-progressed their face to approximately 70 years old. Participants "interacted" with their future selves using virtual reality technology before completing a temporal discounting task. Interacting with the age-progressed picture resulted in participants shifting their temporal discounting behavior, choosing larger sums of money available in the future over smaller rewards available immediately.[7] Hershfield and colleagues showed that effectively conceptualizing the future can facilitate saving.

One advertiser who brilliantly executed the idea of bringing future and current self closer together (though perhaps without knowing the scientific thinking behind it) is Medifast, a weight loss company based in Owings Mills, Maryland. With its agency, Solve, it cleverly filmed people who were overweight as if they were talking to their future, slimmer self about how it feels to be overweight. Then, several months later, they filmed the same (now slimmer) person listening empathetically and encouraging their former self, and telling them how great it feels now that they have succeeded

---

6 Hershfield, H.E., Wimmer, G.E., Knutson, B. (2009) "Saving for the future self: neural measures of future self-continuity predict temporal discounting." *SCAN* 4: 85–92.

7 Hershfield, H.E., Goldstein, D.G., Sharpe, W.F., Fox, J., Yeykelis, L., Carstensen, L.L., Bailenson, J.N. (2011) "Increasing saving behavior through age-progressed renderings of the future self." *J Marketing Res* 48: S23–S37.

in losing weight. The best of the campaign, "Kimberley" feels absolutely authentic, and emotionally touching, as old Kimberley says to her new, slim self "seeing myself this way—now I know it's possible."

Perhaps the authenticity isn't surprising. Kimberley Vandlen, the Kimberley in the commercial, said in a *New York Times* interview,[8] that when she saw the footage of her old self,

> I broke down in tears, because I remember "that" girl, and I remember how badly she was feeling and not wanting to get up from the couch or play with my daughter because my knees would ache or ankles would ache.

Many of the behavioral changes that marketers require of users and choosers are easily postponed for a variety of practical and emotional reasons. In general, people will readily agree to change in the future, or for their future self, but in reality do little or nothing in the present. Recognize something of yourself in this? Rest assured—it's not just you, it's all of us. It's called human nature.

Hyperbolic and temporal discounting experiments demonstrated that the future is worth less than the present, but this doesn't mean that people cannot be encouraged to make decisions in the present that benefit their future selves. Behavioral economists Richard Thaler and Shlomo Benartzi[9] developed an ingenious program called "Save More Tomorrow" that made saving for retirement nearly effortless. Whenever participants received a pay raise, a percentage of the increase goes directly into their 401k every month. Called auto escalation, this manner of saving for retirement requires no additional effort from participants.

Save More Tomorrow is one ninja of a program; it nudges different tendencies at all the right times. As well as using auto-escalation (making the intensifying of the program effortless to the saver) it weaves in different construal levels, first to get agreement to save in advance, when it is a worthy idea rather than a pragmatic choice. But its design ensures concrete contributions to the program, making them less resistible by putting the "pain" of saving money in the future, which negates temporal discounting

---

[8] Newman, A.A. "Poignant Endorsements in Weight-Loss Campaign." *New York Times*, December 19, 2012.

[9] Thaler needs no introduction at this stage. Benartzi is Professor and Co-Chair of the Behavioral Decision-Making Group at UCLA Anderson School of Management.

effects. The *coup de gras* is that Save More Tomorrow takes loss aversion out of the equation by taking a percentage of your raise, before it hits your checking account and becomes money you can think about spending. By not taking money from that you could mentally spend, it makes the savings deduction not feel like a loss.

Forgive me for waxing so lyrically, but Save More Tomorrow is a very beautiful program.

According to Thaler and his confederates, Save More Tomorrow has worked well and has the potential to work even better. In its first implementation, the Save More Tomorrow program helped boost the average participant's 401(k) savings rate from 3.5% to 13.6% in just 3.5 years. A group who received standard financial advice moved from 4.4% to 8.8% over the same period.

In 2004, Thaler suggested that, with wide-scale adoption, Save More Tomorrow had the potential to increase U.S. savings by $125 billion.

The takeaways from this chapter are

- *Construal level theory* (CLT) means we think about the future in an entirely different way to the present. To get someone to **agree** to do something, give the outcome a distant horizon. To get someone to **do** something, give it near horizon. BUT—remember that to get someone to do something, that something needs to be framed in a way that addresses a short-term objective.

- Finish strong—don't forget that the end defines the experience.

- *Hyperbolic* or *temporal discounting* means we value a reward in the future less than we would value if we could have it now. Our preference is for smaller-sooner rather than larger-later.

- When we think about doing things for ourselves in the future it's almost as though we are thinking of someone else. One way of encouraging an action that has benefits in the future rather than now is to close the gap between current and future self.

- *Optimism bias* means we think bad things are less likely to happen to us than to others. Messages of fear and doom, while eliciting an emotional response, may not change behavior. It's almost like we think "Wow! That's scary, but it's going to happen to someone else, not me."

- The more people feel they can delay a decision, the less likely they are to make it. Giving people reasons to act now with time-sensitive messages and offers drives their decision making and helps prevent them from reviewing other options.

What others learned from this chapter:

- "...as a realtor I have transactions that are long and complicated with good moments and terrible. The finish strong idea is probably the most easily teachable marketing technique to retain repeat business."

- "This explains why I come back from holiday having bought clothes I'll never wear again. The problem is that the present-self and future-self are strangers to each other with different needs and even different tastes in clothes..."

8

Loss and Ownership

How people's non-conscious desire to avoid loss affects their choices in many, many ways.

Sometime in the 1890s, T.R Russell of Liverpool made a gold pocket watch. According to an inscription on the movement, Russell was a watchmaker for the Admiralty and the Queen. The watch has a beautiful, clean face and an assertive tick. It is about $1\frac{1}{2}$ inches in diameter and weighs a hefty $4\frac{3}{4}$ ounces. I know this because I weighed it on my kitchen scales a couple of months ago, before entrusting it to a safe deposit box.

I inherited the pocket watch from a great uncle I hardly knew. He was a laborer who had immigrated to England from County Donegal in Ireland in the 1920s. My great uncle worked hard for many years in dusty factories, earning little, spending less, and suffering from asbestosis later in life. No one in our family has any idea how he acquired the watch. It's romantic to think that he won it in a table game in Liverpool after getting off of the boat from Ireland, or cunningly stole it from some dandy. But by all accounts Great Uncle Carey was as clean-living and honest as the day is long, and it's likely the acquisition of the watch involved considerable hard work and financial sacrifice. Given that he lived a frugal life and never had anything in the way of luxuries, there must have been times when he thought of selling or pawning the watch. But he didn't. Whatever it had taken him to acquire the watch made it important for him to keep it. As he neared the end of his life, he gave the pocket watch to my aunt, telling her that he wanted it to stay in the family. She gave it to me.

Today, we live in an age of instant and easy acquisition, from Amazon One-Click to the potential of 3D printing. But just two generations ago, during Great Uncle Carey's life, most of you have relatives like him who struggled to acquire things that they then kept and passed on to the next generation.

If you go back just a few generations more, to the middle of the 18th century, your relatives (and we all, of course, have relatives that lived then, however often we forget we had forebears) would have been staggered by how easily we can get new stuff in the present day. In their time, before the Industrial Revolution, everyday people made goods, which included necessities like clothing. Artisan crafted goods weren't a chic choice; they were the only option. Because sewing machines wouldn't be invented for another hundred years or so, clothing was made entirely by hand, from spinning the thread to hand-stitching the final products.

Possessions came as a result of significant effort, in terms of labor and time. After you had acquired something, you would have been wise to try very hard to hang on to it, and to value it highly—perhaps even more highly than others might offer to pay you for it.

Let's go back further, say 10,000 years, to your ancestors who populated the earth at the dawn of civilization. They would have had virtually nothing in terms of surplus. To them, losing anything would have likely been devastating (and I mean devastating in terms of your ancestors' lives and survival prospects rather than just an emotional reaction). For all but a tiny percentage of human existence, the best strategy for surviving and thriving has been to focus on keeping what you already have before considering gains.

You might be thinking, "But that's ancient history. Things have changed." You might point to the fact that we can't wait to ditch our old iPhones, or that that we live in a disposable society (we seem to love razors, diapers, and product packaging that are all meant to be discarded after little use) because of the unnecessary amount of material we throw away. But remember what anthropologist Dean Falk of "Hobbit Man" fame said about 6,000 years ago being essentially today? Our ancestors' behavior still lives on in us, because while we seem to jettison a lot of stuff, consider the things we *don't* throw away that we could.

When my wife and I first arrived in the U.S. 16 years ago and were looking for somewhere to live, we were amazed by the abundance of storage space in every apartment we saw. And this was in San Francisco, one of the more space-constrained cities in the country. Compared to what we were used to from decades of living in European and Asian cities, what we found in the U.S. was storage heaven.

In spite of all the in-home storage spaces in this country, the American need for personal storage extends beyond the boundaries of the home. On the edges of nearly every town in America, you will find self-storage facilities. According to the Self Storage Association, the trade organization for this growing industry, there are 52,500 facilities across the U.S., for which Americans paid a total of $24 billion to use in 2013. They estimate the total square footage of storage in these facilities is 2.3 billion square feet—more than three times the size of Manhattan Island. Wall Street analysts described the industry as "recession proof." In 2012, Bloomberg ran an article titled "Best U.S. Real Estate Investment with Self Storage: Riskless Return."

With this growth of physical storage and the well-documented growth of data storage, you could say that today we live in a "Storage Society." In 2007, global data storage had grown to 295 billion gigabytes, which is nearly enough for a top-of-the range iPhone for every man, woman, and child on the planet. Andy Warhol is credited as saying: "In the future everyone will be famous for 15 minutes." These days it might be more accurate to say 15 gigabytes.

This need for storage—particularly secure storage—exists for deeply natural reasons and not just for humans, but for squirrels, ants, and woodpeckers as well. Avoiding loss and keeping what we have is instinctual; it's a feeling that drives many aspects of our behavior. By understanding our aversion to losing what we have acquired, you start to see reason in seemingly strange decisions: from those of sports coaches and umpires,[1] investors, medical doctors, shoppers, and even your own.

The cognitive mechanisms behind loss aversion and a number of other biases are encapsulated in *prospect theory*, a groundbreaking idea that emerged from the pioneering work in behavioral economics of academics including psychologists Daniel Kahneman and Amos Tversky and economist Richard Thaler.

Prospect theory won Kahneman a Nobel Memorial Prize for Economic Science in 2002. (His collaborator Tversky had died in 1996, and Nobels are not awarded posthumously.) James Montier, an influential economist, rates the impact of Kahneman and Tversky's seminal work very highly: "Prospect

---

[1] For fans of American sports, *Scorecasting* by Tobias J. Moskowitz and L. Jon Wertheim shows the effect of cognitive biases on players, managers, and umpires through analysis of sports data. They give a number of examples that relate to loss aversion and status quo bias.

theory has probably done more to bring psychology into the heart of economic analysis than any other approach."

The intersection of psychology and economics is Grand Central Station for marketers, and I think prospect theory is something that we should always have in the back of our minds. (A range of mouse mats, business card holders, and other executive tchotchkes with the motto *"Prospect theory is always at work in your customers' minds"* will shortly be available from the author's website.[2])

So what is it? Prospect theory provides a descriptive account of people's decision-making behaviors by considering how gains and losses affected choices. Kahneman and Tversky showed that when making a decision, people weigh the final outcome as less important than potential gains or losses, in contrast to rational economic models of choice. The theory provides rationales for several cognitive biases, such as *loss aversion,* the *endowment effect* and its close relative, *status quo bias,* and the *omission bias.* In this chapter, I aim to explain how these biases affect how people make choices.

The first phenomenon, *loss aversion,* is one of the first and most famous biases Kahneman and Tversky studied. Rationally, we should feel pretty much the same about gaining $100 as we would about losing $100, but their experiments showed we don't. In fact, losing something appears to have twice the psychological impact of gaining something. Sparky Anderson, the baseball coach, was scientifically on the money when he said, "Losing feels twice as bad as winning feels good."

In *Scorecasting,* Tobias J. Moskowitz and L. Jon Wertheim reference an interview in the *New York Times,* where Tiger Woods confessed to the psychological effect of loss aversion:

> Anytime you make big par putts, I think it is more important to make those than birdie puts. You don't want to ever drop a shot. The psychological difference between dropping a shot and making a birdie, I just think it's bigger to make a par putt.

I remember vividly feeling the effects of loss aversion about five years ago. We had just bought a 2010 chili pepper red and white MINI Cooper to replace our previous car—a 2004 chili pepper red and white MINI Cooper. Our original MINI was factory ordered (and thus full-priced) and had two accessory packages, which meant it was pretty well equipped for a 2004 car.

---

[2] Not really.

We bought its replacement off the lot—it came with one package and some other accessories, and was discounted by $2,500.

The new car had a number of cool things the previous one didn't. Bluetooth, a way better stereo, heated front seats, heated mirrors, better head lights, six gears rather than five—and was brand new.

For all of these additional features, there was one thing that the original had that its replacement didn't—a rain-sensing windshield that meant that the windshield wipers turned on automatically after a few drops of rain hit the windshield. In a rant about this innovation, James May, one of the co-presenters of BBC TV's global phenomenon *Top Gear* described rain-sensing windshield wipers as

> ...a prime example of the sort of technology for which no one was clamouring and which has not advanced our happiness one jot since some under-employed electronics nerd dreamt it up.[3]

A couple of days after getting the car, I was happily driving along and it started to rain. Having been flummoxed for a couple of seconds that the windshield wipers didn't turn on, I turned them on myself, an action that, by itself, was neither cognitively or physically taxing. But in my gut, I felt rather put out. Despite May's damning assessment of auto-sensing windshield wipers, and the fact that our new car had a host of goodies our old one didn't, at a visceral level I started to feel bad about our choice. I questioned the entire car. Should we have bought it off the lot—was it really the car we wanted? Should we have just kept the other one for a few more years? Had we made a terrible mistake? It took me a few minutes to realize that I was experiencing loss aversion because I no longer had auto-sensing windshield wipers. By locating the source of this feeling as the effect of a cognitive bias I was able to get over it and enjoy the snuggly comfort of those heated front seats.

Our innate aversion to loss can also explain why we hold onto objects, like that non-functioning first generation iPhone taking up space in your desk drawer.

Our aversion to loss doesn't just lead us to hang on to things, but also to stick with service plans. A friend at a brand consultancy told me of one of his clients who has a subscription model—customers sign up and get one

---

[3] May, J. "As seen on TV: Who needs rain-sensing wipers?" *Daily Telegraph*, March 2005.

service interaction a month. The services roll over if unused, but if a customer cancels their service, they lose all these unused appointments. This is very clever. Logically, if you need service so seldom that you have accumulated a stock of unused service interactions, you might question whether you need the subscription in the first place. But if canceling the subscription means that you will lose these interactions you have stocked up as credits, your intuitions will make the cancelation a very uncomfortable decision. Not surprisingly, the company in question has a very high retention rate.

A natural inference of our compunction to avoid loss is that we overvalue things we already own. This overvaluation is demonstrated by another phenomenon related to prospect theory, called the *endowment effect*. Economist Richard Thaler coined the term *endowment effect* to describe how people assign higher value to items they feel they own compared to identical items they do not own. In a now famous experiment, Thaler and collaborators demonstrated the endowment effect using Cornell University students and coffee mugs.[4] The students were given coffee mugs from the university bookstore and others received nothing. Students who weren't given a mug were asked what they would be willing to pay for such a mug; students who received one were asked how much money they required in order to part company with their mug. The striking finding from this experiment is that the amount of money students said they would accept to sell their mug transpired to be around *twice* the amount of money students without mugs were prepared to pay for a mug.

More recently, Dan Ariely conducted an experiment at Duke University that illustrates the endowment effect.[5] Basketball tickets are highly sought after at Duke, and when demand exceeds supply, student tickets are given out via lottery. Ziv Carmon and Ariely asked students who won tickets through the lottery what price they would sell them for and also asked students who did not win tickets how much they would pay for them. The difference in prices was staggering: Lottery winners wanted $2,400 while the ticketless wanted to pay $170!

One of my favorite examples of the endowment effect (and perhaps of loss aversion) is research by Jane Risen and Thomas Gilovich that demonstrates

---

[4] Kahneman, D., Knetsch, J.L., Thaler, R.H. (1991) "Anomalies: The Endowment Effect, Loss Aversion, and Status Quo Bias." *The Journal of Economic Perspectives*, 5(1): 193–206, Winter.

[5] Carmon, Z., Ariely, D. (2000) "Focusing on the forgone: how value can appear so different to buyers and sellers." *Journal of Consumer Research* 27: 360–370.

people's reluctance to swap a lottery ticket that they have acquired.[6] In one study, the researchers found that 46% of the participants agreed with the statement, "making the trade would make my old number more likely to win," whereas only 4% agreed that, "making the trade would make my old number less likely to win."

Ownership of an object makes us value it differently—not just financially, but emotionally. When Thaler was the victim of theft and had some expensive wines stolen, he told *The Economist* that he was, "now confronted with precisely one of my own experiments: these are bottles I wasn't planning to sell and now I'm going to get a cheque from an insurance company and most of these bottles I will not buy. I'm a good enough economist to know there's a bit of an inconsistency there."

A couple of years ago some fellow practitioners and I were chatting during a break at a conference where some research about the endowment effect had just been presented. We discussed how it helps brand leaders preserve their position more than it helps trailing brands usurp the leader. Our thinking was that the greater frequency of purchase and usage that brand leaders enjoy creates a sense of ownership, thus facilitating people valuing leading brands more highly. Out of the corner of her eye, one of our group, Elina Halonen[7] spotted none other than Richard Thaler, who was filling up his coffee mug just a few feet from us.

Reminiscent of the scene in *Annie Hall* where Woody Allen imagines producing Marshall McLuhan to clarify McLuhan's theories to a bore who is discussing them loudly in a movie theater line, my colleague enticed Dr. Thaler to join our discussion. Thaler seemed to agree with our hypothesis, and suggested that anything a trailing brand could do to create a sense of ownership—from using language that suggested it was yours, to free trials, and other ways to physically get it into people's hands—might help in its battle against the "endowed" market leader.

---

[6] Risen, J.L., Gilovich, T. (2007) "Another Look at Why People Are Reluctant to Exchange Lottery Tickets." *Journal of Personality and Social Psychology*, Cornell University 93(1): 12–22.

[7] Halonen is more involved in building connections between academics who study choice and the marketers who want to influence it than almost anyone else I know. She is a partner of a market research company (the Irrational Agency) that uses behavioral research methods; she is a communications consultant for the Society of Consumer Psychology, and she runs a blog on decision science (http://indecisionblog.com).

Simply having people touch, hold, or try on items seems to have an effect. A 2014 study from Point of Purchase Advertising International (POPAI)[8] revealed that 66% of observed "grabs" led to a purchase. A client who used to work for one of the world's largest clothes retailers told me that if they could get people to try an item on in the dressing room, it would result in a purchase 50% of the time. For the men's brand that she now works with, that number is 70%.

Research by Joann Peck from the University of Wisconsin and Suzanne Shu from the University of California Los Angeles shows that just getting people to touch a product elevates their valuation of it, improves their feelings toward it, and increases their sense of ownership of it.[9] Another recent study shows that more involved physical interactions (ones reminiscent of stroking or hugging) can create a stronger emotional connection to a product.[10] And a study from researchers at Boston College suggests that shopping online using a touchscreen device creates greater feelings of ownership than when using a keyboard and mouse.[11] The suggestion is that simply touching the image of a product with your finger has a similar effect to touching the product itself. The research showed the effect was even more noticeable for what the researchers called "products high in haptic importance," meaning items that you might want to touch and feel before purchase.

Earlier in the book, I mentioned Jodi Beggs' analysis of how cognitive biases affected Homer Simpson's decision making. In *The Simpson's* episode "Little Big Mom," Homer shows his susceptibility to the endowment effect, which Beggs describes:

> [The endowment effect] can lead to irrational behavior, such as when Homer frantically ran down the street to catch the Goodwill truck after Marge donated some old items from the attic:

---

[8] 2012 POPAI Shopper Engagement Study.

[9] Peck, J., Shu, S.B. (2009) "The Effect of Mere Touch on Perceived Ownership." *Journal of Consumer Research* 36(3).

[10] Hadi, R., Valenzuela, A. (2014) "A Meaningful Embrace: Contingent Effects of Embodied Cues of Affection." *Journal of Consumer Psychology* 24(4): 520–532.

[11] Brasel, S.A., Gips, J. (2014) "Tablets, touchscreens, and touchpads: How varying touch interfaces trigger psychological ownership and endowment." *Journal of Consumer Psychology* 24: 226–233.

"That was scary—we came this close to losing our spare Christmas tree stand."

It's pretty unlikely that Homer would have expended the same level of effort to obtain a spare Christmas tree stand that he didn't already own.

Loss aversion applies beyond just economic losses and gains; it is seen as one of the main reasons why moving people away from the status quo is difficult.

Our preference not to move away from the status quo is, predictably enough, called the *status quo bias.*

This bias was demonstrated in another behavioral experiment involving coffee mugs. Students in one group were given a choice between a mug and a bar of Swiss chocolate. In a second group, students were given a coffee mug, but were given the opportunity to exchange their mug for a chocolate bar a little later. A third group of students were given the chocolate bar, and later allowed to exchange it for the mug. Of those in the choice condition (the first group), 56% chose the mug and 44% chose the chocolate bar. While this shows some preference for the mug, it is still a pretty even choice between the two options. So you might expect that, when given the chance, around half of those originally given the mug would have traded it for the chocolate bar, and half of those given the chocolate bar would want to trade it for the mug. But this isn't what happened. Just 11% of those given a mug wanted to trade it for a chocolate bar, and only 10% of those given a chocolate bar decided to trade it for a mug.

A couple of years ago our healthcare agency invited me and Talya Miron-Shatz, a behavioral scientist and the founding director of the Center for Medical Decision Making at Ono Academic College, to participate in a strategic and tactical ideation workshop for a large pharmaceutical company. The workshop incorporated key principles of decision making.

Having made a breakthrough a decade earlier with a drug that had revolutionized treatment of a serious illness, the pharmaceutical company had launched a drug that promised faster results to a wider range of people afflicted by the same disease. Yet despite this, physicians were extremely reticent to prescribe the new drug and continued to prescribe the old one. After reviewing the focus groups and other research that the client had carried out, our conclusion was that the physicians had become "endowed" with the old drug (it had, after all, enabled them to give a lot of patients good news over the years), and what we needed to overcome was status quo bias, which led the physician to favor their existing choice over any new option. Our advice to the client was that while it may be tempting to market the new, superior drug through its differences, and ask physicians to change their choice, we should instead focus on how this was a similar choice to their original decision to choose and prescribe the older drug.

The doctors' reluctance to move from the safety of an existing, even if suboptimal choice, is classic status quo bias, which relates all the way back to Kahneman and Tversky's prospect theory. Dr. Miron-Shatz, CEO of CureMyWay who constantly works with the healthcare industry and with physician choices, describes it this way:

> Physicians are human. So it shouldn't be a surprise that in many cases, they are as influenced, or as biased, as the next person. I have studies showing that when receiving too much information, physician choices become less than optimal. In another study we show that gynecologists' recommendations for amniocentesis reduce dramatically when they hear the woman has become pregnant through IVF treatments. This makes them think of the procedure risk, which is really there all the time, though not necessarily a main consideration for them, until confronted with a "precious pregnancy."

Miron-Shatz believes that, just like with other humans, cognitive biases like the status quo bias drive doctors' decisions more than they realize. She says

> Few doctors will say things like "if I prescribe anything other than the prevailing drug, patients and colleagues may raise their eyebrows, so why should I?" Or "I prefer to play it safe and do what everyone else is doing." Or even "this drug is not great, but I'm used to it and know what to expect. This sense of certainty is important to me, and it also helps me reassure the patient. I realize that the new drug offers more hope, but I'm less familiar with it, and there's less of a sense of certainty, so I really hesitate to prescribe it." Just with any behavior you are trying to change or influence, this can only be done if you know the underlying reason for the behavior. Otherwise, you can show the physicians really good data till the cows come home and still not convince them, because you haven't targeted their biases and emotional preferences.

John Gourville, a Harvard University professor and author of an excellent paper "The Curse of Innovation,"[12] would probably agree with Miron-Shatz. He points out that when marketers try to engineer the behavioral change necessary to get people to try new products, we typically tell people what they might gain, or we emphasize how our product is different and innovative. But we fail to consider and address what people may *lose* by changing their existing behavior.

His paper very elegantly explains the effect of loss aversion on the development of innovations from the perspective of both the people who develop them and the people who may choose them.

Gourville's paper is a must read for anyone in marketing, and a must, must read for anyone involved in innovation. Starting with the often-stated high failure rates of new products failing (estimates vary from 40% to 90% across categories), Gourville has a unique take on why such an alarmingly high amount of products fail. Typically, most innovation focuses on what people will gain from it. Developers become obsessed with how the new product is different from what has gone before it. But many differences driven by innovation require users to change their current behavior, which means giving up an existing behavior and the perceived benefits that go with that. The innovation may be "better," but what might be given up leads to an intuitive feeling of loss and resistance to the new product, as the physicians we described a couple of paragraphs ago experienced. Understanding what you are asking people to change, and particularly what you are asking them to give up by adopting an innovation and thus moving from their status quo, is a critical but often unasked question.

Gourville suggests that after a substantial investment of time, money, and effort in the innovation, the developers tend to see the status quo as their new product. Thus they are often over-optimistic of success, and fail to consider a key point—rather than being focused only on the advantages their product offers, they should also think about how their innovative product is compatible with existing behaviors and choices.

Don't lose out! Leveraging loss aversion to your benefit is possible. Tell people they are going to miss out. Although people like to gain stuff, they really, really, *really* hate to lose it. Loss aversion has a powerful effect when

---

[12] Gourville, J. "The Curse of Innovation: A Theory of Why Innovative New Products Fail in the Marketplace." Harvard Business School Working Paper, No. 06-014, September 2005.

people feel at risk of missing something to which they are entitled. This feeling is something well known to all of us—it is even referred to in popular culture as "fomo," or "fear of missing out." The *Urban Dictionary* gives the following as an example:

> Billy's fomo grew stronger when all of his friends had tickets to the upcoming show! Against all good reasoning, he went to the venue anyway without tickets!

People's fear of missing out is probably most present when people feel that something may be scarce.

"Whatever is rare, uncommon or dwindling in availability—this idea of scarcity—confers value on objects, or even relationships," Robert Cialdini said. On the telephone, people are less likely to remain on hold if they are told, "someone will be available soon" rather than if they are told that "all agents are busy." The first scenario suggests the service is unpopular; the second makes people wait for hard-to-come-by, or scarce, service.

One of Robert Cialdini's "six rules of influence" is the *scarcity principle*, according to which people assign more value to opportunities when they are less available. Scarcity, or sense of rarity of some sort, should be implicit in every luxury brand's narrative. Cues of scarcity can come from descriptions of precious materials or from manufacturing processes that clearly can't keep up with demand ("handmade by a dying breed of artisans in ateliers in the Pyrenees"). Or even blatant marketing approaches such as "limited editions" or time-limited offers where we might know rationally that the scarcity is artificial, but our instincts get the better of us. Ferrari's famous approach of making one car *less* than anticipated demand is a brilliant application of the scarcity principle. Digital environments provide great opportunities to communicate scarcity in real time. If you book flights online, you have probably noticed more and more airlines informing you that there are "only two seats remaining at this price." This is very likely an effective tactic, prompting choosers to be decisive in favor of that airline. But airlines are proof that you have to handle scarcity carefully. In the past they have come under criticism for using the scarcity created by the high demand of peak time travelling periods to ramp up prices. This can lead to *inequity aversion*, which as we saw in Chapter 5, "Getting Familiar," can lead to people walking away from a brand.

The premium spirits market is reliant on products with built-in appeals to scarcity. A "12 Year Old" whiskey is, by definition, a limited supply—you can't turn the clock back and make another batch.

Beam Suntory (or Beam Inc. as it was called, before its takeover by Suntory in early 2014), owner of Laphraoig, Courvoisier, Sauza tequila, Jim Beam, Maker's Mark, Knob Creek, and many other fine spirits know this very well. Knob Creek is aged nine years (significantly more than the legally required minimum of two-years aging for bourbons) and their volume forecasts for 2009, which determined their production in 2000, were way below what demand turned out to be. (Personally, I put this down to the launch of the TV series *Mad Men* in 2007 and the lead character, Don Draper's affection for the bourbon based cocktail, the Old Fashioned. But this may be a case of a *self-serving bias*, leading me to see my occupation as more influential than it really is. The growth of export markets is probably a more important factor.)

In 2007 the team at Maker's Mark planned production for their six-year aged brand. Like Knob Creek four years earlier, Maker's Mark didn't have enough inventory to meet drinkers' demand. (I'll continue with my *Mad Men* hypothesis—2007 was the year the first season started—by 2013 it was a global phenomenon, and a taste-maker for anyone likely to be drinking premium spirits.)

Each brand took a very different approach to deal with its respective shortage. The typical reaction of most marketers to having no product to sell would be to reel in marketing and advertising spend to an absolute minimum. In 2009 Knob Creek did the opposite—running a campaign to celebrate their supply shortage. Ads showing the last drops being poured from an empty bottle ran with a headline saying, "Thanks for nothing." The brand's most loyal drinkers were given T-shirts that said "I survived the drought of 2009" and a letter that thanked them for creating the "'situation' here at the distillery" which had led then to running out of Knob Creek. The well-crafted letter went on to reassure them that normal service would return soon without any compromise to quality:

> Keep in mind that our next batch will be fully matured and ready to go this November (we'd bottle it now to boost supply, but then it wouldn't be aged a full 9 years, and it wouldn't really be Knob Creek).

The letter closed with a final nod to scarcity to stoke anticipation for the new batch.

> Now, hang in there and cherish every drop of Knob Creek like it's the last, because, well, it could be. Until November anyway.

While not having access to sales figures, my guess would be that this approach helped Knob Creek become an even stronger brand when the drought ended and supply and demand were realigned.

Maker's Mark took another route. Realizing that it wouldn't have enough spirit to meet demand, it came up with a strategy to help it boost supply by 6%. Bill Samuels Jr., the son of the brand's founder, announced on February 11, 2013, that they would dilute the spirit from 45% alcohol (90 proof) to 42% alcohol (84 proof). They insisted that drinkers wouldn't notice the change, as "even Maker's Mark's professional taste testers couldn't tell the difference."

One week later, after considerable outcry from their customers, Samuels announced that they were reversing the decision. He noted, in a letter that was posted online:

> The unanticipated dramatic growth rate of Maker's Mark is a good problem to have, and we appreciate some of you telling us you'd even put up with occasional shortages.

Even for the brand's loyal drinkers, waiting was a preferable option to dilution.

This apparent discrepancy—preferring to not have something instead of having a lesser version—reveals another interesting aspect of scarcity. We talked about our desire for "now" earlier, and we'll see later how we find it difficult to muster the self-control to put off consuming things immediately, even when there are benefits in the delay. When a product is in limited supply and people accept that they have to wait, the result can have a surprising emotional upside.

Anticipation is a powerful force. While the anticipation of bad things is often more stressful and painful than the event itself, the anticipation of something positive often trumps how we feel about the actual experience.

Researchers from the Netherlands looked at this phenomenon by measuring the happiness of a sample of "vacation-takers," and compared them to a control group of people who were not taking a vacation over the period of the research.[13]

---

[13] Nawijn, J., Marchand, M.A., Veenhoven, R., Vingerhoets, A.J. (2010) "Vacationers Happier, but Most not Happier After a Holiday." *Applied Research in Quality of Life* 5(1): 35–47.

The broad finding was that the vacationers appeared no happier than the non-vacationers, but they were happier during the period where they *anticipated* the vacation. Jeroen Nawijn, who led the research said in an interview with the *New York Times*:[14]

> The practical lesson for an individual is that you derive most of your happiness from anticipating the holiday trip.... What you can do is try to increase that by taking more trips per year. If you have a two-week holiday you can split it up and have two one-week holidays. You could try to increase the anticipation effect by talking about it more and maybe discussing it online.

While every product experience isn't as much fun to anticipate as a vacation, there are a couple of interesting take-away points for marketers here. As Nawijn suggests, anticipation is increased by discussion, so encouraging potential choosers to discuss what they will do with your product could be a way to increase emotional engagement. Another point is that breaking an experience down comes with emotional benefits. Two one-week vacations will yield more overall happiness than one two-week trip. How can marketers make one block experience of your product a number of smaller or shorter ones?

I think of scarcity almost as a super food in the world of influence strategies. It does many different things. It makes a product seem superior, because it suggests demand outstrips supply. It has implied social proof—because we figure that if something is scarce, demand must have been high. For example, the opening line of the Knob Creek ad I mentioned earlier reads "You see, because we have so many loyal customers out there, demand for Knob Creek Bourbon has finally outstripped supply." Scarcity has the power to get people to think about future consumption and experience it in a positive and emotional way. By appealing to our fear of missing out, scarcity drives action. Not bad for something that has its origins in human nature and our intuitions around loss.

The takeaways from this chapter are

- Prospect theory is a key building block of behavioral economics, and can be found as a force behind many different choices people make.

- Loss aversion means that losses loom larger than gains.

---

14 Parker-Pope, T. "How Vacations Affect Your Happiness" *New York Times* February 18, 2010.

- The endowment effect means we value what we have.

- Status quo bias means that we have a preference for the current state of affairs.

- Appeals to scarcity are very powerful. Scarcity leverages fear of missing out (triggering loss aversion), and suggests the object or service is high quality and demanded (creating implicit social proof). It can also stall instant gratification and make people wait for something, allowing for the emotional benefits of anticipation.

What other people gained from this chapter:

- "The notion that your superior innovation should resist standing apart from the category leader is so counterintuitive, it hurts...and likely doesn't get implemented very often. Overcoming the pain and trying out this neat little piece of jiu-jitsu could prove very productive."

- "In my first working weeks I was taught that the most powerful marketing tool of all is sampling. What I didn't know then was how the endowment effect ascribes greater value to something that people own." (Author's note: While the endowment effect and the sense of ownership it ascribes is one of the things that makes sampling effective, another is likely to be the very powerful evolutionary drive of *reciprocity*.)

9

Make People Feel Smart, Attractive—or Even Lucky...

How people feel at the time of a choice can change the choice they make and how they make it.

Years ago, a copywriter I worked with told me that he was continually surprised by how even the most intelligent people were susceptible to flattery. I was doubly flattered when he then proceeded to flatter me.

Behavioral science backs up my colleague's observation. Even a disembodied voice is capable of effective flattery. A computer voice was used to flatter participants while they completed a quiz, and the flattering comments led people to not only perform better on the quiz but also to report more positive emotions, more positive evaluations of the interaction, and more positive regard for the computer—and all of this happened even though people knew that the flattery from the computer was purely random![1]

As Robert Cialdini said, "We are phenomenal suckers for flattery."

Flattery might not just make us feel better about ourselves but also the person (or entity) who flatters us. It may influence our decisions as well. As the computer flattery study showed, flattery influences us even when we know it is insincere. Another behavioral science research study, tellingly titled "Insincere Flattery Actually Works: A Dual Attitudes Perspective"[2]

---

[1] Fogg, B.J., Nass, C. (1997) "Silicon sycophants: the effects of computers that flatter." *International Journal of Human Computer Studies* 46(5): 551–561.

[2] Chan, E., Sengupta, J. (2010) "Insincere Flattery Actually Works: A Dual Attitudes Perspective." *Journal of Marketing Research* 47: 122–133.

---

demonstrates the effect of flattery in a way that also tells us something about the lasting power of information we acquire non-consciously.

Participants were exposed to an advertisement from a fictitious fashion retailer that flattered their style and fashion sense. When given time to think about the complimentary advertisement, respondents discounted the flattery. The advertisement was impersonal, so how could the flattery be sincere as it wasn't a comment on *their* personal sense of style? And wasn't there clearly an ulterior motive? The store was just trying to get them to part with their cash.

But the researchers looked beyond these considered reactions in two ways. First, they asked themselves, "What would happen if the participants didn't have the time to think about the message (which is, of course, the normal state of affairs when people are exposed to advertising)? Second, they asked, "What would happen after the passage of some time?"

What the researchers found was that the flattery that had been rationally discounted at an explicit level still had a powerful effect. One group of respondents (the explicit state) were given as much time as they needed to indicate how they felt about the store while another group (the implicit state) were required to respond quickly, within five seconds. This technique, measuring response speed to assess the strength of agreement or disagreement with a statement is a form of *implicit association*; we'll discuss this technique in more detail in Chapter 15, "Think Differently about Market Research." Associations made about the store were stronger and more positive by people in the implicit state compared to people in the explicit state, who had more time to consider the ad and their feelings.

The researchers repeated the experiment but added a twist. As a way of saying thank you, participants were offered a coupon from either the store that had served them up the flattering message or from a competing store that didn't deploy flattery in its approach. One group of participants made their choice immediately while the other group was contacted three days later to indicate their choice.

In both cases, participants preferred the choice from the store that had flattered them. This may have been because of the flattery but equally could be because of the effect of familiarity (everyone had been exposed to the flattering store earlier in the experiment) that I discussed earlier, in Chapter 2, "The Ever-Advancing Science of Choice." But what is really interesting is that after the three days elapsed, the number choosing the coupon from the flattering store increased from 64% to 80%. One possible explanation is that the rational moderating of the flattery ("they're just trying to get me to part with my cash") doesn't last as long as the non-conscious appeal of the flattery itself.

When people feel attractive, it affects their behavior and choices. In a paper titled "Of the Bold and the Beautiful"[3] researchers report on six studies where they primed some participants in ways designed to make them feel attractive. In each experiment there was also a control group that had not been conditioned in this way.

In the one experiment, the participants were given the option of a safe choice for a vacation (everything average, nothing exceptional) and a vacation spot that had exceptionally positive aspects but also included some negative ones. Those primed to feel more attractive were more likely to choose the more extreme option.

In other experiments, those primed to feel attractive were more likely to move away from a default choice in a mundane area of public policy (suggesting they were more open to shifting from the status quo); more likely to be optimistic about their future; and more likely to be unrealistic about the date by which they would complete a homework task.

When people feel attractive it seems they make bolder and more extreme choices, suggesting that marketers could use this tactic for a wider range of applications than fashion or skincare.

Allowing people to feel smart, or to feel they have mastery in an area relevant to the choice they are making, can have an effect on choices. Similar to when people feel attractive, feeling smart, competent, or like an expert can also lead them to make quicker and bolder decisions.

Increasing people's confidence makes them act more quickly and feel better about their choice. Confidence can be increased with simple mechanics like quizzes that let people feel they know more about the product category than they thought they did.

Psychologists call this feeling *self-efficacy*. It is the condition we attain when we have confidence in ourselves to achieve a specific goal. It is very much evidence based—we reach a state of self-efficacy when we realize, or it is revealed to us, that we have what it takes to get us to the next level. Unlike

---

[3] "Of the Bold and the Beautiful: How Feeling Beautiful Leads to More Extreme Choices" Margaret Gorlin, Yale School of Management; Zixi Jiang, Guanghua School of Management; Jing Xu, Guanghua School of Management; Ravi Dhar, Yale School of Management.

self-esteem, which is more a general sense of feeling good about ourselves, self-efficacy relates to our performance as it relates to specific skills and processes. In recent years, things that improve self-efficacy, such as praise or reinforcement of actions or process, have been seen to have a more positive effect with both children and athletes than praising the individual. Saying, "You really stuck at that math problem" as opposed to, "You are really good at math" leads to people valuing the process rather than overvaluing their innate gifts. For marketing, helping someone increase their self-efficacy in a particular area is a win-win for both the marketer and the chooser.

One benefit is that if people feel confident in a process they are more likely to put the effort into complete it. An online study[4] shows that website visitors were 23% more likely to enroll in a free trial when the website showed instructions for signing up rather than showing testimonials from satisfied clients.

Another is that when people have been primed to have a sense of their self-efficacy in an area where they will make more daring choices, they are often more decisive and more likely to make decisions that overcome inertia, or go against the default or status quo.[5]

Albert Bandura, one of modern psychology's giants, puts self-efficacy at the heart of his social cognitive theory. He explains that

> People avoid activities and situations they believe exceed their coping capabilities. But they readily undertake challenging activities and select situations they judge themselves capable of handling.[6]

Making the decision to choose your product or service a task that choosers "judge themselves capable of handling" could be a very powerful precursor to choice itself, especially for complex decisions.

Providing experiences that allow people to see that they are acquiring knowledge, discernment, and *savoir-faire* can lead them to be more decisive and to make bolder choices with confidence, which in turn increases their appreciation of the goods they have chosen. Nespresso is a case in point. It

---

4 Weedmark, D. "The Importance of Self-Efficacy in Marketing," Demand Media.

5 Krueger, N., Dickson, P. (1994) "How Believing in Ourselves Increases Risk Taking: Perceived Self-Efficacy and Opportunity Recognition" *Decision Sciences* 25(3): 385–400.

6 Bandura, A. (1993) "Perceived Self-Efficacy in Cognitive Development and Functioning" *Educational Psychologist* 28(2): 117–148.

provides a coded system of names and colors that may appear complex at first but is learned quickly by users, making them feel more expert in the system and about coffee in general. Bike shops that offer bicycle maintenance classes allow their customers to become more confident with bikes. My personal experience is that as I became more confident about repairing bikes, I have spent more on them.

This is probably why high-performance car brand, Mercedes-Benz's AMG, has developed its Driving Academy. During a day-long course at racetracks around the U.S. and other countries, "civilian" drivers are taught how to drive high-performance vehicles. By increasing these drivers' confidence in handling these machines, I would be pretty certain the experience increases the likelihood of their buying high-performance cars in the future.

One thing key to creating a state of self-efficacy among choosers is making information available to help people feel they are making informed choices. "But," you might be saying, "surely the last thing people need in this information-overloaded world is more information?"

Since 2011, the Institute of Decision Making has been involved in a large-scale quantitative study in conjunction with our holding company, Interpublic Group.[7] This study looks at people's attitudes about marketing information in its various forms. Our value in this exercise has been to add a layer of analysis and interpretation to the data, based on learning from behavioral science.

In the study a number of questions ask people how they feel about marketing and product information. Is it helpful? Is there too much of it?

We had confidently expected that consumers would complain about the incessant bombardment of information to which they are subjected, given that information volume has been tracking with Moore's Law[8] since the dawn of the digital age. Every week a journal or news magazine warns of the perils of information overload.

---

[7] "New Realities—Consumer Decision Making in Today's New Information World" is proprietary research that polls attitudes about information sources among several thousand consumers across the world's seven most important economies.

[8] Moore's law is the observation that, over the history of computing hardware, the number of transistors in a dense integrated circuit doubles approximately every two years. The observation is named after Gordon E. Moore, co-founder of the Intel Corporation, who described the trend in his 1965 paper (Wikipedia).

But to our surprise, across every country we surveyed, rather than being overwhelmed or confused by the increase in information from marketers, people generally seemed to consider it helpful.

One explanation may be that we asked specifically about marketing or product information. Most of the headlines in magazines about information overload are about information in its broadest sense (the recurring villain is e-mail, especially in a work context). Marketing information seems to fall into a less troublesome mental bucket, as it doesn't impose an obligation on us in the same way that a boss or colleague might.

Nonetheless, the counterintuitive response from the survey led us to dig a little deeper into the history of information overload.

Scholars have long had concerns of the consequences of too much information on the general population. In the first century CE, Seneca the Elder claimed, "The abundance of books is a distraction." (I'm not sure how many books were in circulation 2,000 years ago, but it can't have been many.) Alvin Toffler coined the actual phrase "information overload" and described its destructive effect on individuals and society in his 1970 book *Future Shock*, which was written while the world was still firmly in the ink and paper era. Nicholas Carr's book *The Shallows* and essay "Is Google Making Us Stupid" takes the concerns into the digital age.

People have been complaining about the effects of too much information for nearly as long as people have been complaining. (By and large the concern is from philosophers or sages, and their beef is the effect of too much information on other, less-learned people rather than themselves.) However, humans seem to have endured this assault of information pretty well.

I think the answer why humans are okay with an abundance of information may lie in the truth that there has *always* been too much information—and we have always filtered most of it out.

Even though information continues to increase exponentially, perhaps one thing greater than technology's ability to generate more information may be the human brain's ability to ignore it. (Remember the description earlier in the book of the human brain as an adept "ignoring machine.") We humans have found ways to manage or ignore the glut of information, be it from Guttenberg or Google, and these days we use technology as well as our innate instincts to filter it out.

Providing plentiful information may be important because other data from New Realities suggests that, when it comes to making good decisions, and being satisfied with brands, consumers seem to think more information is better. The idea of more is better when it comes to quantity of information conflicts with a lot of decision science literature; a wide range of behavioral experiments[9] suggest that more information leads to poorer decisions. Typically, though, these experiments require people to pay attention to and to use the information as they struggle with their choices. However, outside of the lab, and in the real-life world, attention is never a given. My feeling is that for the participants in the New Realities study, their positive responses didn't come from their trying to use all this information to inform choices, but that the mere knowledge that information was available allowed them to approach decision-making with greater confidence.

Recent work from David Faro at the London Business School suggests that the availability of tools improves performance through creating greater perceived self-efficacy, *even if those tools are not used*:

> ...merely having a task-relevant product available for consumption (without actually consuming it) can improve performance. Participants with access to coffee during a reaction-speed task performed better than participants without access to coffee. Participants with access to a dictionary solved more word puzzles than those without access to a dictionary. We propose that having the product available enhances consumers' perceived self-efficacy to cope with a situation or a task. In line with this account, task difficulty and feedback on a preceding task moderate the effect, and a measure of self-efficacy mediates it.[10]

This increased self-efficacy by merely having information available may have important implications on how marketing materials, particularly in the area of product information, are evaluated. Often, marketers consider information effective only if it is shown that consumers have used it. But it is quite possible that materials and information may be at their most influential when they are merely available, rather than used.

While simply executing a data dump is not an advised approach, the issue for marketers may not be volume of information they provide as much as being smart about how they connect and curate it. As Edward Tufte,

---

[9] Including Bastardi, A., Shafir, E. (1998) "On the pursuit and misuse of useless information." *Journal of Personality and Social Psychology* 75(1): 19–32.

[10] Faro, D., Heller, M., Irmak, C. (2011) "Merely Accessible: Products May Be Effective Without Actual Consumption," in *NA - Advances in Consumer Research*, Volume 38, eds. Dahl, D.W., Johar, G.V., van Osselaer, S.M.J. Duluth, MN: *Association for Consumer Research*.

the celebrated authority on information design and data visualization, is reputed to have suggested, the problem isn't so much information overload as organizational underload.

One thing that is as powerful as feeling smart is feeling that you have outsmarted the system. According to our New Realities data, the most positive attribute of marketing information was that it made people feel smarter about their choices. The second most positive was that "it helped them beat the system," which was particularly true in Brazil, India, and China.

Feeling they have beaten, or outsmarted the system is emotionally rewarding for people—even if it takes a little deceit to do so.

In the preface, I referenced Dan Ariely's research about honesty and cheating. (Ariely ended up writing a whole book about the subject: *The Honest Truth about Dishonesty*.) Now, don't judge me on this statement, but I will go as far as to say that lying, while not morally desirable, is entirely natural. In 2011 at South By Southwest (a music, film, and interactive conference and festival held in Austin, Texas, every year), I attended a talk by Genevieve Bell, the director of User Experience at Intel Labs. Bell, who is also well known as an anthropologist, was profound, witty, and touchingly human on the subject "Our Devices: How Smart is too Smart?" One of her key points was that for technology to be completely natural, it had to become smart enough to intuitively keep our secrets and to tell lies for us. Not Bernie Madoff–size lies, but the little lies that lubricate relationships or ease social awkwardness. Or on occasion, the lies that get us something we want, that strictly speaking, we may not be entitled to.

Ever wondered why those friends and family offers (they work really well by the way) get passed around with such glee by people who are neither friends nor family of employees of the company?

Research from Christina I. Anthony and Elizabeth Cowley[11] of the University of Sydney may cast some light on why those offers work. Their findings suggest that there could be benefits in turning a blind eye to, or even encouraging, consumers to be a little "economical with the truth."[12]

---

[11] Anthony, C.I., Cowley, E. (2012) "The Labor of Lies: How Lying for Material Rewards Polarizes Consumers' Outcome Satisfaction." *Journal of Consumer Research* 39(3): 478–492.

[12] A phrase famously used by then UK Cabinet Secretary, Sir Robert Armstrong, during the 1986 Australian "Spycatcher" trial, in defense of a statement he had given. "It contains a misleading impression, not a lie. It was being economical with the truth."

According to Anthony and Cowley, by the time the average person is 60, they will have told 43,800 lies. Their research looked at what happened when people had to be loose with the truth in order to get a product or service they wanted, but that strictly speaking, they weren't entitled to.

In one lab experiment, participants were given the opportunity to misrepresent their usage details during an interaction with a service provider so that they qualified for a small incentive.

If denied, they tended to be less happy, but when they succeeded in qualifying for something, that strictly speaking, they weren't entitled to, they were significantly happier than the consumers who were entitled to it. The psychologist and economist George Loewenstein sees a benefit for brands in the halo of this happiness. "The silver lining for the retailers is that if they are lied to, maybe the consumer is getting away with something they shouldn't but at least they get the benefit of goodwill from the consumer," Loewenstein said.[13]

I think there may be something more informative for marketers in this research, and it relates to the value of surprise that we discussed in Chapter 5, "Getting Familiar." Marketers frequently give discounts or give away free promotional items, but more often these are things to which their customers may feel that they are entitled. Prefacing these offers with phrases like, "As a valued customer…" may make the marketer feel that they are getting more "credit" for the offer, but letting customers feel they are getting the reward because of their smarts, good fortune or even, heaven forbid, their willingness to be a little loose with the truth, may lead to greater satisfaction. That a company has bestowed something on them can make a customer feel good, but if customers think they got that reward due to something innate, because of something special about them, it makes them feel even better.

The takeaways from this chapter are

- Even though people discount flattery at a rational level, it works at an implicit level.

---

[13] Equally, giving people more than makes sense can have a catastrophic effect financially and in terms of brand equity. Upon reading this chapter, a colleague reminded me of the Hoover free flights promotion disaster of 1992. Faced with a huge inventory surplus, Hoover's UK division offered free flights to purchasers who bought more than £100 worth of products. The response for the promotion overwhelmed Hoover, and it ended up costing them £48 million, with court cases continuing for 6 years. You can read the BBC story about "one of the greatest marketing disasters of all time" here: http://news.bbc.co.uk/2/hi/business/3704669.stm.

- Having confidence in one's ability to complete tasks or achieve goals is called *self-efficacy*. Marketing can really help people reach this state, which can be emotionally and functionally beneficial for the end user or chooser. In the past, brands tried to position themselves as the experts. From the perspective of helping people make confident choices, focus more on helping them feel expert.

- If you can make people feel confident in their ability to make a decision they will make it more quickly and more boldly. Quizzes and games can really help with this. Asking them a question (like "which uses the most data, video or audio?") could create a sense of self-efficacy in choosing a wireless data plan.

- Don't always "grant" your choosers benefits and offers. Sometimes you can benefit more by letting them feel that they have acquired them through their own smarts, or even just good fortune.

What this chapter made other extremely intelligent people think:

- "I won't be the only one to read this and wonder whether we should spend less time figuring out how to declare that our brand is a winner, and a lot more making sure it's the customer that feels victorious."

- "...this explains the popularity of the 'hack' that has dominated social media in the past few years. The 'hack' is the social celebration of the consumer having outsmarted the corporate system in a way that fits their life even better than intended. (They 'got away with more' out of the product than anyone intended.)"

10

Make It Easy—For the Mind and the Body

Humans' innate tendency to save physical and mental energy can work for you.

About 20 years ago, I found myself playing soccer with a pig-tailed macaque (a medium-sized monkey) on the Thai island of Phuket. I was working for an advertising agency in Bangkok at the time, and we were shooting a TV commercial for one of our clients, whose marketing program included encouraging Thai kids to play sports and attend sports camps. The commercial's story was about a young boy from the rural south of Thailand who practiced his soccer shooting skills while his pet monkey played goalkeeper. The pig-tailed macaque has been trained and used in the south of Thailand for centuries to harvest coconuts. The monkeys leap around in the coconut palms and bite the coconuts off at the stalk. Because the monkeys then throw the coconuts down to the humans below (who pile the coconuts into trucks for transport), the use of the monkey catching and throwing a soccer ball made sense to the Thai audience.

In the commercial, the monkey's athleticism and reflexes made him a difficult opponent to score against unless the boy managed to shoot low into the corner of the goal. The commercial ends with the boy scoring the winning goal at a tournament in a big city by employing the same tactics against a human goalkeeper.

At one of the many breaks in the shooting of the commercial (and, if you have ever attended a shoot, you will know it is a slow-moving and tedious process filled with many such breaks), I asked the monkey's trainer if I could try and score a goal against the monkey.

The macaque was a very good goalkeeper—his razor-sharp reactions and acrobatic leaps made him almost unbeatable. Any shot within a yard or so to either side of him he didn't just stop, but, diving at the last second, would catch the ball cleanly and then roll it back to me (or at least in my general direction). I noticed after a while that any shot that was even just a little more than a yard away from him beat him every time, but not because he was making a futile effort for the sake of appearances or because that's the norm, as we see professional (human) goalkeepers doing all the time.[1] The monkey simply ignored anything more than a yard away, to the point that it seemed as if a ball flying just beyond his reach didn't even exist. The ball was only of interest when he knew it was catchable, hence the last-minute dives. As soon as it became apparent the catch was easy, he didn't miss an opportunity to act. If the catch was difficult, even just a little difficult, the instinct to act never kicked in. It seemed as binary as that.

From an evolutionary perspective, this binary scenario makes a lot of sense. Effort uses calories (energy), and most animals seem to have an intuitive sense as to when effort exceeds the reward. Going back to Chapter 6, "Thanks for Sharing (Whether You Meant to or Not)," and the gulls who were eyeing the sandwich you were enjoying on a park bench; they would noisily squabble over a large crust you might have thrown them. But if you were to chuck them a small crumb, it would be a different story. An individual bird may deign to eat it, if the crumb lands very close it. But a similar-sized crumb thrown four or five feet from a bird would be ignored.

We, being animals, are just the same. One of the simplest and most accurate ways of predicting whether we pursue one behavior or another is to work out which one, from a cognitive and physical perspective, is the easiest. That's the one we'll choose.

Our ancestors from the Victorian era (a mere five generations ago) might chide us for committing the cardinal sin of sloth for following the path of least resistance. However, from an evolutionary perspective, sloth is simply common sense.

---

[1] A study shows when soccer goalkeepers face a penalty, they are likely to pick a side before the ball is kicked and dive left or right as an extravagant display of effort, even though the probability distribution of kick direction means their best strategy would be to stay in the center of the goal. Bar-Eli, M., Azar, O.H., Ritov, I., Keidar-Levin, Y., Schein, G. (2005) "Action bias among elite soccer goalkeepers: The case of penalty kicks." *Journal of Economic Psychology* 28(2007): 606–621.

For any marketer intent on creating a movement or starting a trend, Duncan Watts' book *Everything is Obvious** *(*once you know the answer)* is well worth reading. By studying huge data sets (Watts is a data scientist *and* a social scientist), Watts pours cold water on the theory that getting a few influencers to do something will trigger a bigger movement in the mainstream population. This theory, popularized by Malcolm Gladwell in *The Tipping Point*, would be wonderfully convenient for marketers (and lucrative for influencers) if it worked with any degree of frequency. Watts' point is that it is very often the less obvious factors, or ones lying deeper in the weeds, that make movements happen. These factors are often difficult to predict (unless you know the answer of course).

In his book, Watts writes about a question he asked Columbia University undergraduates: Why might the rate of people consenting to donate their organs in one European country be as low as 12% and in another as high as 99.9%?[2] This question had students coming up with all manner of explanations: Was such a difference caused by religious reasons? Or were the countries very different politically? Or culturally? When Watts then revealed that these countries were neighbors, with a common language, cultural similarities, and a lot of shared history, explaining the difference became even more difficult. Why might organ donation consent in Austria be a near perfect 99.8%, while the Germans could only muster a measly 12%?

It turns out that this difference is not only observable between Austria and Germany. The question could also be asked about Denmark (4.25% consent rate) and Sweden (85.9% consent rate). As you can see from Figure 10.1, seven countries had consent rates higher than 85.9% (with an average across those seven countries of 97.5%), and four had consent rates lower than 27.5% (with an average of 15.2% across the four).

What divides the seven countries from the four is not some big political or cultural difference. What divides the seven countries from the four is merely a simple administrative procedure on a form.

---

[2] A study of organ donation consent rates across 11 European countries by Dan Goldstein and Eric Johnson was published in *Nature* in 2003. An analysis of the data showed that rates varied from 4.25% for Denmark to 99.91% for France. Spoiler alert: The title of the study is *Do Defaults Save Lives?*

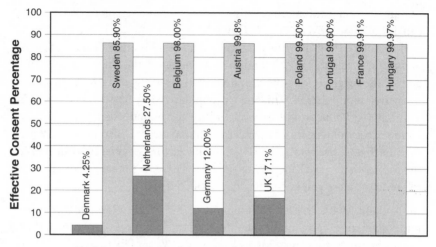

Figure 10.1 Effective organ donation consent rates across 11 European countries

The four countries with the lowest rates all required people to consent to organ donation (that is, they had to check a "yes" box). The seven countries with the highest rates all required that people opt out of organ donation.[3]

The slight physical effort of checking boxes on a form and the more considerable mental effort of making the choice to go against the default means that people naturally gravitate toward the easy choice—the default. This, of course, is "powered" by that incredible force that drives inaction—the status quo bias that we covered a couple of chapters earlier.

Although there seems little doubt that the main agent at work is the default, I think another force, social proof, may also play a part. If something is a default, the implicit message is that this is what most people normally do, and as we discussed earlier, social proof doesn't need definitive statistics to do its work. Often a vague hint suffices.

Another example of the use of defaults comes from a country I have visited many times. Zimbabwe has been devastated by the affects of HIV and

---

[3] There could be political and cultural factors underlying the choice to offer "yes" or "no" as a default. I was discussing this research with a German colleague, Julian Lambertin, who is also fascinated by social and behavioral sciences. His hypothesis was that authorities using "yes" as a default would still be politically unacceptable in Germany as it may be seen to echo the Nazi regime's subversion of free will.

AIDS, with prevalence of the infection at 15% of the adult population.[4] A study conducted in antenatal care clinics[5] in Chitungwiza, a socioeconomically disadvantaged community 25 km south of Harare, looked at the effect of defaults on the percentage of pregnant women that visited the clinics for antenatal care and took part in HIV testing.

The standard procedure in these clinics was for the HIV test to be an "opt-in" (meaning patients had to say they wanted it). In June 2005 that procedure was changed to an "opt-out," with right of refusal.

The researchers measured rates of testing from June–November 2005, the first six months of when the opt-out testing was in place and compared them with a six-month period when women had to opt in for the test.

For the opt-in period, 67% of women attending the clinic agreed to be (and were tested); for the opt-out period that figure rose to 99.9%.

While no official policy is in place, according to a senior health worker in Zimbabwe I spoke to recently, the opt-out approach has become has become the general procedure.

Making something easy has two dimensions: making it physically easy (the earlier example about the impact of the physical act of checking a box may seem a little farfetched) and making it mentally easy. The latter is called *cognitive fluency* by behavioral scientists. However, before we get into the nitty gritty of cognitive fluency, let's talk about the effects of making things physically easy.

Brian Wansink is somebody who has studied the effect of what happens when choices are made easier or more difficult. Wansink is the director of the Cornell University Food and Brand Lab, and he also served as the Executive Director of the U.S. Department of Agriculture's Center for Nutrition Policy and Promotion. His book *Mindless Eating—Why We Eat More Than We Think* explains how the best way to eat more healthily is simply to make healthy eating mindless. Put healthy options in prominent places in school cafeterias. Make healthy food easier to reach. Use lighting to display healthy food more prominently. (In one experiment, simply shining a simple desk

---

4   National AIDS Council of Zimbabwe, Situational Analysis. HIV and AIDS In Zimbabwe, December 2012.

5   Chandisarewa, W., Stranix-Chibanda, L., Chirapa, E., Miller, A., Simoyi, M., Mahomva, A., et al. (2007) "Routine offer of antenatal HIV testing ('opt-out' approach) to prevent mother-to-child transmission of HIV in urban Zimbabwe." *Bull World Health Organ* 85(11): 843-50.

lamp on fruit in a school cafeteria led to more fruit being chosen.) These little changes, or nudges, make the healthy choice the easiest choice.

Wansink and his team are incredibly inventive with their research. At a keynote address at Society of Judgment and Decision Making in 2012, he talked about a research study carried out at all-you-can-eat buffet restaurants. As people walked to the buffet, the researchers surreptitiously calculated their Body Mass Index (BMI) using a mat that weighed people and a laser device that measured their height. Wansink's team then observed how the behavior of those with BMIs above the median differed from those with BMIs below it. Those with lower BMIs scouted out the entire buffet before making their choices. I've started scouting buffets. Before I learned about Wansink's work, I used to follow the habit of those with higher BMIs, which was to walk along the buffet taking everything you fancy. Not planning in advance means you end up piling more and more food on your plate, as the next irresistible offering makes its case for inclusion. People with lower BMIs also tended to choose smaller plates, and whether consciously or not, were more likely to sit further away from the buffet and with their back to it, when they ate.

One of Wansink's most famous studies won him an "Ig Nobel" prize.[6] He rigged up a soup bowl that would secretly refill (via a hose in the bottom) as people ate. Those with the never-empty bowls ate 73% more than those eating from normal bowls...and they didn't even feel fuller! Wansink's work reverses the old saying of, "your eyes are bigger than your belly." His observations are that it is your eyes that tell you when you are full, not your stomach.

In an interview quoted on "Nudge Blog,"[7] Wansink also describes an experiment[8] where a cafeteria freezer containing ice cream was left open some days, and closed on others:

---

[6] According to the Improbable Research website, the "Ig Nobel" prize is awarded to people whose work might first make people laugh but then makes them think. The awards "celebrate the unusual, honor the imaginative—and spur people's interest in science, medicine, and technology." http://www.improbable.com/ig/

[7] *Nudge Blog* was run by John Balz until 2011. Balz is a great example of the application of an academic background in behavioral sciences to practical behavior change, having worked with FCB Chicago, Ideas 42, and most recently Opower.

[8] Rozin, P., Scott, S., Dingley, M., Urbanek, J.K., Jiang, H., Kaltenbach, M. (2011) "Nudge to nobesity: Minor changes in accessibility decrease food intake." *Judgment and Decision Making* 6(4): 323–332.

The ice cream cooler was in the exact same location, and people could always see the ice cream. All that varied was whether they had to go through the effort of opening the lid in order to get it. Even that was too much work for many people. If the lid was closed, only 14% of the diners decided it was worth the modest effort to open it. If the lid was open, 30% decided it was ice cream time.

The requirement of a small amount of effort can make big differences to our choices. It is as important to make eating badly difficult as it is to make eating well easy.

In an interview with Eric Barker on *Barking Up the Wrong Tree,* Dan Ariely describes another example of how effort works in practice:

> Here's an experiment that Google did recently. The M&Ms in their New York office used to be in baskets. So instead they put them in bowls with lids. The lid doesn't require a lot of effort to lift but it reduced the number of M&Ms consumed in their New York office by 3 million a month.

One example where "easy" is really important is for the people who have chosen your product or service to sort out any issues they may have with it. In *The Effortless Experience: Conquering the New Battleground for Customer Loyalty,* Matthew Dixon, Nick Toman, and Rick DeLisi discuss how customer dissatisfaction correlates with the amount of effort the customer has to put into getting the problem resolved. In fact they define the role of customer service as *mitigating disloyalty by reducing customer effort.*

The Effortless Experience gives examples of other ways companies can make doing business easier. Old Navy, for example, has made a number of aspects of the shopping experience easier, especially for moms shopping with kids. They've lowered the height of the racks so that moms can see where their kids are, and they reconfigured the merchandise and displays around an oval track with dressing rooms in the middle, so shoppers don't have to ask where they are or seek them out. Old Navy stores have "quick change" areas for trying on items like jackets and sweaters that don't require potential choosers stripping down to their underwear. And with one of those tiny but brilliant ideas I love, they've labeled the hooks in the changing rooms

"Love It," "Like It," and "Not For Me."[9] Not only do these labels make sorting easy, but I suspect that once something gets put on that "Love It" hook it triggers the endowment effect. (Remember the endowment effect is the force that makes us value things we feel ownership over and is discussed in Chapter 8, "Loss and Ownership.") By simply putting an item on the hook labeled "Love It," you have pretty much decided to buy it.

I think that the Old Navy Hooks are a great example of finding and addressing *channel factors*. This term describes small things that can make a big difference in facilitating a choice. If you think about why you might buy one item of clothing over another, you could go to emotionally rich and subjective areas like self-expression and image management. Yet the small thing that drove the decision to actually purchase it might have been the presence of a simple hook that performed the function of clarifying your choice, and making the next step simple and apparent.

A classic study at Yale University demonstrated a similar effect. Known popularly as Leventhal's Tetanus Experiment[10] it demonstrates the importance of helping people map next steps. Using tetanus inoculation as their experimental model, Leventhal, Singer, and Jones found that merely instilling fear of tetanus in Yale University undergraduates was not enough to encourage them to get vaccinated. When the students were given a specific plan of action, such as a campus map with the student health center circled, they were more likely to be vaccinated for tetanus.

Research also suggests that having people map out how they will go about doing something or doing it in ways that work for them further increases their chances of doing it.[11] We used this approach for a strategy proposed to the Californian Public Utilities Commission for a program to prompt

---

9   A more recent fieldtrip revealed examples where the hooks were labeled "Love It," "Love It," and "Not for Me," suggesting Old Navy is at least experimenting with removing the "Like It" option. This may make sense—removing "Like It" could help reduce uncertainty in the decision process and help shoppers reach quicker, more convicted choices. Also, having two "Love It" hooks for every one "Not for Me" hook could work as a nudge to love more items and buy more items.

10 Leventhal, H., Singer, R., Jones, S. (1965) "Effects of fear and specificity of recommendation upon attitudes and behavior." *Journal of Personality and Social Psychology* 2(1): 20-29.

11 Leutzinger, H. (2005) "Why & How People Change Health Behaviors," Health Improvement Solutions.

greater energy efficiency among Californian homeowners. Social marketing teams (these were largely volunteers who would go door to door in key neighborhoods, encouraging homeowners to take measures to save energy) went with a list of potential actions, and then helped homeowners choose the action(s) that they felt they could achieve. The social marketing team would then ask the homeowner how they might carry out this action, and then would give them additional advice on how to do it.

Just making a process easier can have a dramatic effect on behavior. My colleague Anirban Chaudhuri, the head of strategy at FCB Ulka in India, told me of this powerful example:

> Until recently only about 35.5% of households in India actively maintained bank accounts. Efforts for financial inclusions of the Bottom of the Pyramid (as the largest, but poorest socio-economic group in India is known) in the past didn't yield very much in the way of results until the new Prime Minister launched Pradhan Mantri Jan Dhan Yojana (Prime Minister People Money Scheme) on August 28, 2014. That day alone saw 15 million new savings bank accounts opened, mostly by blue collared workers and their socioeconomic equivalent. One of the most compelling reasons for this overwhelming response was the simplified account opening form that had just a few easy details and relaxed documentary requirement for proof of address, which is often a challenge for migrant workers. In five months (from when the scheme launched up until early January 2015) about 106 million of these savings bank accounts has been opened.

Ease isn't just a physical or process thing. All of us (and it really is *all* of us) who have put off a mentally challenging task know the lengths to avoid the effort involved. Thinking competes with resources that we might use for other (often more immediately rewarding) things. While your laptop's battery might drain more quickly while playing a video than running a word processing program on which you are writing a document, your brain is more likely to drain quicker writing the document than watching the video.

In *Thinking, Fast and Slow* Daniel Kahneman writes about how, if you were taking a relaxed walk (Kahneman is an avid walker) with a friend and you were to ask him to solve a complex math problem, he would probably stop in his tracks.

A recent study from Stanford University found that how a question was phrased could make it easier or harder to answer.[12] Researchers asked a series of hyperbolic discounting (Chapter 7, "Now, and the Future—Different Places with Different Rules) questions to participants while they underwent functional MRI scanning. Participants answered questions in a "hidden zero" format ("Would you like $10 today or $15 next week?") or "explicit zero" format ("Would you like $10 today and $0 next week or $0 today and $15 next week?") The explicit zero format reduced discounting; people preferred the $15 next week over money today. Importantly, the explicit zero format also reduced the amount of work the brain had to do to answer the question.

Processing information, be it a complex math problem while walking or answering a hyperbolic discounting question while in an MRI scanner, requires energy. Scientists refer to this mental effort as *cognitive load*. The term *cognitive load* connotes something heavy, so it's perhaps not surprising that we favor decisions that require us to make less mental effort. Minimizing cognitive load is part of the power of the cognitive biases and heuristics that we have been discussing—that they are shortcuts means they help us avoid excessive mental effort.

Our love of ease goes deeper than just the use of these mechanisms; a lively area of behavioral research suggests that as well as biases making decisions easy, we have a bias for the easy option.

Decision science calls this area of research *cognitive fluency*. An article on the subject in the *Boston Globe* describes it in this appropriately simple way:

> Cognitive fluency is simply a measure of how easy it is to think about something, and it turns out that people prefer things that are easy to think about to those that are hard.[13]

Adam Alter, an associate professor at NYU's Stern School of Business and author of New York Times best seller *Drunk Tank Pink*, and Danny Oppenheimer, an associate professor of psychology at the UCLA Anderson School of Management, are two of the world's experts in the field cognitive fluency. They've investigated the effects of cognitive fluency (and its opposite effect,

---

[12] Magen, E., Kim, B., Dweck, C., Gross, J.J., McClure, S.M. (2014) "Behavioral and neural correlates of increased self-control in the absence of increased willpower." *Proc Natl Acad Sci* 111: 9786–9791.

[13] Bennett, D. "Easy = True—How 'cognitive fluency' shapes what we believe, how we invest, and who will become a supermodel." *Boston Globe*, January 31, 2010.

cognitive disfluency) on things as diverse as stock prices, physical distance, and career prospects in the legal profession.

Fluency effects lead us to favor the easier-to-process option. Often we choose the choice that is easy to evaluate, rather than the one that offers the greatest benefits. So in most cases, marketers should look to make every aspect of their marketing both before and after people buy their products as easy as possible. In *The Effortless Experience: Conquering the New Battleground for Customer Loyalty,* authors Dixon, Toman, and DeLisi put forward the idea of companies evaluating how easy it is for their customers to do business with them and resolve problems with a metric they call the *Customer Effort Score.* I think this approach should be extended to evaluating marketing. A question we should always be considering is "how can I make the path to choosing my brand take less cognitive and physical effort"? Fluency, or cognitive ease, can make the decision to choose your brand a no-brainer.

The importance of "easy" in marketing isn't just about taking complexity out of the chooser's journey. It is absolutely central to what makes brands powerful. A colleague from our Auckland office, Simon Bird, recently wrote a thought-provoking piece called "Marketing Made Easy,"[14] which isn't about making marketing easy for marketers, but about making marketing easy for people to respond to. (Unfortunately, making things easy is seldom easy for the ones that make them so.) Bird writes that famous, popular, or preferred brands give their choosers a great gift. They make choice effortless:

> A German neuroeconomist, Peter Kenning, found when looking at brain scans of shoppers selecting brands, that the area of the brain that lights up when shoppers choose their preferred brand was different to all other brands including their stated number two choice. Furthermore, the brain showed significantly less activity when choosing the number one brand (another example of cortical relief). In other words strong brands help the brain "think" less, which is its default, preferred setting.

We also saw some indication of marketing helping the brain work less in research that the Institute of Decision Making commissioned in the UK

---

14 Bird, S. "Marketing Made Easy." *NZ Marketing* magazine, November/December 2014.

with consumer neuroscience firm MindLab a number of years ago. The research was designed to examine how ads in different digital formats affected donations to charity. We asked participants to split £50 between one of three charities as we showed ads in different formats on a computer screen; participants could adjust their allocation after seeing each ad. There were four kinds of ads:[15]

A: A simple banner ad from the charity

B: A social media message using social proof

C: A social media message using affinity

D: A social media message using celebrity

We tracked the amount of each charitable donation associated with each kind of ad while collecting an electroencephalogram from each participant. Electroencephalography (which is called EEG and is discussed further in Chapter 15, "Think Differently about Market Research") measures electrical activity in the brain through electrodes placed directly on the scalp. EEG robustly measures attention and emotional arousal levels. Our study with MindLab measured the relative amount of attention participants paid each kind of ad.

When we looked at the effect of attention, this is what we saw:

	Attention to Ad	Size of Donation
Ad A	Low	Low
Ad B	High	High
Ad C	Low	Medium
Ad D	High	Medium

Ad B created the best behavioral effect, and also got the most cognitive attention from the participants. Ad D got similar levels of attention but a lower level of donation.

---

[15] For Ad C, the affinity message appeared to come from someone in the participant's social network; for Ad D the message came from a celebrity that the participant followed or would consider following. This information had been obtained in a disguised interview with participants a week before fieldwork.

While we deemed there was too much "noise"[16] in our experimental setup to address the original objective of the study, to draw useful conclusions about which ad formats worked best for capturing attention, we did get an interesting, albeit unexpected, insight about cognitive effort. To measure attention to each ad format shown, continuously collecting EEG measurements while the participants decided how to allocate their £25 was necessary. This data—that we had not originally planned to analyze—revealed how the cognitive effort required for performing the task of allocation differed across the different ad formats.

When we looked at cognitive effort, what we saw was this:

	Attention to Ad	Size of Donation	Attention While Donating
Ad A	Low	Low	High
Ad B	High	High	Low
Ad C	Low	Medium	Low
Ad D	High	Medium	High

Just focusing on the two ads that received the highest amount of attention according to the EEG signal (Ads B and D), we saw that Ad B did better in terms of persuading participants to allocate money to the charity it advocated. Even though Ad B was more persuasive, it actually required people to think less while donating than Ad D did.

There is an interesting implication here: Marketing may be successful when it repays the chooser's investment of cognitive resources.[17]

Ad D made people want to work hard when they saw it, achieved an average behavioral result, and required people to work harder at the moment of decision. Ad B made people want to work hard when they saw it and achieved the greatest behavioral effect, but the choice was relatively effortless. An analogy for the mechanism underlying Ad D's effectiveness might be that we made people put effort in training on a bicycle when the decision task was a running race. The effort put into the exercise didn't really make the decision easier. With Ad B we had people putting the same amount of

---

[16] We felt that the social proof aspect of Ad B gave it an inherent advantage over the other ads.

[17] A related effect was observed in the fMRI study on temporal discounting from Stanford referenced earlier in this chapter.

effort into training on the treadmill, and effort spent training did make the task easier.

The emergence of digital platforms has given marketers more and more opportunities to actively engage people with their brands, whether that is through immersive experiences or by encouraging them to create and submit content. The general view is that when it comes to engagement, more is better, although I remain unconvinced about this as a blanket perspective.

In May 2013, I was one of a group of guest speakers at a discussion on consumer engagement at Georgetown University's Institute for Consumer Research. My argument was that humans are cognitive misers and that marketers should heed advice given to me long ago (by whom I have since forgotten) that "you have a dollar of attention, so spend it wisely." To me this statement works both ways—potential choosers should spend their attention wisely, and marketers should make sure they use the limited attention they can get from people wisely.

The problem, I think, is that marketers have become obsessed with getting as much attention or engagement as they can, rather than designing that engagement to help them achieve behavioral objectives. During the talk, I quoted Charlie Brooker, media correspondent for the UK newspaper *The Guardian*'s colorful take on this idea:[18]

> ...advertising used to work like this: you sat on your sofa while creatives were paid to throw a bucket of s**t in your face. Today you're expected to sit on the bucket, fill it with your own s**t, and tip it over your head while filming yourself on your mobile.

His point, written from the perspective of the consumer, was that in the name of engagement, advertising is asking more and more of people.

I think engagement that facilitates decision-making for people is a great investment—dollars of attention spent well all round. Perhaps this is what we saw happening with the charity ad in our study that required cognitive attention but repaid it by reducing cognitive load at the time of the decision. Attention that simply "burns" cognitive effort without being designed to help achieve specific behavioral objectives isn't just an unwise way to spend dollars of attention. It's probably not the best use of marketing dollars either.

---

[18] Charlie Brooker's Screen Burn, *The Guardian*, December 4, 2009 http://www.theguardian.com/tv-and-radio/2009/dec/05/charlie-brooker-screen-burn

While making things easy and simple is a good rule of thumb in the psychology of consumer decision making, in luxury categories the rules are different. There is a reversal of this effect for luxury products.

According to Adam Alter, people associate more complexity with luxury products and so disfluency, or cognitive difficulty, makes luxury products more appealing. The study *Making Products Feel Special: When Metacognitive Difficulty Enhances Evaluation,*[19] by the appropriately disfluently named Anastasiya Pocheptsova and others, demonstrates that disfluency makes high-end goods seem more special.

Laphroaig Malt Whisky, Louis Vuitton, and Häagen Dazs, for example, all have names that require us to think about how we pronounce them, at least for the first time.

Ornate labels that make type more difficult to read, such as Chivas Regal, or typefaces that are less legible, such as Neiman Marcus, similarly create the need for effort on the part of consumers. All of these things take a bit more effort, creating cognitive disfluency.

Unlike most brands that bend over backward to show they understand us, luxury brands require that we put in the effort to understand them, to become *savoir-faire* on how to use them correctly, to know why their provenance is important and how their story makes them special. From a cognitive perspective, living in the lap of luxury isn't as easy as it is cracked up to be.

The takeaways from this chapter are

- Where possible, make the outcome you want the default. Some observers pin a large amount of Google's success to its early deal that made it the default search engine on the AOL browser.

- The authors of *The Effortless Experience* suggest a Customer Effort Score to measure ease of customer interaction. How can you make your marketing take less effort, and make it easier to act upon? How can you make choice easier? Review the steps to choice. How would you score the ease of each step? What is your Ease of Choice Score?

- Engagement can be powerful, but make sure that the effort you are asking of people in engagement makes the behavior or choice you want easier for users and choosers.

---

[19] Pocheptsova, A., Labroo, A.A., Dhar, R. (2010) "Making Products Feel Special: When Metacognitive Difficulty Enhances Evaluation." *Journal of Marketing Research* 47(6): 1059–1069.

- While everyday brands should do everything to make their marketing and brand experience as *fluent* or cognitively easy as possible, part of luxury brands' cachet rests in being *cognitively disfluent*.

Ideas that this chapter prompted in others:

- "Wanting engagement is common, knowing *why* we want engagement less so. What have we really achieved by getting a few thousand people to share a selfie on Instagram? Instead we should be thinking about how engagement can make things easier for consumers."
- "This is why I shop at the corner store. It costs twice as much as Trader Joe's, but it is twice as close. Thank goodness they don't leave the ice cream cabinet open..."

11

Never Be Above Comparison

People use comparisons as an intuitive form of navigation, and relativity can drive choices.

S weden's Stockholm is a city awash with museums. One of the world's finest museums—the impressive Vasa Museet—houses the preserved wreck of the Vasa, a 226-foot warship that sank less than a mile into her maiden voyage in 1628. The building itself is difficult to miss once you are in its vicinity—a stunning piece of modern architecture topped by a large copper roof with three stylized masts that represent the actual height of the ship. But one museum you might easily overlook, as I certainly would have if I hadn't taken cover at the front door to avoid a summer downpour, is the much less dramatic Royal Coin Cabinet. Tucked away in a courtyard near the Royal Palace, the Royal Coin Cabinet is also known as the National Museum of the Economy. In it, you will find examples of Europe's first paper money and what is generally believed to be one of the world's first coins. Both the paper money and oldest coin, it turns out, have a relatively recent history.

Printed bills were the brainchild of Johan Palmstruch, general manager of the precursor to Sweden's national bank. Paper money was introduced in 1661 as an alternative to Sweden's cumbersome coins. The coins that paper money replaced were essentially plates of copper, many weighing around 10 lbs. The largest coin, with a value of 10 daler (or thaler, which is also the last name of one of the pioneers of Behavioral Economics, who appropriately happens to be an economist), weighed more than 40 lbs. Not surprisingly, Palmstruch's innovation was one that John Gourville would classify as a "home run" (big innovation; little behavior change required). The success of paper money prompted him to print more money than he should have, and he was sentenced to death for irresponsible bookkeeping. Although pardoned, Palmstruch died a couple of years later in 1671.

While Palmstruch's bills were not the first financial currency ever, paper money's history is not that much older. Before the invention of printing, hand-written paper notes were used in parts of China, starting around 600 CE. For the first coins (an example of which the National Museum of the Economy proudly displays) you only have to go back a further thousand years, to 610 BCE and the Lydians of Asia Minor. The Lydians forged (in the metalwork sense) coins from electrum, an alloy made principally from gold and silver.

If, as anthropologist Dean Falk suggests, another 6,000 years or so before the Lydians created their coins is "essentially today" in terms of human brain development, then money is a relatively "new thing" to humankind. Economists describe money as a way of defining value. Like money, the other systems we use to define something's weight, height, length, or volume are also "relatively new." The earliest known standardized measurement system comes from the Indus Valley in the third millennium BCE. While there is little doubt that other less formal systems would have been in place before this time, for most of our existence human judgment relied less on measuring and more on comparing.

Comparisons remain a critical part of how we navigate the options before us. Actually, it might be more accurate to say that the points of reference enabling comparisons are the things that are critical. And sometimes, comparisons and the reference points they rely on can be far more critical to their customers than businesses realize. JCPenney found this out the hard way.

In February 2012, Bloomberg reported that JCPenney had its "lowest sales in decades." In the all-important fourth quarter, its net loss plunged from $87 million for the previous year to $552 million; its annual revenue was $13 billion, which, according to Bloomberg, was "the lowest since 1987."

What went wrong? What did JCP do to engineer a loss like this in one year?

Before I answer these questions, let's review a little JCP history. In November 2011, JCP hired Ron Johnson as its CEO. Johnson was recruited to make the JCP brand an emotional destination rather than just an economic one and to transform the store to a specialty department store rather than just a chain. In his previous job, Johnson was the executive largely responsible for the success of Apple's retail stores. The Apple store redefined the retail experience and achieved what are among the highest sales per square foot in the history of retail. What better place for a tired, frumpy retailer to seek a new leader than Apple?

However, many commentators subsequently suggested this "Apple envy" and "failed imitation" was likely at the root of JCP's problem. In an article in the *New Republic*,[1] Johnson even went on record saying that his new JCP "retail interface" would lead to an experience "just like Apple."

Criticism of Johnson and JCPenney abounded in light of the company's poor performance. Critics suggested that the desire to radically transform the JCP brand led the company to ignore its existing customers, leaving them behind. But in my view, the problem wasn't just that JCP ignored its existing customers with the changes it rolled out after Johnson's hire. It did something far more damaging—it ignored human nature.

So what led JCPenney to do this?

With the best intentions, JCPenney tried to make its pricing more transparent to its customers. A January 2012 *Wall Street Journal* article titled "Merchandise Pricing Changes by JCPenney Could Be Radical" detailed how JCP was reducing complexity in its pricing. Price tags would start to feature round dollar amounts, so an item that would have been priced at $19.99 would now be priced at $20. Discount pricing would be abolished. Items would not be displayed at a higher price and then be reduced after the statutory period, but they would go on the floor at the "discounted" price. Thus, price tags would no longer mention the higher price at which the goods had been sold. Behavioral economists call this higher price a "reference price." These and other changes intended to make pricing transparent were packaged as "Fair and Square Everyday Pricing."

Anybody reasonably well versed in understanding decision sciences, behavioral economics, or an emerging area called cognitive pricing would have doubted that Fair and Square Everyday Pricing would work (even if it was—as is most likely the case—endorsed in focus groups or quantitative studies among customers and prospective customers). While all of these pricing initiatives make sense at a rational level, that's just not how we humans make choices, whether those humans be you, me, longtime JCPenney shoppers, or anybody else on the planet. People will often agree with rational approaches when asked their opinions on them through market research, but don't follow rational approaches when actually making decisions. Who

---

[1] DePillis, L. "A Bite from the Apple Store. What JCPenney's Failed Imitation Says About Retail—and Identity." *New Republic*, March 4, 2014.

would disagree when asked if they wanted more transparent pricing, or low prices all the time, or that the one cent between a $20 and $19.99 price ticket isn't a big deal?

When we think about it—which is what most research asks us to do—we would agree with the principles of the Fair and Square pricing program because we tend to think we will behave rationally, even though we won't. In these cases, traditional market research based on surveys or focus groups doesn't really help, because it simply asks people their reasons for doing something rather than revealing their motivations for doing it. Daniel Kahneman writes about how these pre-conscious motivations dictate our choices but remain hidden from us in his book *Thinking, Fast and Slow*, when he says "...the intuitive system is more influential than your experience tells you, and is the secret author of many of the choices and judgments you make."

Given we all overestimate our own rationality, it's not surprising that executives will too often choose a marketing approach that appeals to consumers' logic or stated preferences over one that appeals to the intuitive mechanisms that have driven human decision-making for hundreds of thousands, if not millions, of years.

Some commentators on the failure of JCPenney's "Fair and Square Everyday Pricing" suggested the program flopped because consumers like complexity in pricing. While finding examples from behavioral economics supporting this idea is possible, this conclusion misses the point. It is not that people like complex prices; we like easy decisions that "feel right." It is ironic, but some things that may seem complex from a rational perspective can make our decision-making easier at an intuitive level, and also make us feel better about our choices.

JCPenney's mistake was that in creating a pricing approach that seemed simple from a *rational* perspective, it erased cues that enabled easy and intuitive decision-making. JCPenney unwittingly suppressed its shoppers' abilities to allow cognitive shortcuts to guide their choices.

The absence of reference prices may have been one of the most significant factors in the failure of JCP's Fair and Square pricing program.[2] Comparisons help us make choices quickly and intuitively.

---

[2] http://www.mediapost.com/publications/article/197734/why-pennies-are-important-for-penney.html?c=109245#axzz2WHVgVFJI

Everything is relative, especially in regards to reaching a decision. We are more comfortable letting our intuitions guide us when we have a reference point to act as a compass to help us navigate our choices.

This intuitive reliance on reference points can lead us to make wildly differing estimates of an object's height, of a person's age, or of something's value.[3] It can make us see something we might normally consider expensive as a bargain, and lead us to change our choices when presented with a selection of products or offers. In behavioral economics, this phenomenon is known as *anchoring*.

Countless experiments have demonstrated the effects of anchoring, but one that describes its essence simply is mentioned in *Thinking, Fast and Slow*. Visitors to the San Francisco Exploratorium (a museum that's not really a museum, and was described by the *New York Times* as "the most important science museum to have opened since the mid-20th century") were asked to estimate the height of the tallest redwood tree. But first they were either asked, "Is the height of the tallest redwood tree more or less than 1,200 feet?" or "Is the height of the tallest redwood tree more or less than 180 feet?" These heights acted as the high and low anchor, respectively. They also had a dramatic effect on the estimates people made—those presented with the anchor of 1,200 feet estimated the tallest redwood tree would be 844 feet in height, while those presented with the anchor of 180 feet estimated the tallest redwood to be 282 feet.

Remarkably, an anchor doesn't even have to be relevant to the decision at hand to have an effect. Behavioral economists Dan Ariely, George Loewenstein, and Drazen Prelec conducted a now classic experiment[4] demonstrating anchoring by using an arbitrary number. Students were shown a range of goods (that included computer accessories, books, and bottles of wine) and were then asked if they would pay a dollar sum equal to the last two digits of their Social Security number for each object. When people were asked to bid on these goods, those whose last two digits were in the highest quintile (that is, 80–99) bid an average of $56 for one item (a cordless keyboard), whereas those who had a Social Security number where the last

---

[3] Kahneman discusses all of these scenarios and more in the chapter *Anchors* in *Thinking, Fast and Slow*.

[4] Ariely, D., Loewenstein, G., Prelec, D. (2003) "Coherent Arbitrariness: Stable Demand Curves Without Stable Preferences." *Quarterly Journal of Economics* 118(1): 73–106.

two digits were between 01 and 20 bid an average of $16 for the *same* item. A similar pattern was observed for bids across all the items.

The last two digits of participants' Social Security numbers was clearly an arbitrary anchor, yet it still had a sizeable effect on what they were prepared to bid. Such is the power of reference points, even irrelevant ones.

Anchoring can be beguilingly persuasive, even outside of academic laboratories.

A couple of years ago, I was in Hamburg, Germany, for a meeting. As I walked back to my hotel in the Neustadt area, I found myself window-shopping at high-end jewelers. I have never spent more than $300 on a watch (the one I wear most days is a Citizen Eco Drive and costs much less than that), so let's take $300 as my reference price or anchor. The display I was looking at was of IWC watches, and one of the models on display was priced at the equivalent of $18,000—more expensive by a factor of 60 than the maximum you might expect me to pay for a watch. There were watches that were $14,000, and some around $12,000. At the bottom of the display was a very simple IWC watch with a beautiful clean face, priced at $4,000... $4,000! Now that is still 13 times more expensive than any watch I have bought or intend to buy, but in the moment the price tag seemed very reasonable—almost a bargain!

Suddenly I found myself thinking about buying something very expensive that, 30 seconds earlier, I hadn't even desired. My anchor had shifted from $300 to $18,000. A $4,000 watch next to $300 watch is outrageously expensive. But, next to an $18,000 watch, the $4,000 one seems like a steal. The jeweler's insight, whether intentional or not, had been to mix the watches up a bit. Common sense suggests that the person in the market for an $18,000 watch isn't the same person as someone in the market for a $4,000 watch. The jeweler could have decided that people shop in price bands (which shoppers would probably tell you they do) and decided to put all the $15,000 to $20,000 watches—across all the brands they carried—in one group; the $10,000 to $15,000 in another group; and so on. By not putting all the very expensive ones together, they had allowed for the very powerful effect of anchoring. The only thing that prevented some serious damage to my credit card balance was that the jeweler was closed. By the time I walked past the store the next day, I was no longer in a buying mood. Time allowed me to deliberate about buying the watch, and my reference point had moved to what my wife would say if I returned home with a $4,000 watch.

A short while after my visit to Hamburg, I was explaining the principle of anchoring at a decision-making workshop in London. One of the attendees, who had worked in marketing at a famous high-end UK retailer, came up to me after my talk and told me a story that shows another powerful effect of anchoring. This particular retailer sold luxury hampers every holiday season—essentially wicker laundry baskets filled with luxury goods, and the retailer had a tradition that any hampers that weren't sold at the end of the holiday season were broken down and they were auctioned off to the staff, with the proceeds going to charity.

The hampers on offer were a premium hamper that retailed for £250 and a super-premium hamper that sold for £500. Normally a couple of dozen hampers remained unsold, making a nice bonus of goodies for the staff. The marketing team came up with a cunning plan—they would create a super-super-premium hamper that was bigger and had some even more high-end goods than the super-premium one and price it at £1,000. Their thinking was that no one would buy the most expensive hampers (they only made up a couple of them) and that they would be able to add some even more luxurious goods to the auction.

Unfortunately, the plan backfired. The presence of even just a small number of £1,000 hampers had an anchoring effect on the £500 one, and as a consequence they sold every single super-premium hamper (it seems likely that people traded up from the entry level £250 version). To rub salt in the wound, they also sold one of the £1,000 hampers as well. This is an example of how an anchor doesn't just change the perception of something's value, but also can change the nature of choice within a selection. This effect has been demonstrated in numerous experiments.[5]

In *Thinking, Fast and Slow*, Kahneman sees anchoring working as a suggestion or prime, and as a form of decision adjustment. He feels (and his late collaborator, Tversky felt) that anchors lead to insufficient adjustments. Take the example of the Redwood trees—the mean estimate for the high anchor condition was, at 844 feet, still way above an accurate estimate for the tallest redwood tree (I just Googled it, and it is just over 370 feet), but it was still an adjustment of the high anchor figure of 1,200 feet. It was just an insufficient one. My adjustment of what I might have paid for a watch

---

[5] Some examples are Dan Ariely's Economist experiment, covered in "The importance of irrelevant alternatives," *The Economist*, May 22, 2009 and Amos Tversky and Itamar Simonson's Minolta camera experiment ("Context-Dependent Preferences," *Management Science*, October 1993).

---

was nearly 80% lower than the high anchor of $18,000, and my wife and my credit card company would certainly have considered that an insufficient adjustment.

Kahneman also talks about how the power of anchoring may be in what psychologists call *associative coherence*. What this means is that it gives you a reference point that makes it easier to connect to different sets of associations and attributes. In a study by German psychologists Thomas Mussweiler and Fritz Strack,[6] participants were either asked whether the annual mean temperature in Germany was higher or lower than 5° Celsius/40° Fahrenheit, or whether it was higher or lower than 20° Celsius/68° Fahrenheit. When they were given the low number as an anchor, they were quicker at identifying "winter words" (like ski, cold, and frost) from a jumbled list that contained winter words, summer words, neutral words, and made-up words. When they were given the high anchor, they were quicker at identifying summer words (like beach, warm, and swim) from the same list.

This is how I think comparisons and reference points work at a broad and emotional level for brands. Even when brands use comparisons with the intention of communicating they are different and better, they rob a little bit of the world of the brand they are comparing themselves to.

Apple effectively encouraged comparison with Microsoft with the "Mac vs. PC" campaign I referred to earlier in the book. By making Windows its frame of reference, Apple didn't just say Macs were better than PCs. It did something that was probably more important for Apple's growth at the time. It made Apple seem more similar to PCs than people thought. Of course, Mac was good at all of those creative kinds of things that seemed uniquely Apple, but now a Mac seemed as good or better than Windows at all of the things that Microsoft does well. Of course, shortly afterward, Apple had the same weapon used against it very effectively by Samsung, who used the iPhone as a point of reference for its Galaxy in its "The Next Big Thing Is Here" campaign.

"The Cadillac of..." is a timeless example of gilt by association (apologies). Hillquist made "the Cadillac of all trim saws," Rock-Ola "the Cadillac of phonographs." The Cadillac "anchor" was used by President Obama to

---

[6] Mussweiler, T., Strack, F. (2000) "The use of category and exemplar knowledge in the solution of anchoring tasks." *Journal of Personality and Social Psychology*, June 78(6): 1038–1052.

describe high cost health care insurance policies in 2009 as "super-gold-plated Cadillac plans."[7]

Contrary to conventional marketing thinking, comparing doesn't dilute who you are—in terms of our non-conscious thinking, comparison makes choices clearer. While brand gurus talk about putting a stake in the ground, behavioral scientists might suggest that lassoing an existing stake is a better approach. As my colleague John Kenny, Chief Strategy Officer of FCB Chicago says, "Better beats best...." His point, which may sound counterintuitive from a traditional marketing perspective, is that from a "decision ease" perspective, being comparable to something is preferable to being above and beyond comparison.

JCPenney's errors went beyond taking away reference prices, and thus putting its goods beyond comparison. By rounding prices up, and by doing away with the pennies, JCPenney made its products feel more expensive.

Leigh Caldwell is an expert on cognitive pricing and partner of The Irrational Agency,[8] who has partnered with the Institute of Decision Making on a number of projects. In his book *The Psychology of Price* Caldwell writes about how being just below the dollar mark (for example, $19.99) means the consumer unconsciously puts your product in the "below $20 band," whereas a price tag of $20 puts you above that band. There is evidence that using "bands" is a shortcut people use a lot.

Even Johnson's previous employer Apple uses this approach, although admittedly with bigger currency units. Every MacBook, iPad, or iPhone is priced at one dollar below the nearest hundred. The $499 Mac Mini on which I am writing this book is in the $400 band, but the addition of a single dollar to the price would have moved it up to the $500 band.

The mechanism of how this pricing mechanism works is interesting. Ben Ambridge, a senior lecturer in psychology at the University of Liverpool and author of the book *Psy-Q*, points to three reasons something priced at $9.99 seems intuitively cheaper than $10.00 (and the reasons go beyond the obvious fact that shouldn't be overlooked, which is that $9.99 actually *is* cheaper). The first may be the recall of a stored memory—we have learned

[7] Zimmer, B. "Cadillac Thrives as a Figure of Speech." *New York Times,* November 5, 2009.

[8] The Irrational Agency is a market research practice that specializes in understanding the non-conscious aspects of consumer decision making.

to associate prices ending in .99 with items that are on offer, so when we see $5.99 or $9.99 it triggers that memory. A second elaborates on Caldwell's explanation, relates to anchoring, and is based on how we read the numbers 9.99. We read from left to right, and the theory is that reading in this direction "anchors" us on the "9." We see $9.99 as being "around $9," whereas $10.00 would be "around $10."

Ambridge's third reason for how intuition influences pricing programs deals with sound symbolism:

> Studies with made-up words show that certain sounds (such as those in "bouba," "malooma") are associated with large (and round) shapes, while others (for example "kiki," "taketi") are associated with small (and angular) shapes. Why? The former force us to open our mouths wide, and are found in words such as large, huge and enormous. The latter involve stretching our lips to make a tiny gap, and are found in words such as little, tiny, mini, petite, itsy-bitsy and teeny-weenie. So when you hear, for example, "one ninety-nine," you are hearing these "tiny" sounds.[9]

As the extent of JCPenney's lost sales became public, Johnson made a public *mea culpa*:

> Experience is making mistakes and learning from them, and I've learned a lot.... We worked really hard and tried many things to help the customer understand that she could shop any time on her terms. But we learned, she prefers a sale. At times, she loves a coupon. And always, she needs a reference price.

In his statement, Johnson showed that he had learned the importance of working *with* the way humans are wired to make choices rather than trying to change human nature, however compelling the logic to do so may be.

But the damage was already done, and Johnson paid with his job. In April 2013, just 16 months after being hired, Johnson was fired as CEO of JCPenney, his first public failure following his extraordinary success with Apple and Target.

If JCPenney's attempt to elevate its brand led to failure, Dos Equis beer can claim the opposite. Dos Equis was an unexceptional mid-market imported

---

[9] What we do with our mouth may affect our choices in other ways. One study suggests that advertising copy that is alliterative leads us to subvocalize the message, increasing our chances of considering the advertised product.

beer from Mexico until it launched "The Most Interesting Man in the World" advertising campaign. It has become an Internet meme and one of America's favorite campaigns.

Like all good advertising, it works for many reasons. Brilliant scriptwriting (every commercial has a gem of a line in it—whether it be, "He once had an awkward moment. Just to see how it feels," or "His organ donation card also lists his beard," or, my personal favorite, "His mother has a tattoo that reads son."[10])

Then there is the disassociation yet cohesion between what is being seen and being said (this may cause a bit of disfluency, which you learned in Chapter 10, "Make It Easy—For the Mind and the Body," is something that makes us pay attention). And with the hitherto unknown Jonathan Goldsmith as the Most Interesting Man in the World, the series has one of the best pieces of casting you will ever see (remember we talked about the importance of facial expressions—Goldsmith's eyes fairly twinkle and his hint of a smile exudes wry confidence). Goldsmith's character comes across as a Latin James Bond of the Sean Connery era.

I also think there is a powerful behavioral mechanism at work in this advertising. The character and the setting seem to conjure up the sense of a classic cocktail occasion rather than beer drinking, with the brilliant line that features in every commercial—"I don't always drink beer, but when I do, I prefer Dos Equis."

By implicitly making its frame of reference expensive, sophisticated cocktails, Dos Equis has succeeded in re-anchoring the brand. Because of the quick, almost heuristic-like power of origin, our natural comparison set for Dos Equis would most likely be Mexican beers such as Sol or Corona. As a category, Mexican imported beers were down 1.3% from 2008 to 2009. Now, thanks to the most interesting man in the world, we might consider Dos Equis more in the context of cocktails like an Old Fashioned or a Manhattan. And given what we know about bourbon sales from our discussion about scarcity in Chapter 8, "Loss and Ownership," that could be a smart move. In an interview on Brandchannel in March 2010,[11] Paul Smailes

---

[10] His mother having a tattoo that reads "son," is a secret wish of this book's author.

[11] Alexander, R. "Dos Equis most—interesting?" Brandchannel, March 31, 2010.

(then Dos Equis's senior brand director) said of this period when Mexican imported beer suffered a decline:

> We jumped from the No. 11 import brand in the country to No. 8 last year (2009) and we grew market share by 22 percent.

Implicitly changing the frame of reference from beer to a suave, cocktail-like occasion was a smart move. But comparisons that are outrageously cheeky can also be effective. Another of my colleagues, John Kenny, had this thought about comparisons:

> Comparisons are good, but comparisons that are out of your league are better.

A tongue-in-cheek ad from the 1980s for the tiny-engined (0.6l) Citroen 2CV compared it favorably with the supercars of the day. The ad claimed that traveling at its top speed of 71.5mph the 2CV could easily overtake a Ferrari Mondial traveling at 65mph; that it had the same number of wheels (four) as the Rolls Royce Silver Spirit that cost 20 times more; and that it had more luggage space than a Porsche.

A few decades on, MINI forced a mischievous comparison with Porsche, by challenging it to a race at Road Atlanta road course,[12] effectively suggesting MINI's performance was closer to a Porsche than the options suggested by a CNN review of MINI alternatives around the same time[13] that included the Kia Soul, the Nissan Cube, and the Ford Fiesta. Porsche didn't accept the challenge. This would have been exactly my advice to the company, as even if the Porsche had comprehensively outraced the MINI, by accepting the challenge, Porsche would only have been perpetuating a comparison that was not in its interest.

One final example of the power of a reference point is a simple one I love from FCB's Auckland office. It is for the Electricity Authority, which is the entity that is responsible for regulation of the New Zealand electricity market. The Electricity Authority started a campaign in 2010 to encourage householders to shop around among electricity providers in order to

---

[12] http://www.autoblog.com/2010/06/10/followup-porsche-turns-down-mini-challenge-at-road-atlanta-w-v/

[13] "6 alternatives to the Mini Cooper—The Mini's great, but these days there are lots of cars that can give you coolness with a small size and price." CNN Money, July 2010.

increase competition. Getting someone to change their electricity provider is a challenge—it's one of those things you never get around to, and that's assuming it was even on your radar in the first place. FCB Auckland used social proof to create a sense that the behavior of reviewing your electricity deal was usual, or a *social norm* through a campaign called "What's My Number," that encouraged people to check out what they might save (that amount being their "number").

The average annual saving from reviewing and switching was NZ$150 (approximately US$120) per household (choosing a larger, annual number rather than a smaller, monthly number was a smart move from an anchoring perspective).

While $120 seems like a big amount in some contexts, it gets dwarfed in the context of larger household expenses, such as the mortgage or property taxes, and thus may not seem a big enough amount to get someone to reevaluate their energy provider.

But an ingenious and inexpensive tactic within the "What's Your Number?" campaign was the use of supermarket coupons as an advertising medium. By running "Save $150" in the style of a coupon next to offers to save $2 off shampoo, and by engaging people when they were in money-saving mode, the task of checking out what people might save from switching providers seemed a much more worthwhile endeavor.

The takeaways from this chapter are

- *Anchoring* is the tendency to attach or "anchor" our thoughts to a reference point, even if it is not directly relevant. Understanding this concept is key to pricing strategies. While anchoring may make our choices seem sometimes irrational, the mechanism also helps us make very quick and efficient decisions rather than calculations that involve a lot of cognitive effort.

- Comparisons provide the anchors that are key to how we navigate choice. When no points of comparison exist, choice becomes difficult and frustrating. Choosers are more reliant on comparisons than they think they are.

- Comparisons can be a quick way to position your brand. They help people intuitively work where you fit on the map. People will often have a default place for you—giving them a fresh and imaginative point of reference can help you bust out of that default.

Thoughts from other people took who read this chapter:

- "A good chunk of my job is facilitating negotiations. Recognizing that points of reference intuitively drive decisions is enormously useful in determining how to make a proposal that will feel good to the other side and engender optimism that the negotiation will be fruitful."

- "Any one who has ever been involved in a naming project knows how difficult it is. Perhaps if we spent more time thinking about mouth feel and less time thinking about names that 'make sense,' there would be many more better names in the world."

12

If Content Is King, Context Is Queen

Marketers focus so much on message, we frequently underestimate the dramatic effect of context.

Marketers have long known the importance of context for their messages, but few harness the full power context has to offer.

Consider online shopping. In early September 2014, I was browsing for digital cameras. The review site I looked at didn't just show customer reviews for different cameras but also carried ads for Best Buy's Labor Day sale, a photo storing service, and links to camera manufacturers and photography retailers. This kind of advertising is known as *contextual targeting,* an approach that uses the reasonable assumption that if I am researching cameras, then I might notice and respond to ads related to cameras.

Later, I visited a UK sports site to read about any developments in the last few hours preceding the "transfer window." (The transfer window is the period when soccer players can move from one club to another, and which, like an eBay auction, often saves its twists and turns for the very end.) The sports site displayed an ad for a photography retailer and one for espresso machine accessories. Both of these ads are examples of *behavioral targeting.* Rather than just matching content, the behavioral targeting approach uses information gleaned from previous behavior, such as visited websites, online searches, clicked-on content, or purchases. I was served up an ad for Fry's Home Electronics, because I'd been browsing for cameras earlier in the day, and an ad from Seattle Coffee Gear because I had bought an espresso machine online two weeks ago.

Yet another approach to place messages in a relevant context is known as *semantic targeting*. This is a more subtle form of contextual targeting that uses data mining and sentiment analysis to identify the mood or point of view that a web page may project. Advertising messages that are in tune with that mood and point of view are then placed automatically on the webpage.

All three targeting examples defined in the online shopping example are based on the idea that messages do not live in isolation; advertisements can work harder when aligned with the context of the situation in which they live.

The notion that "it is not just the message" is not new. In his 1964 book *Understanding Media: The Extensions of Man,* Marshall McLuhan coined the phrase "the medium is the message." (Perhaps, apocryphally, this phrase was the original title of a book he wrote a few years later. The story goes that a typesetter's error on the proof had misspelled the title as *The Medium Is the Massage.*[1] Rather than being annoyed by the mistake, McLuhan's response was "Leave it alone! It's great, and right on target!")

Despite the pervasiveness of McLuhan's sound bite, and notwithstanding the approaches I've just described, the people who pay for, design, and place messages habitually underestimate potential power of the environment surrounding their message. Time and place matter. That isn't to say that marketers (and media planners in particular) don't pay attention to the "where" and "when" associated with their messages; they pay great attention to both. A lot of thought goes into finding a good time and place to *reach* the people they want to influence, rather than understanding *how* the medium that transports the message can affect choice. The broader context enveloping the message can determine how the message affects people's response and ultimately their decisions.

In some ways it seems that marketing has never been more focused on context. Consider the Internet example with which we opened this chapter. The Internet gives marketers the ability to both track individual behavior and send personalized messages, at the times when those messages seem to be most appropriate for influencing the decision process. While this kind of advertising is a step forward in terms of efficiency, it does little more than scratch the surface in terms of how context can affect and influence choice.

---

[1] McLuhan, M., Fiore, Q. *The Medium Is the Massage: An Inventory of Effects.* Penguin, 1967.

As Heather Segal, head of strategic planning at FCB Canada says, "Most contextual relevance is simply just using similarities between content and context. It's little more than matching luggage."

In this chapter, I discuss four different areas of context that dramatically affect the choices people make. I will show that even though it is often said that "content is king," context, as in chess, is the more powerful and potentially game-winning queen.

1. Context Activates Evolutionary Goals

I first came across the work of Vladas Griskevicius (co-author with Douglas Kenrick of *The Rational Animal*) some years ago. I was interviewing Robert Cialdini, who, as we saw in Chapter 5, "Getting Familiar," has led to some of the most interesting experimental work in areas that affect decision making, including the effects of social proof (a book like this would be much less interesting if it couldn't draw on the work of Cialdini and his collaborators).

One of my questions to Cialdini was something that must be in the back of many marketers' minds when they hear about the power of social proof. We're told how the behavior of others drives people to imitate that behavior. Or how, as Cialdini said, "Our intuitions tell us that a given behavior is more correct to the degree that we see other people doing it." So, how can a brand encourage someone to make a choice that makes that individual stand out from the crowd? Do Apple's exhortations to "Think Different," or Levi's appeals to individuality and self-expression fly in the face of the effectiveness of social proof? Would those brands be better off saying "Think the Same" or encouraging people to celebrate homogeneity?

As an answer to my question, Cialdini pointed me toward Griskevicius' work, specifically a paper titled "Fear and Loving in Las Vegas."[2] Griskevicius reports an experiment in which people were shown two different ads for various attractions (one of which was the city of Las Vegas, hence the name of the paper). One version of the ad emphasized the popularity of the attraction, as in "visited by over a million people each year." The other version of the ad positioned the attraction as unique, so that someone visiting might feel they were standing out from the crowd rather than following it.

---

    [2] Griskevicius, V., Goldstein, N.J., Mortensen, C.R., Sundie, J.M., Cialdini, R.B., Kenrick, D.T. (2009) "Fear and Loving in Las Vegas: Evolution, Emotion, and Persuasion." *Journal of Marketing Research* 48: 384–395.

Conventional thinking in marketing would say that the ad suggesting you do what a million others were doing would strike a chord with people whose personality favored blending in, who might be happier making safe choices. The same line of thinking would also say that the ad suggesting you take the road less travelled would resonate with people who have a more independent mindset, those who want to take a little risk and do things without needing a seal of approval. Typical marketing thinking would be that people's choices would be consistent to their personality or mindset.

There was one more important element to Griskevicius et al's study. Prior to viewing the ads, participants were shown a short clip from one of two movies. One movie clip was a few particularly terrifying minutes from the psycho-horror classic *The Shining*. The other clip consisted of a few minutes from the romantic *Before Sunrise*, where two strangers (played by Julie Delpy and Ethan Hawke) who meet on a train traveling through Europe spend an evening connecting intimately in Vienna.

So what happened next (not with the movies, but with the experiment)? In their excellent book, *The Rational Animal*, Griskevicius and co-author Doug Kenrick describe what happened when people viewed *The Shining*:

> When people viewed the ads in between segments of a scary program (clip of *The Shining*), they found the products more attractive when they emphasized the product's popularity.... People who had been viewing the scary film weren't simply drawn to follow the masses, they actively avoided products and experiences that made them stand out from the crowd.

After viewing clips from *Before Sunrise*, people preferred products that were advertised on the basis of their distinctiveness.

Rather than showing that some people are inherently disposed to be conformists while others are inherently disposed to be unique, the study found that the same person will in some circumstances want to conform and in others seek to be unique. We are inconsistent, but with very good reason.

Kenrick and Griskevicius explain these apparently contradictory preferences by suggesting the film clips triggered evolutionary goals that then filtered how people viewed the advertisements. Watching *The Shining* primed the instinct for self-protection, and the subsequent response was to seek the safety of crowds. (Countless wildlife documentaries show, often in gory detail, how being separate from the herd when predators attack generally leads to a better outcome for the hunter than for the hunted.) Watching *Before Sunrise* primed the instinct for mate acquisition, and the subsequent response was differentiation. Our personal experience, or even that from movies, teaches us that standing apart from others in the right ways improves our chances of being noticed and selected by a potential mate.

Mate acquisition behaviors, of course, are not unique to humans; many animals take great risks to attract the attention of the opposite sex. Songbirds sing loudly from prominent perches,[3] while peacocks and many other game birds (that are, ironically a tasty and substantial meal for humans and other predators) have prominent tails that become an eye-catching display to a mate. It would seem likely these features also attract attention to their enemies, and given their bulk (a peacock's tail is often as much as 60% of its entire length) can't make escaping them any easier.[4]

Griskevicius and his collaborators identified two evolutionary drives, self-protection and mate acquisition, at work in the experiment. Evolutionary drives can also be thought of as subsets of the self, and evolutionary psychologists count a total of seven "evolutionary selves" that each drive distinct behaviors. I list all seven evolutionary selves next,[5] but to understand their full context and potential application, I recommend reading *The Rational Animal*.

- **Self-Protection**—Protecting ourselves from enemies and predators
- **Disease Avoidance**—Avoiding infection and disease
- **Affiliation**—Making friends and allies

---

[3] Conspicuous singing has two roles in songbirds. Males sing loudly to assert their territory and to ward off competitive males as much as they do to attract females. The louder they sing may suggest they will defend their territory better, or that they will claim a bigger area, which marks them as prime providers and thus suitable mates to females of their species.

[4] There is some disagreement on the mechanism by which the peacock's tail attracts mates. One theory (Zahavi) is that it uses the handicap principle, that the male with the most prominent tail and thus greatest impediment must have other characteristics that have allowed him to survive. Another (Petrie) is that the number of eyespots in the tail makes the male more attractive, and if these are pruned, the males are of less interest to females. A further suggestion is that the tail isn't about attracting mates, but about intimidating predators and rivals, which has a secondary role in sexual selection.

[5] These are also covered in a number of papers, for example: Neuberg, S.L., Kenrick, D.T., Schaller, M. (2011) "Human Threat Management Systems: Self-Protection and Disease Avoidance." *Neuroscience and biobehavioral reviews* 35(4): 1042-1051.

- **Status**—Gaining respect within a social group
- **Mate Acquisition**—Attracting a romantic partner
- **Mate Retention**—Maintaining a romantic partnership
- **Kin Care**—Caring for offspring and family

In October 2013, I was fortunate enough to collaborate with Griskevicius on a talk we gave at Advertising Week, an industry event in New York City, prior to the launch of *The Rational Animal*. He used a brilliant modern-day analogy to explain how human behavior serves these seven evolutionary selves. Griskevicius suggested that rather than thinking of our brain as a powerful computer that can process huge amounts of information and work on complex tasks simultaneously, we should think of it more as a smartphone with seven different apps.

When a smartphone is in navigation mode and giving you directions it "behaves" quite differently from when you are taking a picture or playing Candy Crush. In navigation mode the screen displays maps, the speaker clearly gives audio directions, and other parts of the phone, like the GPS chip, are used more than they are when you're setting a new high score in Candy Crush. In camera mode, the screen serves as a real-time viewfinder, the speaker imitates the sound of an old-fashioned shutter, and the camera lens, instead of the GPS chip, plays a critical role (the GPS chip plays a useful but non-critical role by providing a geo-tag for the photograph). Griskevicius's point with this metaphor is that, when activated in different apps or modes, the phone performs quite differently.

It seems the human brain does the same. When primed into Self-Protection mode by something scary like a clip from *The Shining*, the brain guides us toward the safety of crowds. When in Mate Acquisition mode, the brain drives us to throw caution to the winds and stand out from the crowd.

The idea that different evolutionary subselves impact brain function and behavior has huge implications for marketers because these distinct selves are activated by the priming effect of context.

When it comes to context, conventional marketing and media thinking fall short in two ways. The first is the classic approach of matching content and context. For years, the advice I have either given or been given is to put ads that tap into a certain emotion into content that mirrors that emotion. Griskevicius's work suggests that may sometimes be exactly the wrong approach. Putting an ad for a scary movie in a scary movie or TV show might seem to be a good idea in terms of reaching the right audience at an appropriate time, but that media context could be priming viewers in a way that makes the commercial's message ineffective. It is better, perhaps, to use that media opportunity to tell them about a feel-good, feel-safe comedy. Or an alarm system for their house.

The second is more systemic, which is our flawed, but understandable, impulse as marketers to see the world as revolving around our brand and our messages.[6] We consider what we have to say—be that 15 seconds of video or a handful of square inches—on a screen or in print as the most important single thing in affecting consumers' decisions, and we discount how their preceding experience, whatever it may be, prepares them to respond to our message.

This idea of media as not just a way of reaching, but *preparing* consumers reveals an opportunity to position advertising messages in a way that is of greater value to businesses and brands. If media owners can move beyond selling media as way to deliver an audience who may be interested in a brand to showing how their content can prime different evolutionary goals, then they transition from the reach business to the influence business. Media context that prepares your target audience to be instinctively open to your message is going to do a lot more for your brand than context that simply matches it.

In a nutshell, what people see before your ad could be as important in influencing their decision as the ad itself.

2. How People Get Labeled Affects Their Behavior and Others' Behavior Toward Them

Earlier, I wrote about how observing the behavior of others acts as an important driver of our own behavior in ways of which we aren't always aware. It's not surprising then, that how we feel others see, or expect to see, us imperceptibly affects our choices and actions. This rubbing together of identity and culture has a profound and often limiting effect on how we behave, due to social forces such as the *stereotype effect* or *stereotype threat*.

---

[6] When a brand gets mentioned in social media, it often gets described as a "brand conversation." My colleague Kim Lundgren is always quick to point out "conversations are really about people, not brands." People's motivations are generally more self-serving than brand-serving—a brand recommendation isn't as much about the brand as the recommender saying "look how savvy/knowledgeable/helpful I am."

One example of a stereotype effect is gender labeling. A question I am often asked is, "How are men and women different in their decision-making?" I think when people ask this question they are expecting to hear definitive tales from neuroscience and behavioral science confirming the female and male archetypes popularized in non-scientific books like *Men Are from Mars, Women Are from Venus.*

So what's the answer? Should marketers think of men and women as different or similar?

The answer is simply, "It depends."

The topic of gender differences is a very charged one. But again I am in the fortunate position of not wanting to make a politically correct point, nor a politically incorrect one. My only interest is, "When should marketers think of men as being different from women, and when should they think of them simply as humans?" I am not looking for a deep truth; I am just trying to understand what insights from human nature marketers can use to develop strategies of influence.

It's just as well that I'm not looking for the truth, because gender differences are an excellent example of how fluid science is. As with any loaded debate, the gender differences literature is pretty divided, especially when it comes to what is innately different between the biological sexes. Opinions vary. Louann Brizendine, author of *The Male Brain* and *The Female Brain* paints a picture that sometimes makes you question whether men and women might be two different, but related species (this perception is, of course, reinforced by her devoting a separate book to each gender). Others, like Cordelia Fine, author of *Delusions of Gender* point more to similarities. As Fine says "the male brain is like nothing in the world so much as a female brain."

Science suggests less of a gender schism than women being from Venus and men from Mars. Certainly, most behavioral studies referenced in this book do not report statistically significant gender differences. That said, many of these studies look at the general effect of cognitive biases on our choices and are not designed to reveal differences by gender.

For pretty much every study stressing similarities between male and female brains or behavior there is another arguing that gender differences are indeed significant. This academic debate echoes the idea from earlier in the book about science being a work in progress; disagreement is what moves science forward.

Finding agreement on the effect of biological gender on choice is difficult, but a broad consensus among experts exists about how gender as a *stereotype* affects our decisions.

The gender stereotype effect happens for several reasons. First, obvious and fundamental differences between males and females exist that clearly go beyond physiology to cognition and behavior. One obvious difference is the female menstrual cycle; it results in hormone fluctuations that are not present in men. In addition to changes in mood, females also show significant differences in how they make decisions at different points in their menstrual cycles. When ovulating, females are more likely to choose larger-later options in a temporal discounting experiments (we talked about how in other contexts, humans have a tendency to take smaller rewards now in Chapter 7, "Now, and the Future—Different Places with Different Rules").[7] We humans extrapolate from these obvious biological differences to gender stereotypes.

Second, we have absorbed very deep-rooted and vivid *schema* of how we expect men to behave and how we expect women to behave. Schemas are processes and cultural cues absorbed from early childhood through which we build stereotypes. They influence how we think about each other and typically emphasize differences while discounting similarities. Schemas affect gender perceptions and behavior toward others, but they also affect how men or women may perceive their own skills and performance.

A unique perspective on the effect of the female gender schema comes from Jan Morris. Morris is a brilliant writer best known for books about traveling, first as James Morris and after gender reassignment in the 1970s, as Jan Morris. In her autobiographical book describing her post-transition experiences, she wrote:

> The more I was treated as a woman, the more woman I became. If I was assumed to be incompetent at reversing cars, oddly incompetent I found myself becoming. If a case was thought too heavy for me, inexplicably I found it so myself.

Debbie Chachra, Associate Professor of Materials Science at the Franklin W. Olin College of Engineering, finds in her own research phenomena similar to what Morris wrote about in her autobiography. Chachra has

---

[7] Smith, C.T., Sierra, Y., Oppler, S.H., Boettiger, C.A. (2014) "Ovarian cycle effects on immediate reward selection bias in humans: a role for estradiol." *J Neurosci* 34: 5468–5476.

published research looking at how male and female engineering students rate themselves in terms of confidence. Although both genders performed equally in term of academic achievement, after four years studying engineering (and getting grades on average equal to the male students over that time), female students' confidence levels in terms of being good at math and at solving were significantly lower than their male peers. This is a demonstration of what is known as a *stereotype threat*, where people feel themselves to be at risk of confirming negative stereotypes about a group they belong to and identify with.

A number of other research studies show that females and males perform equally at various mathematics tests; in a study in France amongst 7-8 year old boys and girls,[8] the girls performed less well on difficult math problems when they were reminded they were girls, than if not reminded. The boys' performance was indifferent to their gender identity being activated. Another study among adults with above-average mathematical ability introduced a simple stereotype threat to a subset of participants by stating up front that the math test was part of research to understand whether men or women are better at math. Women exposed to this stereotype threat performed worse than women who weren't.[9]

As we've said, despite the gender differences that seem obvious to us every day, outside of the predictable areas that relate to reproduction, there seems to be less gender differences than one would expect in many everyday aspects of behavior. An evolutionary psychologist told me his theory that men scan the horizon and are more alert to movement than women, because of men's evolutionary role of protecting territory and mates. What a wonderful excuse for the men among us when constantly distracted by the game on the screen at a bar! "I'm pre-programmed to scan for danger in the distance...I'm really just protecting you!" Whether this theory is true or not, it doesn't extend to retail. I asked a shopper marketing expert, and someone who has been involved in scores of eye-tracking tests to investigate where people look in retail environments. His answer: "No...in pretty much every test we've seen, everyone is looking down."

---

[8] Neuville, E., Croizet, J-C. (2007) "Can salience of gender identity impair math performance among 7–8 years old girls? The moderating role of task difficulty." *European Journal of Psychology of Education* 22(3): 307–316.

[9] Spencer, S.J., Steele, C.M., Quinn, D.M. (1999) "Stereotype Threat and Women's Math Performance." *Journal of Experimental Social Psychology*, January 35(1): 4–28.

Wherever marketers or scientists land on gender differences (or similarities), here is the most important thing: As a marketer, it doesn't really matter whether gender schemas are true, as long as you know *why* you are tapping into them. If men relate to a schema about men—say that men make rational decisions rather than emotional ones—by all means feed that back to your target audience. Exaggerate it, make it comedic, or make it poignant to get your target nodding along with you. You would probably be wasting money trying to persuade them otherwise, even if the opposite is the truth.

There is also a broadly held belief that women are better at multi-tasking than men. This was seemingly confirmed by a global study commissioned by Nokia published in 2007 with the headline "Survey results confirm it: Women are better multi-taskers than men."[10] However, all the Nokia survey really did was to ask respondents who they *thought* were better multi-taskers, and both men and women thought that women were. It turns out that this research simply shows the power of an inaccurate schema in shaping our beliefs. The scientific evidence is far from conclusive on this issue, and it seems quite likely that men and women are equally bad at multi-tasking. However, as a marketer, making a connection through the cultural belief that women are better multi-taskers may be very powerful.

When it comes to putting your marketing together, remember that just like with women, emotional and instinctual aspects account for the vast majority of male decision-making processes, and while you may be praising their rationality, you need to appeal to their hearts. Also remember that even if people believe women are better multi-taskers, don't design a digital experience that assumes that they are. *Understand how your consumer sees the world in order to make a connection, but understand the realities of their behavior before you construct marketing plans.*

Whether or not gender schemas are accurate, gender itself is a label. Another interesting, and unexpected, label is your name. In Chapter 5, I wrote about the cocktail party effect. The cocktail party effect demonstrates how special names are—we immediately hear our name over an airport public announcement system or if someone across the room at a crowded party says it.

---

[10] http://company.nokia.com/en/news/press-releases/2007/11/22/survey-results-confirm-it-women-are-better-multi-taskers-than-men

A couple of years ago I collaborated with Adam Alter for a talk at the Cannes Festival of Creativity. Alter is a psychologist by training and Associate Professor of Marketing at New York University's Stern School of Business. At the time, Alter had just published his book *Drunk Tank Pink: And Other Unexpected Forces That Shape How We Think, Feel, and Behave*, which examines how features of the world shape our thoughts and feelings beyond our control. Alter captivated the audience in Cannes, and his book deservedly became a *New York Times* bestseller.

In *Drunk Tank Pink* Alter writes about how our names—things we have been given or saddled with, rather than chosen—have an effect on our behavior, our life decisions, and decisions others make about us. While the effect of your name isn't generally as extreme or obvious as it was for the subject of Johnny Cash's song "A Boy Named Sue," Alter makes a convincing argument that names do make a difference.

One place where the effect of your name on your life may come into play is in the distinctly non-scientific but rather fun area of *aptronyms* (also spelled *aptonym*). An aptronym is a name that seems particularly suited to its owner. One example I've already given in Chapter 8, "Loss and Ownership," is the economist and behavioral economics pioneer Richard Thaler; *thaler* is an old German word for "dollar." Other examples include friends of mine in San Francisco who use a podiatrist called Dr. Knee. Alter refers to the urologist team of Drs. Weedon and Splatt, the Aussie Rules footballer Derek Kickett, and Israeli tennis player Anna Smashnova. Research examining *nominative determinism*—that your name influences your profession or other aspects of your life—suggests that there are more people whose first name begins with "Den" in the dental profession than found in the population at large.[11] However, the notion of nominative determinism is currently being challenged.[12]

Scientifically valid or not, aptronyms seem to crop up regularly. This may be, because they create a vivid connection, names that match an occupation or interest are particularly sticky, so we over-estimate their actual incidence. Perhaps a memory bias called the *context effect* is at play. The context

---

[11] Pelham, B.W., Mirenberg, M.C., Jones, J.T. (2002) "Why Susie sells seashells by the seashore: Implicit egotism and major life decisions." *Journal of Personality and Social Psychology* 82(4): 469–487.

[12] Simonsohn, U. (2010) "Spurious? Name Similarity Effects (Implicit Egotism) in Marriage, Job and Moving Decisions." *Journal of Personality and Social Psychology* 101: 1–24.

effect occurs as things that are "in-context" (rather than out-of-context) are easier to retrieve.

So I'm not sure I would recommend a targeting strategy for a baking goods company that assumed a particularly high percentage of people named Baker are in fact bakers, or even remotely interested in baking—although this phenomenon may explain why Arsenal Football Club hired a Frenchman named Arsene Wenger as their coach, and after great initial success still stuck with him over a period of nine trophyless years (the trophy drought ended in 2013, with victory over Hull City in the FA Cup final).

Aptronyms may be a bit of a stretch, but Alter does convincingly demonstrate that names have an important influence on our lives. Names are, literally, our identity. He points to a number of studies that show how people's names affect others' behavior toward them and how names can even, insidiously, affect how employable that person is considered.[13] Perhaps more importantly for marketing, Alter shows how names have a hidden effect on the behavior of the person who carries that name.

The work of the late Belgian psychologist Jozef M. Nuttin showed how people prefer the letters in their own names, choosing these over other letters in choice tasks, and selecting them more frequently when listing their top six favorite letters. Nuttin described this as the effect of *mere ownership*.

Alter also points to an interesting analysis of real-life behavior that shows that we don't just *like* the letters in our names but we are also likely to give financial favor to an option that begins with one of our initials over one that doesn't. Using donation records of a chapter of the Red Cross in the Midwest, a team of researchers from University of Michigan[14] investigated whether the "name letter effect" influenced donations to hurricane relief. Specifically, they were looking to see whether people who shared an initial with the hurricane were over-represented as donors to that hurricane. They found that this was the case—people whose names began with "K" were more likely to donate at the time of Hurricane Katrina relief than

---

[13] "Are Emily and Greg More Employable than Lakisha and Jamal? A Field Experiment on Labor Market Discrimination" by Marianne Bertrand, Sendhil Mullainathan and published by the National of Economic Research found that a resume with a white-sounding name had a 1 in 10 chance of getting a callback, but for an identical resume with a black-sounding name that number dropped to 1 in 15.

[14] Chandler, J., Griffin, T.M., Sorensen, N. "In the "I" of the storm: Shared initials increase disaster donations," Department of Psychology, University of Michigan.

they were to other hurricane relief efforts, and people whose names began with "M" were more likely to give within the period of Hurricane Mitch relief. A friend of mine who is Filipina was particularly moved to respond to the effects of Typhoon Haiyan on her homeland, raising many thousands of dollars for relief through her network of friends, something she had not attempted before. In the Philippines Typhoon Haiyan was known as Yolanda. My friend's name is Yumi.

Alter's "back of a napkin" calculations based on the findings of this research suggest that simply naming hurricanes with initials found in the most popular names in the U.S. (for the record, that is "J" for men and "M" for women) could have raised an additional $700,000,000 for aid agencies since the year 2000.

It's a little ironic that marketers gather huge amounts of hard-to-get data on consumers, but using the most public information about someone—their name—has not been used often as a marketing technique. One exception is a highly successful campaign for Coca-Cola that started in Australia in 2011. Under the umbrella of "Share a Coke," the company printed 150 of Australia's most popular names on bottles and cans. The campaign took off like wildfire, and in Australia, a country of 23 million people, Coke sold 250 million cans and bottles with names on them, and various media reports suggest the campaign boosted consumption by 7%—an impressive amount for such a large brand. The idea has spread to 70 countries. In the UK, market research firm YouGov reported that "Consumer perception of Coca-Cola, Diet Coke and Coke Zero improved substantially on virtually every measure for those who were exposed to Share a Coke TV adverts," and *The Grocer*, a UK trade magazine, quoted Nielsen data that showed a 10% increase year over year.

A version of the campaign reached Coke's homeland in 2014, and according to the *Wall Street Journal*, the campaign halted an 11-year decline for Coke in the U.S., and increased sales by 2%.

Appeals to implicit egotism aren't just limited to names. In a 1989 study, students were given a short biography of Rasputin (the Russian mystic who had a hypnotic hold over Tsarina Alexandra, and whom legend portrays as evil and demonic[15]). Some students were given an altered biography so

---

[15] Legend also portrays him as an inveterate womanizer, giving credence to Boney M's claim that he was "Russia's greatest love machine" in their 1978 song *Ra Ra Rasputin*.

that they shared a birthday with Rasputin. Those students who "shared" a birthday with Rasputin regarded him less negatively than students who read a biography that included Rasputin's actual birthday.[16]

The appeal of connections like sharing a name, a letter, or a birthday gives opportunities for brands to build empathy, connections, and nudges to action with consumers. In an age where there are rightly concerns about marketers using data that consumers consider to be private, we may be overlooking the power that lies in some of the most public data about people—their names and birthdays.

3. From Macro to Micro, Our Environment Affects Our Choices

Adam Alter is an expert not just on names but also on context in many of its forms. When we at FCB's Institute for Decision Making interviewed him in 2010, he explained how context can have effects as broad as the weather:

> [Even broadest level aspects of the environment] like the weather, whether it's a sunny day or a rainy day, influence whether people are likely to purchase products. It influences whether people are likely to purchase stocks. Researchers have found that, when you look at the performance of the stock market on days when it's sunny, the stock market tends to appreciate. In general, people buy more stocks. They're also happy to buy products, so you get the same basic effect for financial stocks and for products.

Where something happens is often as important as what happens. James Hallatt, the global head of GlaxoSmithKline's Oral Health Category, told me of the importance of sampling for one of his global brands, Sensodyne:

> Being given a sample for Sensodyne by a dentist in his or her surgery for a sensitive teeth sufferer is clearly a powerful recommendation because it comes from a professional. But the surgery environment, the patient's full orientation to their oral care whilst lying in the surgery chair and the dentist's one-to-one attention all add context to the moment and further endorse the message in a profound manner.

---

[16] Cialdini, R.B., Finch, J.F. "Another Indirect Tactic of (Self-) Image Management," Arizona State University.

Other research shows retail effects of low versus bright lighting, of scents, and even of the amount of space between displays. (Research shows that shoppers "placed in a narrow, confining aisle seek greater variety in their candy-bar choices than people placed in a wide aisle."[17]) A study looking at wine selection in a supermarket in the UK showed the dramatic effect that different types of background music had on how people chose.[18] French and German wines that were similar in price and quantity were displayed. Music played from the display, and it varied on alternate days. One day stereotypically French accordion music was played, but on the next day, wine shoppers heard recognizably German brass Oom-pah music. When the French accordion music was played, nearly 8 out of 10 bottles sold were French wine. When the Oom-pah music was played, just over 7 out of 10 bottles sold were German wine. After their purchase, shoppers completed a questionnaire. Responses to the questionnaire suggested that customers were unaware that the music played a part in their choice; 86% reported music had no effect on their choice. In marketing, we focus so much on the foreground but forget what a difference the background can make to people's choices.

4. How We Feel—The Unrelated Emotions That Individuals Bring to Their Decisions

We've all experienced the feeling when it seems someone has been a little short with us or seems irritated by our greeting. Often, our first reaction is to question what we did to earn this reaction. "What is wrong with me?" we ask ourselves. Or we simply attribute their behavior to their personality and think the worse of them. More often than not, though, a subsequent conversation reveals that something entirely unrelated—an argument with a family member, a frustrating experience with a customer service representative, a worry about health or finances—was what really affected their behavior toward you.

Your brand will often find itself in the same position. However you have set out its stall with your marketing, you are at the mercy of a shopper's personal previous context, something that is often beyond your control. Previous contexts can have a profound effect on the choices people make.

---

17 Levav, J., Zhu, R. (2009) "Seeking Freedom through Variety." *Journal of Consumer Research* 36(4): 600–610.

18 North, A.C., Hargreaves, D.J., McKendrick, J. (1999) "The influence of in-store music on wine selections." *Journal of Applied Psychology* 84(2): 271–276.

Take, for example, a famous experiment from the 1970s that took place at Princeton University. The study is known as "The Good Samaritan Study,"[19] after the New Testament parable about a man who has been beaten, robbed, and left at the side of the rode for dead by his assailants. In the parable, two people with religious backgrounds—first a priest and then a Levite—subsequently passed by the injured man without stopping to help. Finally, a man from Samara, who had no vocational reason to help, stopped and assisted the victim, patching up his wounds and paying for his stay at an inn while he recovered.

In the Good Samaritan experiment, students at Princeton Theological Seminary were asked to prepare a short talk to give to a group of people in a building a short walk away. Some participants were asked to speak about job prospects for seminarians, while others were asked to speak about the parable of The Good Samaritan. To gauge the likelihood that they would offer help to others, all students were also asked to complete a short personality test with some specific questions asking how they felt about religion.

Students were then asked to walk to the building where they were to give the talk. Before the students left, the researchers spoke to them. To one-third of the students, the researchers said, "Oh, you're late. They were expecting you a few minutes ago. We'd better get moving..." To another third of the students, the researchers said, "The assistant is ready for you, so please go right over." To the final third, the researchers said, "It'll be a few minutes before they're ready for you, but you might as well head on over...."

On the way to the building where they were to give their talk, all students passed by someone who appeared to be in distress (this person was actually a research confederate) but only a handful of them actually stopped and offered help.

Interestingly, neither the rather heavy-handed prime of drafting a speech about the Good Samaritan parable nor the results of the personality test indicating whether the individual was likely to help others predicted the students' behavior. It was only the third variable—the state of hurriedness the students felt before walking to the building where they were to give their speech—that determined whether the students offered help. Those students not in a hurry were more likely to stop and help.

---

[19] Darley, J.M., Batson, C.D. (1973) "From Jerusalem to Jericho: A study of Situational and Dispositional Variables in Helping Behavior." *Journal of Personality and Social Psychology* 27(1): 100–108.

The study leaders, John Darley and C. Daniel Batson wrote in their paper:

> Thinking about the Good Samaritan did not increase helping behavior, but being in a hurry decreased it. It is difficult not to conclude from this that the frequently cited explanation that ethics becomes a luxury as the speed of our daily lives increases is at least an accurate description.

In short, being in a state of hurry not only had a more significant effect on participant's behavior than their philosophy or sense of values did, but it also beat out a very recent reminder of the importance of offering help, writing about the Good Samaritan parable, which should have been very persuasive to the theological seminarians who took part in this study.

Having some understanding of a potential chooser's state of mind when he or she is getting your message or making a choice is important. Accounting for state of mind is one of the factors behind the success of the discipline of *shopper marketing*. People behave differently enough in a retail environment (actually, even from one retail environment to another) to require a different sort of expertise to market to them. The traditional view of brand marketing is that the differences between people's psychographics and demographics underlie their behavior. What we have learned from evolutionary psychology and behavioral science would suggest that people's state of mind at the time of the choice makes a more significant difference.

Context, in its broadest sense, makes a big difference in how people choose. As marketers we fixate on content, and see it as king, because it seems easier for us to control. However, that is an illusion. Context can either nullify or turbocharge content in terms of how it influences choice. Your content is only as good as the context that surrounds it allows it to be. The king isn't dead, but long live the queen.

The takeaways from this chapter are

- Everything about how people reach decisions is context dependent. It's so important, I'll say it again. Everything about how people make decisions is context dependent.

- The context that surrounds a choice primes powerful evolutionary goals. These (sometimes subtle) situational differences can make the same person make very different choices.

- Humans use *schemas* and *stereotypes* to help us make quick evaluations that are (often inaccurate) extrapolations of actual behavior. Marketers, being human, do this as well. We need to make sure that we understand that stereotypes aren't predictors of actual behavior.

- We tend to favor things that have connections with us. Sharing a birthday or an initial makes us feel more warmly toward that person or entity. If you are a fundraiser, don't just send your appeals from one person—recruit a panel of people and match the names or initials of senders to the recipients.

A couple of thoughts other people had when they read this chapter:

- "It's not just about saying the right thing. Say it in the right place. In the right way. Context is what drives the insight and content."

- "...thinking about content without context verges on pointless."

13

Same and Different; Nature and Nurture

Both nature and nurture drive people's choices, so marketers need to factor both into their thinking.

L et's go back, for a minute, to Professor Louis Levy, Woody Allen's fictional psychologist and philosopher from the film *Crime and Misdemeanors* whom I introduced in Part I of this book. Levy tells us how our lives are shaped by our choices, how we are "the sum total" of them.

But what shapes our choices? Universal aspects of behavior? Our individual biological differences? The effect of our cultural context? Our personal experiences?

The answer is, of course, all the above.

So, conveniently, we don't need to get into a debate about whether our choices are driven by nature or nurture. The answer is both. In the last chapter, we saw how the social context of gender differences affects behavior, and I discussed how context molds our choices, leading us to choose differently in different circumstances.

However, aren't there also innate differences between individuals that affect their choices?

When I first became interested in the application of behavioral science to marketing, I was struck by how many of the experiments in the various fields focused on the average effect across the sample of participants rather than considering why that effect is more or less observable in some individuals. To be honest, you could read a number of the brilliant books that have popularized the discipline of behavioral economics and be left scratching your head and wondering whether you are any different from your neighbor, from a taxi driver in Tokyo, or a teacher in Hamburg. Of course, in so many ways you aren't different from them, but there are also so many ways in which you are.

A prominent focus of behavioral economics (especially in pioneering studies) has been establishing the existence of cognitive biases in humans rather than revealing what range of effects these biases may have. As discussed in Chapter 8, "Loss and Ownership," prospect theory suggests that a loss has approximately twice the negative psychological impact as an equivalent gain has a positive psychological impact. Pretty much every time I have run a workshop with or given a presentation to marketing professionals I've been asked the question, "Is that number true of everyone?"

It's a good question, and the answer is no.[1] It's a question marketers ask because so much of marketing thinking focuses on the differences between people rather than similarities. We look to target different people with different products. We divide our users into different groups. We buy media based on the demographic and psychographic differences of the audience it attracts. We come up with "handles" for groups born after a certain year and before another—Boomers, Gen Xers, Millennials—and ascribe to them completely different attitudes, beliefs, and even behaviors. Sometimes it seems like we make our brother and sister humans seem like a collection of different species.

Marketers spend considerable sums of money trying to find differences. Every large client I have worked with has invested heavily in a segmentation study, the purpose of which is to divide the total market into groups that are similar in their differences. These groups (or segments) can then be assessed for their potential value to the brand, their addressability, and whether they should be a priority target. Typical criteria used to form these segments might be how one group's needs from the category or brand may differ from other groups; how their claimed behavior differs; demographics and psychographics; or how a group's media use is different, how group attitudes and emotional needs may lead them to be more or less receptive to a particular product or message than the other groups.

---

[1] Research amongst a sample of 660 Germans across a range of age and socioeconomic groups showed older participants were more loss averse, and more educated participants were less loss averse. Gaechter, S., Johnson, E. J., Herrmann, A. (July 2007) "Individual-Level Loss Aversion in Riskless and Risky Choices." *IZA Discussion Paper* No. 2961.

Segmentation studies don't run cheap—a thorough one including analysis can run anywhere from $300,000 to $1 million, or more, depending on the scope, size, and number of countries covered. That's just the beginning of it—segmentation often directly influences marketing investments that cost tens or hundreds of times the cost of fielding the study.

Individual differences are important to marketers (this chapter suggests some novel areas of individual difference that are directly related to behavior), and from a practitioner's perspective may seem rather less important to behavioral scientists. My view is that marketers often place too much emphasis on perceived differences and that behavioral scientists (from the perspective of the application of their work to marketing) place too little emphasis on them. Behavioral experiments are generally designed to suggest an effect at a population level. In contrast, segmentation studies, while incredibly valuable, always have the effect of magnifying differences, which may or may not be useful. One way the head of consumer insights for one of our largest clients gets around this magnification is by identifying individuals who fit into the key groups described by the segmentation study and then making mini-documentaries about their lives and their tastes. The consumer insights team even finds individual consumers who are representative of the groups identified in the segmentation study and has them come to key briefing meetings with the broader marketing and product teams. While this personal approach helps people see differences between the segments, it also subtly reinforces the importance of more universal human motivations and desires that a segmentation study can lead marketers to ignore.

The lack of discussion I found in much judgment and decision-making research about the potential effect of culture on people's choices also perplexed me. Marketers, particularly advertising agencies, are *obsessed* with culture—and for good reason (as Engel, Blackwell, and Miniard say in their book *Consumer Behavior*, "a marketer with a defective knowledge of culture is doomed"). In the previous chapter I wrote about how stereotypes can create cognitive consonance—things that we implicitly agree with and get us figuratively nodding along. Ideas and themes that have cultural resonance probably do the same thing. From the receiver's perspective, an idea that connects with what people are talking about, what they are watching and listening to, what they are interacting with and sharing is probably worth acknowledging.

As often as not, the effect of a culturally relevant theme or meme[2] in marketing is less a mechanism that will trigger a decision or behavior and more a hook to get people to become attentive and engaged. What actually moves the chooser to make a choice is the connection between a feeling a message creates and innate behavioral tendencies, many of which I covered in the preceding chapters of this book.

For example, let's look back into the archives of advertising at a commercial that ran more than 40 years ago and that in 2007, the UK marketing trade magazine *Campaign,* called "one of the best-loved and most influential ads in TV history." The commercial, featuring hundreds of young people singing "I'd like to buy the world a Coke,"[3] nailed the *zeitgeist* (a term borrowed from the German for "ghost or spirit of the times"). When the commercial aired, American troops had already been fighting in the Vietnam War for six years with no end in sight, and the Cold War was dividing almost the entire world. The commercial, as many people from Coca-Cola have said, quickly became more than an ad; it became a rallying message of tolerance and hope.

Coke's commercial had a huge cultural effect at the time—100,000 people wrote to the Coca-Cola Company (at a time when writing to a company involved a lot more effort than clicking the "Like" button on the company's Facebook page), and radio stations were inundated with requests to play the jingle as a song. (Incidentally, the song was recorded shortly thereafter, but without a mention of Coke in the lyrics, by The New Seekers. It reached number 1 and number 7 in the UK and U.S. charts, respectively.)

Although the commercial's message of tolerance and the cultural impact it had are a large part of what made it a much-loved ad, the behavioral engine that made it effective may lie more in its brilliant and positive use of social proof. By finding an artful and meaningful way of showing so many people holding Coke bottles, the commercial didn't just remind viewers that Coke was popular, that it was something many people with whom viewers could

---

[2] A meme is "an idea, behavior, style, or usage that spreads from person to person within a culture," and was coined by Richard Dawkins in his 1976 book *The Selfish Gene.*

[3] I'm sure you've seen this commercial—it is actually called "Hillside." As the titles at the end read "On a hilltop in Italy we assembled young people from all over the world to bring you this message...." It is my, and many other people's all-time favorite TV commercial. A written description won't do it justice, so if you haven't seen it go and watch it on YouTube. If you do know it, give yourself a treat by watching it again.

identify were buying and drinking. Because social proof is a powerful way of activating the innate behavioral tendency to do what others do, it made choosing Coke an intuitive behavior. It made Coke a natural choice.

What's happening in society or in pop culture or how congruent something is with an individual's values or tastes are all important in shaping how people choose. While human nature operates—by definition—at a timeless and universal level, what about things that are more individual or anchored in a specific time? What about the things that make us different from the people around us and the people who came before us?

Differences between individuals exist for many reasons. Some are inherited in the form of genes that have helped a homogeneous group fare better in their common environment. For example, indigenous Scandinavians have adapted to get the most out of the little sunlight available in northern latitudes and thus get the benefits of vitamin D3 (vital for strong bone growth, immune response, and functioning of the brain) from the sun. Adaptations include not just fair skin that maximizes absorption but also a culture of sun-seeking behavior (tourists in Stockholm are often amused that deck chairs outside bars and in public places are arranged in neat rows, angled precisely to catch the maximum rays at a certain time of the day).

Other individual differences may occur because a mix of personalities and behaviors in a population benefits the population as a whole. A study published in 2013[4] reported the discovery of a "leadership gene" and created a frenzy in the popular press. One of the authors, Dr. Jan-Emmanuel De Neve reported,

> We have identified a genotype, called rs4950, which appears to be associated with the passing of leadership ability down through generations...the conventional wisdom—that leadership is a skill—remains largely true, but we show it is also, in part, a genetic trait.

If leadership is to have societal value, then not everyone can have that role. Whether people are destined to be leaders or followers gets into a moral discussion which is not within the scope of this book (but could be an interesting conversation over a pint of beer), but the idea that a society may fare better when its population has diverse but complementary strengths is an

---

4   De Neve, J.-E., Mikhaylov, S., Dawes, C.T., Christakis, N.A., Fowler, J.H. (2003) "Born to lead? A twin design and genetic association study of leadership role occupancy." *The Leadership Quarterly* 24 (1): 45.

interesting and welcome one. The point for marketers is that while human nature is universal, it comes in different strains.

In order to grasp how nature and nurture and how population similarities and individual differences play into how we choose, I developed a map a couple of years ago, and although it doesn't completely answer the questions about how our background and environments affect our decisions, it at least allows one to plot a wide range of influences on human choice. (Way bigger brains than mine continue to debate how nature and nurture affect choice. In any case, the answers, if they are ever discovered will be more interesting to philosophers and scientists than marketers.) I find Figure 13.1 useful as a framework to help visualize the latent variables impacting choosers' behavior.

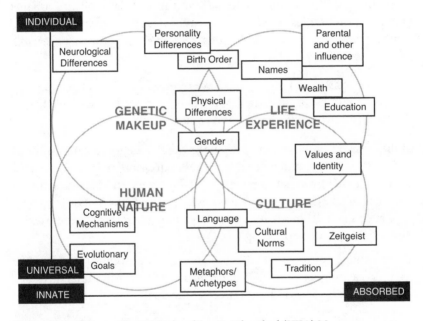

Figure 13.1 Universal/Individual and Innate/Absorbed (UIIA) Map

Let's look at the quadrants one by one.

Human Nature

The Human Nature quadrant lives at the intersection of Universal and Innate and is really what many of the chapters of this book have been about. This space is all about the shortcuts all humans use and how our intuitions have evolved over thousands of years. These factors are near to universal and, as we've said before, they are the bedrock of human decision making. But as we've discussed, and will discuss more in this chapter, context, culture, and an individual's experience of life can all moderate these installed tendencies, a little, a lot, or not at all.

Genetic Makeup

Moving up to where Innate and Individual meet, our Genetic Makeup dictates many of our physical differences, so it should come as no surprise that genes also play a role in differences in brain structure and thus in our behavior and our choices. Genetic influences on behavior are an area of research that has received increased attention in the last few years. As recently as 2010, Itamar Simonsen and Aner Sela published a paper examining similarities and differences in the decision-making behavior of identical and fraternal twins.[5] Simonsen and Sela begin their paper with the observation:

> While constructed preferences have received a great deal of attention, there has been virtually no research regarding the genetic basis of consumer judgment and choice.

In their paper, Simonsen and Sela suggest that genetics research will lead to discoveries about individual differences in decision making. Despite the advances made by genetics researchers, Simonsen and Sela nonetheless think it may take decades before it is possible to find "the links among heritable effects and the mechanisms underlying such effects on things such as risk aversion, divorce, or liking jazz."[6]

There is no doubt that we will start to see more findings from genetic research casting light on what underpins differences in preferences and decision-making approaches between individuals (the "leadership gene"

---

[5] Simonson, I., Sela, A. (2011) "On the Heritability of Consumer Decision Making: An Exploratory Approach for Studying Genetic Effects on Judgment and Choice." *Journal of Consumer Research*, April, 37(6): 951–966.

[6] Although it may be decades before we get an extensive picture on genetic differences affecting choice, it is something researchers are tackling already. A study I reference later in the book ("Dopaminergic genes predict individual differences in susceptibility to confirmation bias" Doll, Hutchison, and Frank, *Journal of Neuroscience* 2011) suggests that people with a polymorphism of a certain gene are more affected by the confirmation bias.

mentioned earlier in this chapter is an example). The issue for marketers will be how addressable these insights will be—targeting people on the basis of their genetic makeup may not just be a technology challenge but more importantly, an ethical one. De Neve, one of the authors of the "leadership gene" study "Born to lead? A twin design and genetic association study of leadership role occupancy," states the ethical hazards of genetic tests for leadership selection and assessment, and the potential for this to lead to genetic discrimination in the labor market.

An obvious and observable individual trait where genetic differences affect behavior of a sizeable minority of the population (between 9% and 11% in the U.S.) is right- or left-handedness. One dirty little secret of neuroscience is that almost all studies (both academic and commercial) use right-hand dominant people as research subjects[7] because significant differences in brain organization, many of which are not yet fully understood, exist between right- and left-handers. It isn't simply a question of flipping brain images around and using a mirror image of a right-handers brain to interpret left-handers activity!

As marketers, we don't have to delve deep into the neuroscience of these differences (though it is a fascinating area of research), but we can think of its effects in the real world. One obvious effect in terms of physical brand and retail experiences is to make sure that, wherever possible, they are as easy for left-handers as right-handers. However, a real opportunity presents itself in digital environments.

A 2012 paper by Ryan Elder and Aradhna Krishna[8] reports on their research into the visual depiction of cues in advertising and their likely effect on behavior. In one test, the researchers showed participants three versions of an ad. One had a bowl of yogurt with a spoon on the right-hand side (the spoon serves as a cue to consumption or action), another had the spoon on the left-hand side, and a third had no spoon at all. For other tests they showed two versions of ads, one version showing cues that were right-handed (including forks, a hand holding a burger or mug handles), the other showing left-hand cues.

---

[7] Willems, R.M., Van der Haegen, L., Fisher, S.E., Francks, C. (2014) "On the other hand: including left-handers in cognitive neuroscience and neurogenetics." *Nature Reviews Neuroscience* February, 15: 193–201.

[8] Elder, R.S., Krishna, A. (2012) "The 'Visual Depiction Effect' in Advertising: Facilitating Embodied Mental Simulation through Product Orientation." *Journal of Consumer Research* April, 38(6): 988–1003.

Across these studies, the findings showed an increase in purchase intent when participants' own hand-dominance matched the image they were shown (so right-handers responded better when the spoon was on the right-hand side of the plate, or when the coffee mug handle was turned to the right).

This research shows two things. The first is a reminder of the importance of visual cues as a path to action. If there is a way of showing a cue that relates to the action you want people to take—be that an eating utensil, a button on a screen, a bottle opener, a keypad, dial pad, or pen—there's a pretty good chance that featuring it will give will nudge your audience a little closer to action.

However, what interested me most about Elder and Krishna's work was the opportunity to address people with different hand dominance in different ways in digital media.

If one could identify whether the person being served ads is left- or right-handed with some degree of accuracy, through different keystrokes, mouse or touch screen actions and gestures (just as a handwriting analyst can determine whether someone is right- or left-handed), serving ads designed to appeal specifically to lefties or righties would be possible. As mentioned earlier, left-handers account for around 11% of the population, which is bigger than every cultural minority in the U.S. except for African Americans (13.6%) and Latinos (17%). By ignoring the differences innate in left-handers we run the risk of serving that 11% of the population suboptimal advertising. In a battle of increments, that could make a difference.

Culture

As we move from left to right at the bottom of the framework, we look at how what people experience at a group level may affect their choices. Without debating the existence of a "collective unconscious" there are some ideas that seem to fall somewhere between "innate" and "absorbed." Archetypes are just one example. Some argue that the archetypes described by Carl Jung and others are so deeply rooted as to be as instinctual as cognitive biases. Others argue they are learned or absorbed. Many marketers are very familiar with archetypes as a way to distill a brand's meaning, largely due to Margaret Mark and Carol Pearson's book *The Hero and the Outlaw*. Mark and Pearson have adapted the archetypes made famous by Jung and built upon by Joseph Campbell in a way that can be applied to the roles that brands inhabit. For example, American Express and Mercedes may be seen as fitting with the archetype of "The Ruler," whereas Nike and the brand of the U.S. Marines might be seen as embodying "The Hero" archetype. Although the scientific validity of brands as archetypes in consumers' minds is debated, archetypes are nonetheless a useful way of thinking about what territory a brand occupies and as a tool to guide brand activity and imagery that is consistent with that territory.

Similarly, some experts believe metaphors operate at an unconscious level. Gerald Zaltman, the Joseph C. Wilson Professor Emeritus at Harvard Business School and the author of *How Customers Think* and *Marketing Metaphoria,* sees the surface metaphors used in everyday conversation as connecting to frameworks that are familiar to everyone and that relate to us in very deep ways.

Language also lives in this space. In *The Language Instinct,* Steven Pinker argues convincingly that language is not entirely learned but is instinctual as a concept. (Probably the simplest way to say this is that we have an instinct for *language,* but that *languages* are learned.) Pinker uses the example that children's mistakes when talking come from their own constructions; they do not memorize and copy what their parents say. An example that Pinker gives is that a young child may say, "He teared the paper and then he sticked it," which it is unlikely to be how their parents speak. Children grasp the *idea* of language before learning the specifics of their native tongue. That said, the details and idiosyncrasies of your home language, which are learned, can influence your behavior. The Chief Strategy Officer of our New York office, Kofi Amoo-Gottfried, was born and raised in Ghana, and at one stage in his career, he ran the Accra office of a global advertising agency network. According to Kofi (and he is as loyal to his country as anyone), Ghanaians have a reputation for a flexible notion of punctuality. Kofi believes that this might be partly due to the fact that there isn't a pejorative connotation to the concept of "lateness" in Ashanti, the language spoken by many Ghanaians, nor is there a directly translatable word. As Kofi says, "Rather than saying 'you're late' we say, 'it's taken you a while' and that doesn't carry the same sense of admonishment."

While at the 2014 Society for Judgment and Decision Making conference in Long Beach, California, I had a chance to chat about this hypothesis with someone who is studying similar effects. Andrea Weihrauch of KU Leuven pointed me toward an interesting paper by Keith Chen[9] at the University

---

[9] Chen, K.M. (2013) "The Effect of Language on Economic Behavior: Evidence from Savings Rates, Health Behaviors, and Retirement Assets." *American Economic Review* 103(2): 690–731.

of California, Los Angeles. Chen's paper looks at the effect of languages that have differences in how they require future events to be grammatically marked when making predictions. Languages that require more "marking" are considered strong in "future-time reference" (FTR), while those that require less are considered weak FTR languages. Chen writes:

> ...a German speaker predicting rain can naturally do so in the present tense, saying: *Morgen regnet es* which translates to "It rains tomorrow." In contrast, English would require the use of a future marker like "will" or "is going to," as in: "It will rain tomorrow." In this way, English requires speakers to encode a distinction between present and future events, while German does not.

This makes English a strong FTR language, and German a weak FTR language. Now before English speakers start doing celebratory laps on the basis of their language being stronger than German, in terms of leading to what should be considered better and healthier behaviors, having a strong FTR language isn't necessarily a good thing. In this respect, a strong FTR language is like having a high score in a golf tournament.

Chen's analysis using Organization for Economic Co-operation and Development (OECD) data shows that member countries of that organization whose population mainly speaks strong-FTR languages save 4.75% less on average than those member countries whose member population mainly speaks weak-FTR languages. While it is impossible to say how much of this effect is driven by language, it is safe to say that language, culture, and behavior are all intertwined.

It also seems the tense in which something is expressed may have an effect on how we react to it. Weihrauch, a native German speaker, is currently investigating the role of tense in the context of advertising claims and social interactions, and she is particularly interested in the power of the present continuous tense. Her research shows that the use of present continuous versus present tense can affect judgments of product use duration (for example, how long a battery will provide power before needing to be recharged), which translates into more favorable attitudes toward products and brands.

Closer to the far right of the map, as we move from "individual" to "many," we get into the effect of culture. Culture has a huge impact on our behavior and choices, and any decent exploration of the subject is beyond the scope and constraints of this book. It's a huge topic, not just because of the number of cultures in the world, but also because culture is constantly changing.[10] Richard Nisbett, author of *The Geography of Thought*, has looked at these both on an international and intranational level. His research covers the effects of culture on behavior, showing differences between males who have grown up in the Southern states of the U.S. and those brought up in the Northern states,[11] and how Eastern and Western cultures affect people's perception of self and others, and thus their choices. I interviewed Nisbett after his keynote at the Society of Judgment and Decision Making conference in St. Louis, and asked him specifically how he thought these differences might affect global brands and their marketing strategy. His suggestion was that rather than one size fitting all, you might want to consider at least two sizes...

MW: What might global brands learn from the work that you've done in terms of how different cultures actually go about making decisions and thinking about things?

RN: One (finding) is that some cultures are much more interdependent and others are much more independent. Interdependent people have closer ties to other people, especially those who are in some direct relationship with them like friends and family and company. They have more to do with them, they care more about them, they're more sensitive to socio-emotional cues than the independent people.

Independent people have wider circles of acquaintances where they deal with people who are typically in a wider range of occupations, of businesses, and there is a big difference in how likely you are to trust someone in the in group versus the out group. Interdependent people trust completely in the in group, people

---

10 The work of Geert Hofstede and his *Cultural Dimensions Theory* is a widely used resource. *The Hofstede Centre* provides courses and tools based on Geert Hofstede's research. One interesting tool lets you compare the cultures of 102 countries across six key dimensions: power distance, individualism, masculinity (meaning a culture driven more by competition than cooperation), uncertainty avoidance, pragmatism, and indulgence (which in this context means a society that allows relatively free gratification of basic and natural human drives related to enjoying life and having fun). The tool can be found at http://geert-hofstede.com/countries.html.

11 Cohen, D., Nisbett, R.E., Bowdle, B.F., Schwarz, N. (1996) "Insult, aggression, and the southern culture of honor: An 'experimental ethnography.'" *Journal of Personality and Social Psychology* May, 70(5): 945–960.

---

that they've gotten to know well, that they feel like they understand what makes them tick. Independent people cast a much wider net; they trust a much wider range of people and sources.

MW: So brands should perhaps think about a strategy for inter-dependent societies, and a different strategy for independent societies?

RN: For marketing, almost surely, there are examples of ads that show the difference of what people believe to be more effective in interdependent societies, which include East Asians in partic-ular, probably South Asians. Eastern Europeans are more inter-dependent than Western Europeans. Continental Europeans are more interdependent than Americans. Basically, the further West you move, the more independent people are as opposed to interdependent.

Although global brands may not want to address every cultural difference (it would be both expensive and create a more fragmented brand), I do think the idea of considering global strategy in terms of how it might sepa-rately address independent and interdependent mindsets an intriguing idea.

One potent area of culture is religion. Asking people about their religious beliefs in market research is either taboo or prohibited in many western countries (in France, for example, you cannot ask people about religious beliefs in screening questionnaires to recruit respondents for focus groups). But, not surprisingly, given the depth of its role in many people's lives, dif-ferent beliefs lead to different choices—beyond spiritual ones.

My colleague Ambi Parameswaran's book[12] *For God's Sake* is about how religion, brands, and business can become intertwined. He says

> Mining cultural differences provides fertile opportunities for prod-uct and service innovations; in high religiosity countries like India, we have seen products and services exploiting religious differences to build large businesses.

Beyond different religions, the degree of religiosity has been found to have an effect on consumer behavior. In a study amongst Muslims, Buddhists, Hindus, and Christians in Kuala Lumpur, Malaysia,[13] people with higher

---

12 Parameswaran, A. *For God's Sake: An Adman on the Business of Religion.* Penguin, 2014.

13 Mokhlis, S. (2009) "Relevancy and Measurement of Religiosity in Consumer Behavior Research." *International Business Research* 2(3): 75–84.

levels of religiosity were found to be more price and quality conscious and less likely to make an impulsive purchase.

Life Experience

As we move up the y-axis from culture we see how individual experiences may impact the choices we make. In *The Rational Animal*, Griskevicius and Kenrick discuss how the experience we have growing up affects our choices through our lives. To answer the question as to why so many people from underprivileged backgrounds who make substantial amounts of money often end up bankrupt (sometimes multiple times), Griskevicius and others conducted research[14] that suggests that thinking from evolutionary biology known as *Life History Theory* may point to an explanation.

Life History Theory suggests animals use one of two reproductive strategies—*Fast,* which means having as many offspring as possible as early as possible; *Slow,* which means focusing on a higher quality upbringing for fewer offspring. This varies by species (some species of frogs lay 20,000 eggs at a time, and invest very little in them; humans take the opposite approach), but we also see differences within species. At times in history and places in the world today where life expectancy is, or has been, shorter and the environment more uncertain and dangerous, humans have had more offspring—the fast strategy. As the environment feels more certain, people adopt a slower strategy, which includes having children later. Two or three generations ago, the number of children an Irish woman bore in her lifetime was often near double digits. World Bank data for Ireland in 2012 puts that figure now at an average of 2.0. A quick glance through this data for the rest of the world[15] shows a statistically significant and directional decline in births per woman from 1990 to 2012 for virtually every country outside of Western Europe. In Kenya the number has gone down from 6.0 to 4.5, in Iran from 4.8 to 1.9, in Paraguay from 4.5 to 2.9 and in the Lao PDR from 6.2 to 3.1.

Getting back to those who start with little, make a fortune, and then lose it, the hypothesis that Griskevicius et al wanted to test was whether an unstable

---

[14] Griskevicius, V., Tybur, J.M., Delton, A.W., Robertson, T.E. (2014) "The Influence of Mortality and Socioeconomic Status on Risk and Delayed Rewards: A Life History Theory Approach." *Journal of Personality and Social Psychology* December, 100(6): 1015–1026.

[15] World Bank, World Development Indicators: Reproductive Health http://wdi.worldbank.org/table/2.17

upbringing leads people to intuitively follow "fast strategies," even if they are successful in later life.

Griskevicius et al's research looked at how people who have experienced uncertainty and resource shortages when they were growing up differ in certain aspects of their decision making later as adults. When people from lower socioeconomic status (SES) groups were primed into a stressful and uncertain condition, they tended to make decisions that would result in getting a smaller reward immediately rather than a larger reward in the future. Participants from higher SES groups, or participants from lower groups who were not primed for stress and uncertainty were less impulsive and more future-oriented in their choices.

Our experiences, especially those early in life, do shape our choices. Our experiences with brands when we are young stick with us. Most people's preference for Coke or Pepsi wasn't something they developed in their 20s or 30s. Specialty grocery stores in San Francisco do a nice line in selling foreign candy bars[16] at premium prices (ToffeeCrisp, Aero, Double Decker, and Twirl, to name just a few) that transplants like me grew up on, and many decades later happily pay that premium when we feel an urge for sweet nostalgia.

Now, still in the top half of the framework (the part that is labeled "Individual") we drift back from the right-hand side. Here at the intersection of nature and nurture are some interesting areas that can lead to different behavior. We covered gender to some extent in the previous chapter, so I won't dwell on it now.

The effects of birth order are a common topic of conversation among parents as they notice differences between their oldest, their youngest, and even the children in between. Science supports their observations, and it seems that these differences endure beyond performance in the seventh grade classroom and pecking order in the tussle of the playground.

Frank Sulloway, Visiting Scholar in the Institute of Personality and Social Research at the University of California, Berkeley, and author of "Born to Rebel" would agree:

---

[16] Not what we call them. We use the rather quaint word *confectionery*, or call them *sweets*. Reading books like *The Hardy Boys* or *Nancy Drew*, I was always puzzled and intrigued by the mysterious substance *candy*.

Birth order is the single most obvious factor that makes the shared family environment different for each sibling. Birth order sums up several variables, not just one. It is a surrogate for differences in age, size, power, and privilege among siblings.

A paper by David Rink[17] suggests that this could spill over to purchase decisions made in later life. Rink reviews previous research (including Sulloway's) and hypothesizes that being firstborn may lead to different behaviors during the decision-making, buying, and post-purchase processes. From his analysis and interpretation he concludes that in terms of seeking information, firstborns may tend toward more adult-oriented or authoritative sources and look at more sources, while later-borns may tend to favor peer-oriented sources, and look at fewer overall. Post-purchase Rink suggests that firstborns may require more confirmation that the purchase is the correct decision than later-borns. Rink also posits that later-borns will be more likely to be early adopters than firstborns. In *The Consuming Instinct*, Gad Saad points to further work by Sulloway that suggests that younger siblings are more prone to base stealing in baseball.[18]

Age is also a factor in how we choose. There is some truth that we become "set in our ways," or certainly more defined by our experience, as we get older. Two aspects of general intelligence, *fluid intelligence* (solving problems in novel situations, and independent of acquired knowledge) and *crystalized intelligence* (the ability to use skills and knowledge that we have acquired) play a part in this. With age, fluid declines and crystalized intelligence increases. The optimal intersection of both is estimated to be when we are in our late 40s and early 50s.

However, every passing year doesn't affect our behavior and decisions in the same way. Some milestones seem to affect us in different ways. An interesting and ingenious analysis of data[19] from a number of sources by Adam

---

[17] Rink, D.R. (2010) "The impact of birth order upon consumers' decision-making, buying, and post-purchase processes: a conceptualization." *Innovative Marketing* 6(4): 71–79.

[18] Sulloway, F.J., Zweigenhaft, R.L. (2010) "Birth Order and Risk Taking in Athletics: A Meta-Analysis and Study of Major League Baseball," *Personality and Social Psychology Review* 14(4): 402–416.

[19] Alter, A.L., Hershfield, H.E. (2014) "People search for meaning when they approach a new decade in chronological age." *PNAS,* October, 111(48): 17066–17070.

Alter and Hal Hershfield looked at what happens when people's ages end in nine, whether that is 29, 39, 49, or 59.

Their analysis suggested that, unfortunately, when people reach this milestone they are

- a little more likely to commit suicide (at 15.05 per 100,000 of population in the U.S., versus 14.71 in a control of 25–64-year-olds)

- more likely to run a marathon for the first time (among 25–64-year-old first-time marathon runners, "9-enders" were over-represented by 48%)

- likely to run a marathon more quickly (people aged 29 and 39 had a mean completion time of 3h:15m:18s, versus a time of 3h:18m:32s for people two years before or after those ages)

- (for males between 25 and 64 with a 9 ending) nearly 18% more likely to be registered on a website for people seeking extra-marital affairs than the total of registered users in the same age bracket

The implication is that "9-enders" might be more interested in acquiring products that might symbolize defiance of the passing years or be more open to experiences that may give them a sense of meaning as they enter the new decade.

So if you are marketing sports cars, adventure travel, or anything else (a certain kind of website perhaps?) that might relate to what Alter and Hershfield call "a search for, or crisis of meaning," you might want to eschew the traditional age target of looking at a spread (25–44 year olds) and focus instead on 29-, 39-, and 49-year-olds.

Our choices are an extension of us. And all of us are a blend of how our genes makes us similar or different, and how our environment and experiences lead us to behave like others, and yet differently from others. Knowing that our choices are part individual, part universal, part innate, and part absorbed can help us not just understand people's choices, but also be a little more understanding of them.

The takeaways from this chapter are

- Many things affect our choices, from deep-seated and universal human instincts to our individual physical and cognitive differences, to our upbringing and personal experience.

- Existing Segmentation studies tend to look at self-reported behavior. Including questions in areas like birth-order and life history can help provide insight into areas of differences that have a non-conscious effect on choices

- Differences in native language may lead to different behaviors and choices. For global marketers, language provides an insight into cultural differences that drive behavior.

- Culture can lead to a huge amount of behavioral differences from group to group, but one large macro division, between cultures where an interdependent mindset dominates versus one where an independent one dominates, is something global advertisers might want to pay attention to.

- Middle-classes in developing countries may increasingly adopt "slow" strategies as increases in wealth and certainty become seen as a norm rather than a windfall.

- Don't just think of your potential users in broad age bands. Being more specific is sometimes helpful. Behavioral research and neuroscience reveal differences that may be predictive of choice that marketers have traditionally not focused on: birth order, dominant handedness, and being of an age ending in "9."

What other people said after reading this chapter:

- "I find I'm either in 'same' mode (thinking how an audience is similar), or in 'different' mode (hyper focusing on differences between groups). I'm going to try to hang on to this duality of 'same and different' when I'm thinking about my target groups."

- "I'm going to be 49 next year—I'm going to be very aware of what might be driving some of my choices now!"

14

The Power of Affirmation

Marketing shouldn't just be about getting people to make a decision to buy your product—it should also be about helping them feel good about their choice

It's not about your brand, but their decision to choose it.

I'm never sure whether the preceding statement is blindingly obvious or a profound insight.[1] Assuming it is the latter, it could make you think of marketing not as brand-centric, or even consumer-centric, but *decision-centric*.

This insight (I'm going with it being one) was revealed to us through the New Realities a global survey that we conduct with our holding company, the Interpublic Group.[2] Specifically, we studied the answer to a question that marketers don't often ask consumers: Do you pay attention to or seek out information about a brand *after* a purchase? The answer was a resounding "yes" in all countries where we conducted surveys. In the U.S. 82% of respondents seek information in hindsight, whereas in India and Russia the figure increases to 90%. Brazil tops the pile at 92%.

We also know that consumers actively seek out information about purchases they have already made from another source. The Georgetown Institute for Consumer Research[3] found that 78% of consumers sought out

---

[1] A wry definition of an *insight*: something that is blindingly obvious to the man (or woman) in the street but a revelation to both agency and client.

[2] Interpublic Group, FCB Institute of Decision Making proprietary research, 2011/12.

[3] "A New Model of Consumer Engagement," Georgetown Institute for Consumer Research and the FCB Institute of Decision Making; Matthew Willcox, Christopher Hydock, Kurt Carlson, Ishani Banerji; GICR Research Brief, October 2014. https://msb.georgetown.edu/sites/default/files/Issue%2038-%20GICR-Research%20Brief-Wilcox-ANewModelofEngagement.pdf.

information about their brand or product after making a purchase (including information from product packaging and product manuals). Further, 47% of consumers sought out information from sources other than the product packaging or manual, such as ads, online information from third parties, or online information from the original brand.

Of those searching for more information, 67% agreed with the statement that they were looking to reaffirm their purchase decision. Additionally, 88% agreed with the statement that they wanted to learn more about the product, and 65% wanted to learn more about the brand.

Rationally, this makes little sense: Why invest further attention in a decision that you have already made?

Typically, as marketers we tend to put this tendency down to conscious affirmation of the purchase decision. However, findings from neuroeconomics and behavioral psychology suggest that this behavior could be the result of some powerful instinctual mechanisms.

Decision science research shows how our brains are selectively tuned into information that reinforces decisions we've already made. Essentially, anything that makes us feel good about a choice, whether that choice is the new car we just bought or the toothpaste we have used every day for the last 30 years, doesn't just make us feel good about our decisions but makes us feel good about ourselves.

After we make a decision, a phenomenon called the *confirmation bias* occurs. The confirmation bias is our tendency to selectively seek information that supports our decisions. We discount all but the most overwhelming suggestions that we have made the wrong choice, and, importantly, we inflate evidence and memories that support our choice.

Neuroscience work suggests that the confirmation bias is mediated, at least in part, by the neurotransmitter dopamine.[4] Dopamine is memorably known as "the brain's pleasure chemical," but dopamine's role in the brain exceeds just tracking pleasure. Dopamine release communicates information about expected rewards—what we got compared to what we thought we would get. (Dopamine's role in tracking rewards is important because reward accumulation drives decision making. Remember in Chapter 5,

---

4   Doll, B.B., Hutchison, K.E., Frank, M.J. (2011) "Dopaminergic genes predict individual differences in susceptibility to confirmation bias." *Journal of Neuroscience* 31(16): 6188-6198.

"Getting Familiar," I wrote that neuroscientists and psychologists would classify a "good decision" as one that maximized rewards.)

The flipside of the confirmation bias is that we also tend to hold on to preconceived notions, and sometimes it can be a roadblock. Dopamine helps our prefrontal cortex signal the rest of our brain to perseverate on things we already know—even if that information is obviously incorrect.

Not only do we seek validation, but we also want to preserve the feeling that we have made the right decision. (The sense that we have made the wrong decision is an inordinately big downer.) Making the "right" decision feels good...so when we feel we have done so, we don't want to spoil the party in our heads. Confirmation is rewarding. No wonder we try to get as much of that feeling as we can by seeking out affirmation of our decisions.

The confirmation bias is at play even when we're seeking advice. This may seem a little odd, because the rational utility of advice is to give us a perspective other than our own. But often it seems that another perspective isn't what we actually want from those advising us.

In a recent study[5] researchers looked at how people rated a financial advisor on the quality of their advice across a number of scenarios. The researchers reported that

> When consumers had a positive opinion towards life insurance, they ascribed higher epistemic authority (EA) to the advisor who recommended purchasing it. Epistemic authority is defined as the extent to which individuals are inclined to treat a source of information as an incontrovertible evidence for their judgment and decision-making.
>
> However, when the clients' opinion was negative, the results revealed a reversed pattern: Recommendation "against" led to assigning a higher EA than recommendation "pro."

Essentially, when a financial advisor's recommendation was in line with the previously held views of the client, the client rated them more highly.

Reinforcing a good decision and the confirmation bias are important because they suggest that, at its best, marketing isn't just about influencing

---

[5] "Confirmation bias in the consumer perception of financial expertise," Tomasz Zaleskiewicz and Agata Gasiorowska, University of Social Sciences and Humanities, Wroclaw; Yoram Bar-Tal, Tel-Aviv University; Katarzyna Stasiuk and Renata Maksymiuk, Maria Curie Sklodowska University.

decisions, or just about making people feel good about your brand. Instead, marketing is about making choosers feel good about *their* decision to choose *your* brand.

There is wonderful simplicity and deep consumer-centricity (or chooser-centricity) in this notion…it is about their decision, rather than your brand.

And taking this a step further, it is not brands that have the greatest potential to make people feel good: it's people's decision to choose them.

Just as we all know that feeling in the pit of our stomachs when we feel we have made a bad decision—be it a sandwich in a meeting room lunch that disappointed, or not taking the damage waiver insurance on a rental car and then scratching it as you return it to the lot—we also know that near-euphoric feeling when we get confirmation that we have made a good one. This happy feeling in turn creates feelings of greater confidence in the choice we have made, which is not just emotionally valuable to consumers, but financially valuable to brands.

How is this good news for marketers?

Research specifically into how people feel about their choice process (rather than the product they chose) shows that when people feel confident about the way they have chosen, they show greater persistence with that decision, meaning they are more likely to repeat their purchase of that product.[6]

Stanford's Baba Shiv suggests that when people feel confident in their choices, they get more utility out of the product, and they also feel good about the brand. But this confidence in choice is not just a powerful form of brand equity. The real payoff may be how decision confidence translates choosers into influencers. Shiv believes that people who are truly confident about their choices are more contagious as recommenders and advocates.

There are some important things for marketers to take from Shiv's perspective. One is that an individual's satisfaction with a product or brand doesn't just come from its performance, but also from how good purchasers feel about their decision. In most cases if it *feels* like the right decision, our emotions and experiences tell us it is. People might run faster in their new running shoes when their choice has been affirmed as a good one or enjoy wine more if they feel they made a smart decision in selecting it.

---

[6] Muthukrishnan, M.V., Wathieu, L. (2007) "Superfluous Choices and the Persistence of Preference." *Journal of Consumer Research* 33: 454–460.

Another is that when a decision feels good, it's contagious. We often feel compelled to let people know about our great choices. It certainly boosts self-esteem. Perhaps contagiously spreading a good decision with others has evolutionary roots—sharing a good decision might have benefitted both the individual (in terms of social standing) and their community (in terms of others in the community benefitting from that decision by making a similar choice). Pinterest and Amazon tap into this desire to share our choices, by offering you the option to share what you just bought online.

Traditionally, marketing has focused directly on influencing an initial decision. But in a world where the opinions of "others" is the greatest influence, investing a little more effort in helping people who have already bought your brand feel good about their choice could bolster their instinct for spreading that feeling.

An interesting finding from research by scientists at University College London is that the more we think about a good choice, the better that choice becomes. In an experiment in which participants imagined taking a holiday while their brain activity was monitored, participants were shown the names of 80 locations around the world and asked to imagine spending next year's vacation in each of those destinations. They then rated (using a keypad with a scale of 1-5) how happy they would be to vacation at each of the 80 locations. In a second brain scan participants were shown two options they had rated similarly. (Let's say they had rated both Thailand and Greece at 5 on the scale.) They were asked to imagine vacationing in these two locations they had rated equally.

When asked to choose between the two options, people chose the destination that most activated the caudate nucleus, which is a brain area important for anticipating rewards and for learning. In fact, activity in the caudate predicted which destination would eventually be chosen from a selection of similarly rated alternatives.

After making their choice, participants once again rated the two destinations (remember—they had rated both of these equally in the previous round). If Thailand was chosen over Greece, it was subsequently rated higher while Greece was rated lower. And activity in the caudate measured by the brain scan tracked with the re-evaluation: Activity increased for Thailand and decreased for Greece.

University College London professor Tali Sharot, the expert on the optimism bias whose work we mentioned in Chapter 7, "Now, and the Future—Different Places with Different Rules," led the study. Sharot said

Re-evaluating our options post-choice may serve an adaptive purpose by increasing an individual's commitment to the action taken. In the absence of a rapid update of value that concurs with choice, we are likely to second-guess our decisions and actions.

Affirming our decisions helps us derive heightened pleasure from choices that might actually be neutral, which in terms of net human happiness must be a good thing. Without affirmation, our lives might well be filled with second-guessing. Have we done the right thing? Should we change our mind? We would find ourselves stuck, overcome by indecision and unable to move forward—and from an evolutionary perspective, that would be a very, very bad thing.

The takeaways from this chapter are

- It's not about *your* brand, but *the chooser's* decision to choose it. Our choices can make us feel very good, or very bad. When someone feels good about a choosing your brand, it is not so much *your brand* that triggers the feeling as it is *their choice*.

- *Confirmation bias* and *choice affirmative bias* make us feel good about choices we have made. Our brain doesn't want us dithering over choices—it wants us to either stick or switch and will do what it can to make us feel good about whichever we choose.

- Don't think of marketing as being just about influencing decisions. How can you make people feel good about their choices? When they do, they are more likely to get more out of the product, to buy it again, and tell other people about it. Remember, though, they aren't really telling others about your brand, they are really telling them about their great choice.

What other people felt when they read this chapter:

- "I run an e-commerce site. I am going to test sending links to articles that praise particular products AFTER people own them."

- "...this chapter emphasizes that we're in a relationship with our customers. Why would anyone stay friends with someone or continue to be someone's partner if that other person didn't make them feel good about themselves and their decision?"

PART III
Looking Forward

15

Think Differently about Market Research

What people think or say they will do are poor predictors of actual behavior.

W hen Steve Jobs was asked if Apple had used consumer research to help design and launch the iPad, he replied, "No." And when asked why not, Jobs said, "It's not the consumer's job to know what they want."

While many of us might not want, or might not be well advised, to trust our guts to the extent that Jobs did when he oversaw the creation of the iPad and iPhone, we could learn from his skepticism toward people knowing what they really want. Actually, a better answer for Jobs to have given would have been, "Consumers aren't very good at telling you what they really want."

Nonetheless, a lot of marketing research is based on asking people what they think about products, brands, or ideas, whether through questioning them in focus groups or having them answer direct questions in quantitative research.

At the 2012 ESOMAR (European Society for Opinion and Market Research) Congress, Tom Ewing, chief culture officer of market research firm Brainjuicer, and Bob Pankauskas, Director of Consumer Insights at Allstate Insurance, presented a paper, "Research in a world without questions," that addressed this. The paper is well worth a read[1] and I will come back to some of its conclusions later in the chapter.

---

[1] "Research in a world without questions," by Tom Ewing and Bob Pankauskas is available at Brainjuicer's website: http://media.brainjuicer.com/media/files/ESOMAR_Congress_2012_Research_in_a_World_Without_Questions_1.pdf.

Although I wouldn't go as far as Gregory House, M.D., the character for whom the very popular TV show *House* is named, when he says, "I don't ask why patients lie, I just assume they all do," we marketers really shouldn't take everything people tell us in research at face value. There is increasing opportunity to use methods that don't force our potential choosers to unnaturally deliberate questions regarding decisions that they will make intuitively.

There are many reasons why people aren't good at telling you what they want, or what influences them, especially in traditional research situations. I discuss a few of these reasons next.

The first is that traditional qualitative and quantitative research can make people pay attention differently than they do in the real world.

Robert Heath, professor at the University of Bath Management School and author of *The Hidden Power of Advertising*, has written a lot about the theory that we tend to be in one of two modes when we are processing information. One mode is *high involvement processing*, which is when we are actively paying attention to something, and the other mode is *low involvement processing*, which is when our attention is running in the background. (Low involvement processing and high involvement processing can be seen as alternative descriptions of what Kahneman refers to as System 1 and System 2, respectively.) According to Heath, these two modes work in quite different ways from each other. High involvement processing enables us to remember logical detail and recall limited amounts of it very accurately but often only for a short period of time. Memories recalled during high involvement processing are triggered voluntarily. Low involvement processing seems to seed memories that can be subsequently triggered involuntarily by external episodes with which the memory has some association. These types of memories are often more emotional, last longer, and feel more powerful. They are also formed without deliberative attention. But when we are primed to be in high involvement processing mode, we may miss noticing these incidental, but potentially important, events or details.

The very famous "Invisible Gorilla" experiment,[2] conducted by Chris Chabris and Dan Simon while they were at Harvard University (later, they published a book with the same name), demonstrates this effect beautifully. Without spoiling the book or experiment (you can find the test and take it

---

[2] http://www.theinvisiblegorilla.com. Like Brian Wansink and his bottomless soup bowl in 2007, Chabris and co-author Dan Simons were recipients for an Ig Nobel prize for psychology in 2004.

yourself at the URL in the footnote at the bottom of this page, and if you haven't taken it you may want to now, before reading any further), Chabris and Simon's research shows that if people are primed to pay attention to a piece of film and then given a memory task, they will recall detail from the memory task but likely will miss non-primed events that may be more significant in a broader context and more emotionally loaded (like failing to notice a large primate in the midst of a group of people). We seem to pick up emotions better when we aren't actively paying attention.

Robert Heath points out two important aspects of how humans pay attention that are relevant to advertising, and in particular to how we research it. Heath's first point is that much consumer research puts respondents in a high involvement processing mode and gives them high involvement processing tasks like detail recall, or having to abstract meaning from an advertisement. However, the nature of much of the media exposure that our brands get is likely to be consumed via low involvement processing. The second point Heath emphasizes is that for many brands, entering memory through low involvement processing may be more helpful for marketers. Low involvement processing allows the brand to forge emotional connections, and external associations can trigger these memories at a later date. Research that—implicitly or explicitly—asks respondents to pay attention to advertisements might be putting too much emphasis on what they perceive through high involvement processing and might fail to get a measure on what information is being retained by low involvement processing. Unfortunately, the former is likely to contribute less to the advertisements effectiveness than the latter.

Another pitfall in asking people direct questions in research is that we are not as rational as we want to think we are. When asked to explain a decision or a preference, we want to feel (and want others to feel) that we were consciously aware of each of the steps of that choice. No one wants to say, "I don't know why I like that" or "I just chose it without thinking about it." The store we place on rational intelligence in education and culture makes this seem an admission of stupidity.

But as a reminder (though I'm sure none is needed), most aspects of most of our choices are not deliberative. Gerald Zaltman, whose work in the field of metaphors we discussed in Chapter 13, "Same and Different; Nature and Nurture," believes that 95% of decision making is non-conscious. Gary Klein, whose research pioneered the field of naturalistic decision making and whose findings led to significant changes in military training, estimates that 90% of the critical decisions we make are based on intuition. In *Thinking, Fast and Slow* Daniel Kahneman tells us, "Although System

2 (deliberative thinking) believes itself to be where the action is, the automatic System 1 is the hero of this book."

This is obviously important for marketing, but it is really, really important for how we should think about research. I've already mentioned Leigh Caldwell and Elina Halonen and their well-named market research company, *The Irrational Agency*. They specialize in understanding how market research can take into account our non-conscious processes. They presented an excellent paper on this and more at the ESOMAR 2014 Congress[3] that captures this point well:

> To understand decisions in full, we must understand all the factors that contribute to them. Some of these are conscious and can be articulated clearly by respondents; but many are not. Indeed, some estimates say that 90% or more of the work of a decision is made beneath the conscious level. We cannot, therefore, gain a clear picture of why consumers do things, or how to change their behavior, without understanding the non-conscious as well as the conscious aspects.

Getting people to reveal the non-conscious aspects is the tricky bit. People see their choices, and want others to see them as a result of their rational thinking. The science fiction writer Robert Heinlein famously said, "Man is not a rational animal, but a rationalizing animal." But, as we've discussed earlier in this chapter, we just don't see ourselves that way.

Dan Ariely dissects the mismatch of how rational we think we are and how rational we actually are in his excellent books *Predictably Irrational* and *The Upside of Irrationality*. Ariely writes that we hate to see ourselves as irrational, which explains why research participants often choose a more rational advertising approach or one that is easy to rationalize when asked to make a choice. The reasons we attribute to our decisions are very often not really the reasons at all. Social and political psychologist Robert Abelsen said we are "very well trained and very good at finding reasons for what we do, but not very good at doing what we find reasons for."

We routinely post-rationalize emotional or instinctual decision-making processes, making them appear, on reflection, rational; these intuitive processes were not understood by experts 50 years ago and are only just

---

[3] Caldwell, L., Halonen, E. "Escaping the Chains: How Our Unconscious Limits and Frees Us...And How to Measure It in Market Research," upcoming, Research World 2015.

starting to filter their way into how marketing research is designed and executed (and at this stage only by the more progressive and enlightened research and marketing companies). Even behavioral economists and other academic experts can find it hard to explain their own behavior in the heat of the moment. Yet billions of dollars are spent in market research asking respondents to do exactly that.

Research very often asks people to explain why they prefer one option to another. This seemingly necessary and innocuous line of questioning is a great example of how research that delves into people's "reasons" for doing things can lead a marketer down the wrong path. When people have to explain a choice (which much research either explicitly asks them to do or implicitly makes them feel they have to), it affects the choice they make.

In a famous study by Timothy Wilson and Douglas Lisle from the University of Virginia,[4] two groups of participants were asked to evaluate a poster from a selection of five. Poster images varied from *Les Irises Saint Remy* by Dutch post-impressionist Vincent van Gogh to more literal images, such as a photograph of a cat looking at a fence with a caption "One Step at a Time." Participants in both groups were given a questionnaire that asked them to rate each poster on a nine point scale, but one group was given additional questions asking them to give the reasons why they liked or disliked each poster. All participants were told that they could return their poster if they didn't like it, but before selecting a poster, one group was told that they would be asked to explain why they liked the poster they chose. There was a notable difference in the types of posters chosen by each group. The group that didn't have to give the reasons behind their choice were more likely to select the more artistic options, like the Van Gogh print, with 95% of them choosing one of the art posters. Only 64% of the group that did have to give their reasons selected the art posters.

The requirement to explain our choice leads us to make choices that we can explain. The image of the cat looking at the fence can be explained as, "I used to have a cat like that," whereas a preference for a van Gogh print is more difficult to put into words.

Perhaps the most interesting finding was revealed when the respondents were contacted two to three weeks later to see whether they were happy with their posters. *The respondents who had to explain the reasons behind*

---

[4] Wilson, T., Lisle, D., Schooler, J., Hodges, S.D., Klaaren, K.J., LaFleur, S.J. (1993) "Introspecting about Reasons can Reduce Post-Choice Satisfaction." *Personality and Social Psychology Bulletin* 19: 331-339.

their poster choice were significantly less satisfied with their choice. Wilson and Lisle summarized their findings:

> When people think about reasons, they appear to focus on attributes of the stimulus that are easy to verbalize and seem like plausible reasons but may not be important causes of their initial evaluations. When these attributes imply a new evaluation of the stimulus, people change their attitudes and base their choices on these new attitudes. Over time, however, people's initial evaluation of the stimulus seems to return, and they come to regret choices based on the new attitudes.

It's not just that people can't tell you why they might make a certain choice. If they know that you are going to ask them *why* (like we do so often in focus groups), they may make a different choice—and, crucially, that choice may be one that they end up being less happy with!

What People Say They Like Can Change... Unintentionally

What people say in a research setting is dictated by their mental and physical state at the time; it is not always ecologically valid. (Remember "ecologically valid" is the phrase scientists use to indicate that the research environment might not be a good proxy for real life.)

The majority of market research doesn't happen near the actual time of choice. Participants are often asked what they will purchase when they next go shopping or how a healthy meal option in a fast food restaurant might appeal to them next time they visit.

However, different time horizons change how we perceive things and the nature of our decisions (remember *construal level theory* in Chapter 7, "Now, and the Future—Different Places with Different Rules"?), adding a dimension of unreality to much research. Typically, we are asking people what they will do in the future, and as we've seen, how we think we will behave in the future is often very different from how we do behave.

In a study in the Netherlands,[5] researchers asked participants to select one of four snacks for a meeting they would be attending in one week's

---

[5] Weijzen, P.L., de Graaf, C., Dijksterhuis, G.B. (2008) "Discrepancy between Snack Choice Intentions and Behavior." *Journal of Nutrition Education and Behavior* 40(5):311–316.

time—an apple, a banana, a candy bar, and a molasses waffle; 49% of the participants indicated they would choose the apple or banana. However, when presented with the actual snacks a week later, 27% of those who had said they would pick a healthy one switched to the candy bar or waffle.

Neuroscience shows that, perhaps not surprisingly, when people are hungry, they respond differently to images of food than when they are sated.[6] Research shows (and personal experience confirms) that our stress levels affect how we respond to information. A bland research room with office furniture may be more stressful than your couch at home but less stressful than trying to navigate the aisles of a supermarket with two screaming kids in tow.

On top of this, people may state one preference, and a short time later indicate exactly the opposite.

In an interview with Knowledge@Wharton, Sheena Iyengar, author of *The Art of Choosing*, describes an experiment where perception is affected by awareness. Participants were shown pictures of two attractive women—one blonde and one brunette:

> ...(participants) were shown a whole set of different pairs of female pictures, and asked which ones they thought were prettier. They were then shown the pictures they chose again and asked why they picked them. In some cases though, unbeknownst to the respondent, the images were switched—if they had chosen the brunette they were sometimes shown the blonde. What did they do—87% of the time they didn't even notice. They simply said, "Oh, I prefer blondes"...even though they had actually chosen the brunette!

At the beginning of this chapter, I referenced "Research in a world without questions," a paper by Tom Ewing and Bob Pankauskas. Their conclusion of that paper seems to be a good way to end this section and introduce the remainder of this chapter.

> Research without questions is not a novelty or another option— it's essential if we're to truly understand consumer decisions. It's also more exciting, innovative, faster in many cases and more actionable than direct research has been. A world entirely without questions is not on the horizon—but the reign of the question in

---

6 LaBar, K.S., Gitelman, D.R., Parrish, T.B., Kim, Y.-H., Nobre, A.C., Mesulam, M.M. (2001) "Hunger selectively modulates corticolimbic activation to food stimuli in humans." *Behavioral Neuroscience* 115: 493–500.

research has ended, and we should celebrate that. Our industry is finally aligning itself around what consumers do, not what they say.

What Might Lead Us to Better Marketing Research, Then?

It seems that asking people to reveal how they make decisions and what may influence them isn't always going to help us make the best decisions as to how to market to them. Fortunately, the science that has revealed this to us also led to the development and improvement of tools and thinking that can make us less dependent on asking people questions that require deliberation to answer. I review some of these in the next sections.

Better Understanding of the Cognitive Biases and Heuristics that Drive the Pre-Conscious Aspects of Decision Making

I really believe that anybody involved in market research should be a keen student of human nature. These days that means working to maintain an understanding of behavioral science. This can help with more enlightened research and questionnaire design, and can even help marketers and researchers to get a lot more out of traditional research, by providing a framework for further interpretation. An understanding of heuristics and cognitive biases can enhance your perspective on quantitative research, as we showed by adding a behavioral layer onto the New Realities research we discussed in Chapters 9 and 14. It can also help provide a filter for qualitative research. The best qualitative researchers do this intuitively. Arnie Jacobson, one of the founding partners of the Qualitative Research Center (QRC) talks about how he takes in people's body language and facial expressions as much as the literal meaning of what they say.

Implicit Association Measures

Implicit association covers a range of techniques where response time is used to study how readily a respondent connects two words, terms, objects, or images. A straightforward implicit association test uses the speed with which people respond to make assumptions about the strength with which people agree with or feel affinity toward something. A faster response means the stimulus is accessing feelings that are more intuitive, and it is

---

believed, are more positive. This has huge potential for logo and packaging research—many of you might have had the experience of having people agonize over the meaning of a logo in a focus group. Implicit association tests have attracted a lot of attention and some criticism, which has been magnified because of their association with societally important areas.[7] Two of the proponents of the technique[8] run a free-to-use online test called Project Implicit, where anyone can take a number of IATs that measure implicit associations that are believed to indicate non-conscious biases in areas like race, sexuality, gender, and disability. The major criticism of IATs is that the analysis of the associations has not been shown to have a causal connection to real-world behaviors. However, for a number of marketing applications (for example, assessing logos) this may not be such an important issue, as IATs do seem to add some real value in measuring non-conscious associations, so although making a direct link between a logo or advertisement and desired behavior may not be possible, IATs do provide a useful way of measuring whether the non-conscious associations revealed fit with the brand strategy.

I think it is an interesting area for marketers to experiment with, not least because it is relatively inexpensive and, because it can be deployed online, fieldwork can be conducted and results analyzed reasonably quickly.

Facial Expression Recognition

A number of copy testing firms have started using a technique where, instead of asking people to respond to how a commercial makes them feel using words, they have them point to a range of emoticons. To me this seems an interesting approach, because it avoids people mediating their feelings through verbalization. There is also evidence that these emoticons work across languages and cultures.

Another technique that holds great promise is automatic facial emotional expression recognition.[9] Of all the techniques that seek to evaluate an

---

[7] Azar, B. "IAT: Fad or fabulous? Psychologists debate whether the Implicit Association Test needs more solid psychometric footing before it enters the public sphere," *Monitor on Psychology* (APA) July/August 2008.

[8] Anthony Greenwald of the University of Washington and Mahzarin Banaji of Harvard University.

[9] Kodra, E., Senechal, T., McDuff, D., el Kaliouby, R. "From Dials to Facial Coding: Automated Detection of Spontaneous Facial Expressions for Media Research."

emotional response, I find this one particularly intriguing. As the technology becomes portable and pervasive, the opportunity exists for getting people to opt in at "ecologically valid" times—for example, when they are looking at a display in a retail environment, or sitting in front of their screen at home. A camera captures their facial expressions, and these expressions are then "recognized" as emotional reactions by computer analysis.

One very robust system for measuring and analyzing facial expressions in real time is the Computer Expression Recognition Toolbox (CERT).[10] This system has been brought to market by a company called Emotient, which was born out of the Machine Perception Lab at University of California, San Diego. Emotient works with large organizations such as Proctor and Gamble and the U.S. Air Force.

Eye Tracking and Pupillometry

Eye tracking measures where a person is looking, and *pupillometry* tracks the size of the pupil. Both kinds of data can be collected using the same equipment but eye tracking is an indicator of where attention is directed whereas pupil size suggests arousal levels.[11]

Using eye-tracking data from people viewing a display of snack foods (chips), neuroscientists from the California Institute of Technology modeled how objective measures and subjective measures influenced attention.[12] The objective measure was how visually salient a product was, and the subjective measure was how much the subject valued each product in the test display. Models that included both visual salience and subjective value fit the eye-tracking data better than models just including visual properties or subjective value alone. Such models can accurately predict choice based on a given display and also guide product display design.

---

[10] Littlewort, G., Whitehill, J., Wu, T., Fasel, I., Frank, M., Movellan, J., Bartlett, M. "The computer expression recognition toolbox (CERT)," *2011 IEEE International Conference on Automatic Face & Gesture Recognition and Workshops (FG 2011)*, 298(305): 21-25. (March 2011).

[11] Gilzenrat M.S., Nieuwenhuis, S., Jepma, M., Cohen, J.D. (2010) "Pupil diameter tracks changes in control state predicted by the adaptive gain theory of locus coeruleus function." *Cogn Affect Behav Neurosci* 10: 252–269.

[12] Towal, R.B., Mormann, M., Koch, C. (2013) "Simultaneous modeling of visual saliency and value computation improves predictions of economic choice." *Proc Natl Acad Sci* 110: E3858-E3867.

Neuroimaging and Analysis

Neuroscience started as a medical discipline but the use of neuroimaging has "emerged from medical analysis identifying abnormalities and dysfunctions to delving into lie detection and decision making."[13]

Its use in market research is sometimes known as *neuromarketing*, though that is a term I don't like at all—it conjures up images of planting messages in people's minds or activating their (non-existent) "buy buttons" via neuroprobes. A number of companies that have used this term in the past prefer to now use *neuromarketing research* or *consumer neuroscience*.

The use of neuroimaging in understanding decision making is known as *neuroeconomics*. Neuroeconomics applies neuroscience methods to economic problems and choice tasks; for example, using biometric measures, like neuroimaging, to understand cognitive load and arousal to stimuli or choices. Neuroeconomics is a field where many wild claims are made. We remain convinced there is value in the field, but it may be at its greatest in areas outside of neuro-copytesting, which has been the mainstay of the work in neuromarketing.

One of the helpful things about neuroscience is that it allows us to put language to one side, so there's no need to debate whether something is rational or intuitive, but simply see what happens in terms of activity in the brain—what parts are activated, what connections are made, and so on. Freud foreshadowed this possibility in his landmark essay "Beyond the Pleasure Principle":

> The deficiencies in our description (of the mind) would probably vanish if we were already in a position to replace the psychological terms with physiological or chemical ones.... We may expect [physiology and chemistry] to give the most surprising information and we cannot guess what answers it will return in a few dozen years of questions we have put to it. They may be of a kind that will blow away the whole of our artificial structure of hypothesis.

Neuroscience is having an impact on marketing, and as Freud predicted, brain imaging does show physical and chemical responses to stimulus.

While neuromarketing has already become somewhat established in the area of market research it has had success mainly as a way to evaluate messages and products.

---

[13] Ken Strutin, "Neurolaw and Criminal Justice," llrx.com. December 2008.

We see the potential more from neuroeconomics as a field because it combines a number of disciplines including neuroscience and behavioral economics. It explores fundamental questions about how people make decisions, by providing an understanding of what areas of the brain and neural processes are involved in different aspects of decision making. From the perspective of advertising and marketing strategists, it can be seen more like exploratory research that helps you find the insights to base creative ideas on, rather than another form of copy-testing, which is what neuromarketing has become synonymous with for many marketers.

There are some examples of what you could call "neuro-insights" that can be gleaned from the work of academics in this area. One of our favorites comes from research by Hal Hershfield, covered to some extent in Chapter 7 that investigated how thinking of ourselves in the future may inhibit our likelihood to save for that very same future.

Hershfield's research used functional magnetic resonance imaging (fMRI)—a technique that indicates what part of the brain is being used in a certain task by showing where the oxygenated blood is flowing. He found that the part of the brain—the rostral anterior cingulate cortex (rACC)—that is believed to be linked to concepts relating to self showed relatively little activity when thinking about ourselves in the future. In fact, the activity was more similar to levels he saw when people were thinking of another person than it was to when they were thinking about themselves in the present! Not surprising then, that we would rather spend the money now than invest it for our retirement, because as far as our brain is concerned, our future self is more like someone else—an insight any creative strategist in an advertising agency might be proud of.

Another example is some interesting research[14] by Hilke Plassmann, Baba Shiv, and colleagues. In this study, people tasted a selection of wines that they were told sold at different prices. However, unbeknownst to them, the wine was in many instances the same. When respondents were told the wine sold at $90 the researchers saw significantly increased activity in an area of the brain associated with pleasant experiences than when the respondents were told the exact same wine cost $10. At a neural level when people were told the wine was more expensive, there was evidence that they enjoyed it more. There is an interesting implication for luxury brands

---

[14] Plassmann, H., O'Doherty, J., Shiv, B., Rangel, A. (2008) "Marketing actions can modulate neural representations of experienced pleasantness." *PNAS* 105(3): 1050-1054.

here, which is that pricing information isn't just important at the time when make their choice, but it can also help create a better experience when people use and consume the brand. In the UK, some years before Plassman's research, Stella Artois, the Belgian lager brand, had a long-running slogan "Reassuringly Expensive" (they ran a similar, but less inspired line, "Perfection Has Its Price" in the U.S.). I'd say this is a good example of advertising creatives not just being unwitting psychologists, but being unwitting neuroeconomists.

The brain-imaging techniques discussed next are the most relevant to marketers.

Functional Magnetic Resonance Imaging (fMRI)

Magnetic resonance imaging (MRI) scanners measure how the body responds to the presence of a strong magnetic field and then use those differences to generate an image of inside the body. MRI is widely used clinically for the entire body, and because it is non-invasive, it is especially useful for studying the human brain. MRI scanners can be found in the basements of neuroscience, psychology, and even marketing departments of universities across the globe.

In the brain, gray matter (neuron cell bodies) and white matter (axons, or the "wires" connecting neurons to each other) respond differently to the magnetic field and therefore show up as separable regions on an MR image.

When MRI is used to study how the brain works, it is called functional MRI (fMRI). fMRI exploits how, when, and where the brain consumes oxygen to visualize what the brain is doing, which areas are active when and under which conditions. When a brain area is active, its oxygen consumption increases. For reasons that will fascinate chemistry and physics aficionados but probably not marketers, increased oxygen consumption in a brain region causes nearby water to be less magnetic. Active brain regions can therefore be identified by a decrease in MR signal. The results of fMRI experiments are colorful brain pictures even though the brain is truly a peach color and regions do not "light up" when active. The pictures are color-coded to identify brain areas that cross a statistical threshold.

As a technique for marketing, fMRI is both powerful and problematic. It is powerful because it is non-invasive and allows an unprecedented view into how the human brain works, but it is problematic because it is incredibly expensive and currently is most useful to study aggregate, not segmented, brain activity. There's also the small matter of it seeming like a medical procedure—participants have to lie perfectly still while in a noisy, claustrophobic tube.

An fMRI study from Baylor College of Medicine in Houston, Texas, sparked the creation of the field of neuroeconomics; this study was the first to lift the lid on how the human brain perceives brands.[15]

The study was a modified version of the "Pepsi Challenge." In the MRI scanner, participants viewed cues, or pictures, that told them whether they were about to drink a squirt of Coke or Pepsi. In a first experiment, a squirt of Coke followed a red circle while Pepsi followed a yellow circle. Brain regions that process rewards, such as the striatum and regions of prefrontal cortex, pay close attention to cues that predict rewards. When the cues were just colored circles, their brains treated the squirts of Coke or Pepsi the same; regions of the medial prefrontal cortex responded to the colored circles in agreement with stated drink preferences.

When the researchers changed the cues from circles to pictures of a Coke can or Pepsi can, what happened in the brain was remarkable. Brain response diverged from stated behavioral preferences. There was no brain response to the Pepsi can image at all, but there was a robust response to the Coke can image in the prefrontal cortex and the hippocampus.

"We know that the hippocampus and DLPFC together are involved in direct memory recall, so it makes sense that they'd be determining what you think of the brand," said Samuel McClure, lead author of the study, who is now a professor at Stanford University and one of the academics who has been particularly helpful to the author and the Institute of Decision Making.

Another example of the power of fMRI for marketing comes from a study that showed brain responses from a small group of people can predict the behavior of an entire population.[16] Researchers from the University of California, Los Angeles, collected fMRI data from smokers as they watched several different smoking cessation advertisements. The group of subjects were also asked which advertisements they felt would be most effective.

[15] McClure, S.M., Li, J., Tomlin, D., Cypert, K.S., Montague, L.M., Montague, P.R. (2004) "Neural correlates of behavioral preference for culturally familiar drinks." *Neuron* 44: 379–387.

[16] Falk, E.B., Berkman, E.T., Lieberman, M.D. (2012) "From neural responses to population behavior: neural focus group predicts population-level media effects." *Psychol Sci* 23: 439-445.

Researchers focused on the response in the medial prefrontal cortex, which had been shown previously to be involved in behavioral change. It was the response of medial prefrontal cortex—not what subjects thought about the commercials—that predicted which anti-smoking advertisements were the most successful across the country.

Electroencephalography (EEG)

Electroencephalography (EEG) is another non-invasive technique used to measure what the brain is doing. As its full name suggests, EEG measures the brain's electrical activity, but it is only capable of measuring activity from brain areas on the surface (adjacent to the skull) or near the surface. While fMRI brings more precision for spatial information (which brain areas are active), it is sluggish temporally compared to EEG. fMRI measures brain activity on a timescale of seconds; EEG measures brain activity on a timescale of milliseconds.

EEG is a useful technique for marketing because it is non-invasive, inexpensive, and portable. It reliably measures arousal levels, cognitive load or effort, and also directed attention. The electrical wave that occurs around 300 milliseconds following a stimulus is a hallmark of directed attention; this wave is called the "P300" (where "P" stands for positive and "300" for 300 milliseconds). Differences in arousal levels show up as differences in the frequencies of the EEG typically from electrodes placed along the brain's midline.

A unique benefit of EEG compared to fMRI for marketing research is collecting data both in real-time and in ecologically valid situations. EEG data can be collected from a person sitting on his living room couch watching the Super Bowl; this simply is not possible with other neuroimaging techniques. (fMRI data for the same situation would require the person to be lying flat on his back in the MRI scanner.) As we discussed in Chapter 5, "Getting Familiar," EEG is used to assess Super Bowl commercials each year. EEG data is combined with physiological measures, such as eye tracking, heart rate, and skin conductance, into an index that reflects how engaging at a neural level the commercial is and also how emotionally engaging it might be.[17]

---

[17] Sands Research calls its index the "neural engagement score" (NES); it has used the NES to assess many commercials. http://www.sandsresearch.com/Neuro_Engagement_Score.aspx.

Many commercials that are neurally engaging are successful from a business standpoint (like Volkswagen's "The Force"), while other commercials might receive a failing neural index but succeed from a business standpoint (like certain GoDaddy commercials showing a well-endowed model with wardrobe malfunctions).

Measured neural, or emotional, engagement does not always translate to success from a business standpoint. This mismatch between neural measures and business success does not mean that neuromarketing will not ever be able to predict business success (indeed a number of companies claim they can already, although I have not reviewed their supporting data for these claims in detail enough to support or dispute these claims). It is important to remember that application of neuroscience to marketing research is still in its infancy; this applies to neuroeconomics as well. Neuroscience itself is hundreds of years old, yet we still do not have a complete understanding of the brain.

But with labs now dedicated to neuroeconomics in many leading schools (including McClure's lab at Stanford, and Ming Hsu's lab at UC Berkeley), we will see an increase in research that will give us a deeper understanding of how people reach their decisions. Not all of this will be useful, but every year a few gems will emerge. Rather than looking at this as validation, I believe the opportunity for marketers and their agencies is to find ways to translate these into powerful insights—and thus use what we see going on in other people's brains to inspire creative ideas in our own.

The takeaways from this chapter are

- The fact that most of our choices are unconscious means we have to think differently about how we do market research. Rather than ask people to consciously think about what they might do, we need to explore methods that can give insight into the unconscious aspects of choice, and help us understand how our marketing efforts can affect this.

- People don't always know what they want, and if you ask them to describe why they like something they will default to what is easy to explain.

- People's choices are extremely context sensitive. Research too often removes context from x equation.

- Emerging techniques, such as the various forms of brain imaging, will transform research, but these are really still at the experimental stage. Developments in techniques such as implicit awareness tests, eye-tracking, and facial expression analysis provide additional opportunities to get beyond people's "reasons" for choice, and get us closer to understanding the underlying motivations.

- The best way to learn about these new techniques is to take a small percentage of your insights budget and experiment with these emerging methods. Compare what they tell you with more traditional measures or with market place performance.

- And, if nothing else, apply a behavioral sciences eye to your traditional research. Can you design questioning and lines of enquiry that truly reflect how people make choices? Simply bringing an understanding of human nature to research design and interpretation will go a long way.

Some thoughts this chapter sparked with other people:

- "...interesting that so much market research tries to access conscious decision making processes when so much of our decision making process is pre-conscious. Is most of that research a waste of money? And is there a Texas sharpshooter fallacy at play here in that we measure what people can tell us about and make 100% of our decisions on 5% of the data?"

- "This reinforces for me how ingrained we are in old research habits. This chapter is a wake-up call to challenge the conventional methods we use and to become more thoughtful in the design of research that will break through to the unexpected, fresh, and game-changing insights that are hidden in the depths of the unconscious mind."

16

Think Differently about How You Work

Marketers can employ an understanding of decision making to their decisions as marketers.

Most of what *The Business of Choice* has suggested so far is how an understanding of the non-conscious mechanisms that people use to make choices can be helpful to marketers trying to influence those choices. However, this is the point where I shift the focus of the investigation...to me and you.

The cognitive mechanisms discussed in this book are used by all of us—mostly, as we've seen, to make quick and efficient decisions that are good enough most of the time. However, sometimes our choices will be revealed to have not had the results we or our organizations desire, whether that is victory in the marketplace or on the battlefield.

Innate tendencies don't just drive people to choose a certain brand or offer, they affect human decision making on subjects that have far greater consequences. An understanding of cognitive biases has been used to look retrospectively at military and foreign policy decisions, with suggestions that these biases played a part in leading the great powers blindly into the First World War.[1] The optimism bias certainly seems to have played a role, with all the powers claiming the conflict "would be over by Christmas," presumably with themselves as victors.

Loss aversion has been suggested as a cause behind the Union Army's General George McClellan and his failure to take Richmond, Virginia, in the American Civil War. Historian Robert Pois and educational psychologist

---

[1] Jonathan Renshon, in an interview with *Harvard Magazine*, June 2007 about his book *Why Leaders Choose War: The Psychology of Prevention*.

Robert Langer wrote that McClellan was "was less concerned with winning then he was with avoiding failure."[2] There is evidence that attributes the German's decision not to invade Cyprus after they had captured Crete in the Second World War to anchoring.[3] The British used deception to convince the Germans that there were 20,000 troops garrisoned on Cyprus when in fact there were only 4,000. Despite subsequent reports and analyses showing that the British number was too high, post-war documents revealed that the Germans anchored on the higher number, believing it "almost without question."

Others have written about how cognitive biases affected decision making in the planning and execution of more recent conflicts such as the Suez Crisis of 1956 or America's war in Iraq in 2003.

If our innate biases can color decisions about actions that involve many thousands of human lives and the fate of cultures and nations—decisions that normally involve a meticulous level of planning and the threat of accountability—then we can be pretty sure the same biases affect the professional decisions of marketers.

There is a particular irony in marketers, who have the goal of trying to influence the decisions of others, themselves making flawed decisions.

Intuitions—or gut reactions—are a critically important part of all decision making, and so they absolutely do have a very important role in the decisions marketers make. Without our gut instincts, we would be significantly less decisive than we are. But when our instincts come calling, we need, as best as we can, to think about where they are coming from.

Note that awareness of a cognitive bias will not make you immune to it—even if you are Daniel Kahneman. "It's not a case of, 'Read this book and then you'll think differently.' I've *written* this book, and I don't think differently" he says, of *Thinking, Fast and Slow.*

During a short interview with Dan Ariely a couple of years ago, he made a very good point about intuitions: Our non-conscious thinking can be shockingly well informed. What we have learned through experience as a marketer may lead us to an instinctive decision and action (just as a firefighter or pilot will automatically follow training in emergency situations).

---

[2] Lieutenant Colonel Michael J. Janser, "Cognitive Biases in Military Decision Making," U.S. Army War College, 2007.

[3] Major Blair S. Williams, "Heuristics and Biases in Military Decision Making," U.S. Army, *Military Review*, September–October 2010.

Following our gut instincts will probably lead to good outcomes most of the time. But marketers, being human, are subject to the cognitive shortcuts described in Part II. For example, even if the market situation requires moving away from an established campaign, the *endowment effect* may make us feel intuitively bad about doing this, because it leads us to emotionally over-value that campaign. Loss aversion may make us, like General McClellan, too concerned about losing. The latest action by a competitor may drive us to deviate from a long-term plan, because the *recency bias* makes the competitor's action seem more significant. Or we may find ourselves as the victims of the Curse of Innovation, so well described by John Gourville, by focusing too much on the exciting gains our new product can bring consumers, rather than thinking about what we need to do to make them feel good about what they're giving up. In these four example scenarios, we should try to ignore the nagging, inner voice of our intuitions.

David Thomason is the Chief Strategy Officer of FCB Auckland and has been a key player in their development of highly effective programs that have changed behavior. Some of the behaviors targeted by Thomason's programs are reducing session (or binge) drinking in New Zealand, getting people to reevaluate their energy provider (which as we mentioned in an earlier chapter is a task that most of us would gladly put off forever, if we even got around to considering doing it in the first place), and helping men in New Zealand cope with depression.[4] Thomason wrote an excellent piece[5] that compared how marketers' susceptibility to short-term thinking is comparable to the inability to delay gratification in Walter Mischel's famous experiment involving children and marshmallows:

> It's the 1960s. Four year-old Craig is sitting alone in a small room staring at a marshmallow. The woman who placed it there has promised she'll be back in fifteen minutes. If he can't wait, he can ring a bell. Then she'll return and let him eat the marshmallow. But, she explained, if he waits the whole fifteen minutes then he

---

[4] FCB Auckland's work for the National Depression Initiative has received global attention among mental health professionals and won the gold award for international campaigns in one of the most prestigious marketing effectiveness awards. In the submission, it was noted that the program had a return on marketing investment (RoMI) of 5, but that "...More importantly, some users reported that it saved their life." http://www.ipa.co.uk/effectiveness/entry/entrant/600.

[5] Thomason, D. "Don't Eat the Marshmallow." *NZ Marketing Magazine*, March/April 2014.

can have *two* marshmallows. It's his choice; a small reward now or a bigger reward later. Craig doesn't bother to ring the bell. He gobbles up the marshmallow thirty seconds after the researcher leaves the room.

On average the children in that Stanford University experiment waited less than three minutes. The true significance only became apparent years later. The children who had waited longer demonstrated remarkable advantages. They achieved higher academic scores. They were more mature, and less likely to be aggressive and misbehave. They were also less likely to be overweight, have drug problems, or get divorced. Many experts now believe that an ability to delay gratification is the single greatest predictor of a happy and successful life.

Thomason observes that the same aspect of human nature is evident with marketers; they are driven by short-term goals that serve financial markets rather than the people who buy their products. Thomason writes that perhaps there is a lesson for marketers from the strategy employed by kids who were able to resist temptation and went on to be more successful in later life.

> (Mischel) saw the kids could wait longer if they distracted themselves by covering their eyes, hiding under the desk, or singing. It's difficult to imagine a marketer employing these techniques when faced by a disappointing quarterly result.

Essentially, the children were blocking out the pull of the short term. Thomason goes on to suggest that Unilever managed to do exactly the same thing—block out the short term, but without covering its eyes, hiding under desks, or singing:

> Paul Polman took the reins as CEO at Unilever in January 2009. Despite the recession, he declared in 2010, "It's easy to be a short-term hero, to get tremendous results very short-term and be off sailing in the Bahamas. But the goal for this company—and it's very difficult to do—is to follow a four- or five-year process."

> At the heart of Polman's strategy was a particularly bold masterstroke. He moved away from quarterly reports, stating that "since we don't operate on a 90-day cycle for advertising, marketing, or investment, why do so for reporting?" Polman proved he was serious when he stopped offering earnings guidance to the stock

market. Not everyone took this well and Unilever dropped 6% to £13 a share. Within a year (the business equivalent of 15 minutes of marshmallow time) it was back at £20.

But what about the long-term? In a November 2013 interview Polman said, "When others were cutting costs, shutting down factories, we were investing. Now we are 4–5 years further, our business is up 30 percent; our share price has more than doubled."

As childish as it sounds, "blocking out" the measures that reward and motivate short-term thinking helped drive business growth.

As we've seen, thinking about the future can be difficult.

In workshops where the goal is to get people to think about long-term objectives, I use an exercise that is designed to make it a little easier. I introduce the exercise by talking about how human nature is a poor judge of the future, and how the short term dominates our thinking, not because we as individuals have shortcomings, but simply because that is the way our brains and decision-making systems have evolved. With the right conditions, we do have the capacity to take ourselves out of the immediate and then we can be quite effective at conceiving the future. One way to do this is rather than having people think from now to the future, have them think backward. The following is an example of how I get people in workshops to do this:

> It is 2020 (or whatever it will be five years from now). Your PR department has scored a coup with *Business Week* (I change magazine title, depending on the workshop goals), who are putting together a series covering successful brands. *Business Week* chose [your brand] for the cover story!

> If 2020, five years in the future, seems a long way off, think of it like this. Five years ago was only 2010. It isn't difficult to think back to how you got from then to where you are today...

Imagine the article:

- What would the headline be?
- What would the main themes of that story be?
- How would the article describe the brand and its approach?
- How would the article summarize what the brand had achieved in business and culture in the five years leading up to 2020?

- What was the realization that sparked the change leading to the brand's success?

- What might the article say about changes in the culture and changes in how people thought within the organization?

- What milestones would the article identify?

- The article includes an inset box, with five bullet points labeled "If you want your brand to succeed like brand x you should..." What would those five points be?

- What else would you want the article to include about your brand?

This exercise is just one way you can put make your intuitions cooperate with rather than impede your planning and decision making.

Exercises like this may not be necessary for the true marketing greats, who—like Steve Jobs—seem to have a natural alignment between their personal intuitions and their brand purpose. The rest of us need to pause and examine the motivational roots of our intuitive or gut response.

Norman Maier, who was an experimental psychologist creator of the famous "two rope problem"[6] suggested one way of putting our intuitions on hold: "Do not propose solutions until the problem has been discussed as thoroughly as possible without suggesting any."

Or as the German poet Rainer Maria Rilke rather less tersely advised a protégé,

> Do not now seek the answers, which cannot be given you because you would not be able to live them. And the point is, to live everything. Live the questions now. Perhaps you will then gradually, without noticing it, live along some distant day into the answer.

I'm the worst offender in the respect of leaping to answers, of jumping to conclusions. I have to physically bite my tongue to stop myself from

---

[6] This is a test where two ropes are hanging down from the ceiling and the research participants are told they have to tie them together; however they quickly realize that the two ropes are too far apart from each other to be both grasped at once. If they haven't found a solution after ten minutes or so, a researcher comes into the room and "accidentally" brushes against one of the ropes making it swing. This cue leads almost all participants to the solution of making one rope swing, but almost none of them attribute it to seeing the researcher making the rope swing.

offering solutions before a problem is even fully explained. My let-off is that this is just really human nature. The role of our intuitions is to propose a quick solution rather than having us ponder, to push us toward taking action (or not, in the case of the status quo bias). Our intuitions want us to reach a conclusion, but sometimes, to reach the best decision, we need to pause a little.

Nigel Jones, Global Chief Strategy Officer of FCB started playing chess semi-professionally at the age of seven (he and two of his brothers were all semi-professional chess players at one stage). When we were chatting about intuitions and decision making recently, Nigel told me that when playing chess he (and, he believes most other decent chess players) see the right move almost immediately that it is their move. The weaker players then make that move. On the other hand, the stronger—and more success-ful—players think for 10 minutes about it before moving. That period of 10 minutes' heavy deliberation is critical. He says,

> Nine times out of ten, after thinking about it, I will make the move that came to mind immediately. It's nearly always the right one, but every so often I will realize that after examining it closely it was flawed or there was a better move. My initial (intuitive) thought would get it right nine times out of ten, but by thinking about it a little longer I can get closer to getting it right 99 times out of a hundred. And that's the difference between winning at the top level or losing.

This is a great example of our fast, intuitive processes allowing us to get it right most of the time. But moderated with a little consciousness, we can get it right more often.

In his excellent book, *Incognito: The Secret Lives of the Brain*, neuroscientist David Eagleman writes, "consciousness developed because it was advanta-geous, but advantageous only in limited amounts." It is the auditor of our intuitions, not a replacement for them (maybe an auditor from before the Sarbanes-Oxley era... it signs off our choices without too much scrutiny. Kahneman describes the deliberative system as "an endorser rather than an enforcer").

The Institute for Decision Making runs sessions not just about brands and marketing, but also about how the unconscious affects hiring and personnel issues, and how it can be used in negotiations by our finance and procure-ment people. The latter sessions are, of course, geared toward managers and HR and can be a great help to people we work with in everyday life.

Though we will never be immune to the effects of cognitive biases, seeking to understand biases can help mitigate their effects, whether they be in responding to an advertisement or how we navigate office politics. Or, at least the knowledge could make us feel better and not so stupid about our own "irrationality."

I've written extensively about how an understanding of behavioral science can help you influence the choices of others and also about how it can improve your own choices as a marketer. A bonus is that an interest in behavioral science also brings you into contact with the work of academics studying creativity, and just as marketers don't spend enough time learning from those who study choice, creative businesses seem to largely ignore the work of scientists who seek to understand the conditions that lead to creative thinking and problem solving.

Some of it is pretty obvious but useful. I relish the opportunity to brief creative teams either on a Friday or before a holiday, simply because the best time to lodge a problem in someone's mind to solve is when they are about to be doing things that will send the problem to the back of their mind rather than having it require conscious attention at the front. Archimedes was reportedly taking a bath when the Eureka! moment came to him. Sleep helps as well. It is much better to ask people to come back to you tomorrow with ideas rather than asking them to come back today. Or at least, as research by Sara Mednick,[7] Assistant Professor of the Department of Psychology at the University of California, Riverside and author of *Take a Nap! Change Your Life* suggests that people are more likely to have solved problems after a sleep where they have dreamed. Her theory is that rapid eye movement (REM) sleep primes associative networks, meaning we make connections that we might not while we are awake.

Other techniques can help you get more creativity out of people. I'm sure you have been in a brainstorming session where the facilitator states at the beginning "all ideas are good ideas" and asks that participants only make positive comments. The thinking is that from a feeling of safety and being free of criticism, great ideas will flow. Research by Charlan Nemeth suggests that this might not be the optimal state for getting the most original thinking from people. In a paper titled "The liberating role of conflict in group creativity," Nemeth found that instructing participants in a group to debate

---

[7] Cai, D.J., Sarnoff, A.M., Harrison, E.M., Kanady, J.C., Mednick, S.C. (2009) "REM, not incubation, improves creativity by priming associative networks." *Proc Natl Acad Sci* 106: 10130–10134.

and criticize each other's ideas led to that group coming up with more ideas—both before the brainstorming session and after it—than groups that had been told not to criticize.

A rather charming technique to boost creativity is to get people thinking like kids. Darya Zabelina and Michael Robinson conducted research[8] in which they had two groups of participants (who were mainly freshmen or sophomores at North Dakota State University) imagine that school was canceled for the day. They asked them to write down what they would do, think, and feel—but for one group, they added the short phrase, "You are 7 years old." After this exercise, participants then completed a version of the Torrance Test for Creative Thinking, which measures creative performance. Those in the group who had been primed to think of themselves as seven-year-olds scored much higher.

Another way to prime creativity is one that is of personal interest to me, as someone who works in a multi-national company, with teams from around the globe, has lived and worked on three continents, and is married to an Italian.

Angela Leung is a professor at Singapore Management University, and has developed a specific research interest in the effects of a multicultural perspective on creativity. In a 2008 article in *American Psychologist*,[9] Leung and her co-authors show through their research that a slideshow that makes people think about and compare different cultural contexts tends to lead to increased levels of individual creativity in a subsequent writing task, versus participants exposed to a slideshow that shows only one culture.

In Leung and her collaborators' experiments, the effect of seeing cultures juxtaposed led to creativity that went beyond just synthesizing the imagery from American and Chinese culture that they were shown. One of the tasks that was used to measure the multicultural effect had nothing to do with either cultures: It was to write a version of the *Cinderella* story for Turkish children. The participants who had been exposed to a juxtaposition of cultures wrote stories that were judged to be more creative than those exposed to only one culture.

---

[8] Zabelina, D.L., Robinson, M.D. (2010) "Child's Play: Facilitating the Originality of Creative Output by a Priming Manipulation." North Dakota State University; Psychology of Aesthetics, Creativity, and the Arts.

[9] Leung, A.K., Maddux, W.W., Galinsky, A.D., Chiu, C. (2008) "Multicultural Experience Enhances Creativity—The When and How." *American Psychologist* 63(3): 169–181.

The mechanism may be that this juxtaposition creates a little bit of discomfort (earlier we talked about how a little dissent in brainstorming session might have the same effect).

Many companies go to great lengths to promote cultural diversity within their organizations. Leung's work suggests that a benefit of doing this could lead to an increase in personal creativity. Creative organizations that have footprints in different cultures could use this thinking to create conditions that foster greater creativity around their networks. Juxtaposing cultures rather than melding them is important. In a telephone interview with Leung in 2013, she told me that to get the benefits of a multicultural experience, companies should embrace a cosmopolitan mindset rather than a globalizing one. *Cosmopolitan* suggests drawing from different cultures, rather than sitting above them, and it sounds way cooler than *global*. I currently have *global* in my job title—I think I may try to change it to *cosmopolitan*.

Finally, if like me you find yourself over-committing and under-delivering, here is a practical tip to help you avoid the stress that comes with that.

How often do you find yourself scrambling for a deadline because you underestimated how long a task would take? Or find that people you are relying on to do things haven't allowed themselves enough time to do them in?

This human trait is caused by cognitive bias called the *planning fallacy* giving us the tendency to underestimate task-completion times.[10] For example, university students were asked to estimate how long it would take them to finish writing their theses. Their average estimate was 33.9 days. Students also estimated how long it would take "if everything went as well as it possibly could" (the answer was 27.4 days) and how long it would take "if everything went as poorly as it possibly could" (the answer was 48.6 days). In reality, the actual completion time averaged 55.5 days, and only around 30% of the students completed their thesis in the amount of time they predicted.

One suggestion is that optimism bias is one of the things behind these inaccurate estimates. You can make yourself a little immune to this by taking your belief in your own superpowers out of the equation. Instead of thinking "how long will it take *me* to do this?" think instead "how long will it take

---

10 Buehler, R., Griffin, D., Ross, M. (1994) "Exploring the 'planning fallacy': Why people underestimate their task completion times." *Journal of Personality and Social Psychology* 67: 366-381.

someone like me to do this?" To get better estimates from your colleagues about completion times, don't ask them how long it will take them to do the task, but ask how long it will take *someone* to do it.

Understanding human nature is the key to understanding how we can influence choice and behaviors, which make us better marketers, but it also helps us understand how intuitions shape our own choices—so that we can make better calls when it comes to making marketing decisions.

The takeaways from this chapter are

- Marketers are human! We use the same decision-making shortcuts as the people we want to influence. Sometimes our intuitions don't lead us to the best marketing decisions.

- Short-term goals are more appealing to us as humans than longer term ones. This isn't always good for the brands we manage. *Status quo bias* can lead us to not change what we should.

- Learning from behavioral and related sciences can also help you and your partners be more creative.

How this chapter made other people think differently about how they work:

- "There are tons of tips and tricks lurking in this book. In this chapter, I liked the idea of taking a nap, briefing on Fridays, and logging what your gut says first, then doing the homework with a willingness to change (if one can become aware of biases just a tad more)..."

- "Priming and framing are magical tools for unlocking creativity. How you frame tasks (for yourself or your team) can make all the difference."

Conclusion

Typically we think of marketing as benefiting marketers and their objectives. But over the last few years, in the process of learning more about how people make choices, I have come to believe that it can do much more than that. Marketing's next evolution should be to always benefit the people it seeks to influence.

There are obvious areas where marketing can do this—using what has been learned from behavioral science we can design and construct marketing programs that will be more effective at encouraging healthy behaviors, better financial habits, and actions that are good for society and the environment.

However, the benefits shouldn't stop there. For every choice we seek to influence that is as profound and as important as the preceding areas, hundreds of choices exist that are not going to save a life or the planet, but even these choices can be addressed by marketing in ways that benefit the chooser.

The first way is something we covered in detail in Chapter 10, "Make It Easy—For the Mind and the Body," which is the benefit of making choices easy. We've talked about how our brains favor easier choices and more "evaluable" ones, and that is what I believe marketers should seek to provide—first because it works for marketers, but second, time is too precious and attention too limited to be making what could be simple decisions more cumbersome than they should be. There are times when creating some decision uncertainty in a category may be a good strategy from a business perspective, where the natural decision may be to choose an established brand leader. But rather than throwing choosers through cognitive loops, wouldn't it be better to start by trying to find ways to make your brand an easier, more natural choice than the established one? Unintentionally creating marketing that is not aligned with how the brain works and how humans intuitively make choices is not going to best serve the brand or business. And intentionally making a choice more complex, more difficult, or more confusing than it need be is not marketing's best service to humanity.[1] When choices are difficult, the effort of reconciling them puts unnecessary strain on people. It makes them feel less competent, and it distracts them from other things that may be important for their well-being and happiness. Life is too short for any of us to spend large amounts of time in decision paralysis over everyday choices. For these kinds of decisions, easier choices equal happier chooser and happier marketer.

A second area is the upside of the emotions around choice. Our fictional friend Professor Louis Levy told us of the importance of choices in our lives. It is quite remarkable how the feelings around our choices affect our moods—the absence of auto-sensing windshield wipers, a pretty trivial car accessory—briefly clouded my entire new car experience. Equally, when people affirm my choice of a Brompton folding bicycle by saying how cool it is, I pedal off with whatever the pedaling equivalent is of a spring in my step. One of the best compliments you can give someone is one that compliments a choice they have made. Perhaps the best strategy in marketing and in life is to do just that.

But then, people like you who've had the curiosity to buy this book, and made the choice to stick with it to the very last word know that already...

---

[1] Of course, an exception to this is for choices that are harmful. Making the decision to buy cigarettes less cognitively fluent and less automatic is a good role for communication and point-of-sale as we know through the work our New York office does for teen anti-smoking on behalf of the FDA.

Appendix
Reading List and Resources

Conferences

A number of excellent conferences exist where academics present their research, either through paper sessions, which are typically short 15-minute presentations, or poster sessions, which are generally held in a large hall at the conference where hundreds of researchers pin a summary of their research on a board in the form of a poster and discuss it with anyone who is interested. Even if the research seems daunting at first, academics are generally very happy to discuss it in a less hardcore scientific manner. I've learned a huge amount from poster sessions as they are a little more intimate, and generally the exhibitor is less time pressed.

I try to attend three annual North American conferences—the Society of Judgment and Decision Making (SJDM), the Association of Consumer Research (ACR), and the Society of Consumer Psychology (SCP). Other North American conferences on my wish list are the Society of Neuro-economics Conference and the Boulder Summer Conference on Consumer Financial Decision Making. In Europe, the Research Conference on Subjective Probability, Utility and Decision Making (SPUDM) is held every second year.

Blogs, Feeds, and Digests I Like

With so much research and thinking being generated almost daily into the hows and whys of human behavior and decision making, blogs and email digests are invaluable in keeping up to speed. Here are a dozen that give me a regular dose of discovery:

- The Inquisitive Mind (and its "In-Mind" blog)
- In-Decision Blog

- British Psychological Society's Research Digest e-mail
- Decision Sciences News
- Brain Juicer Blog
- Nudge Blog (although it hadn't been updated for some months at time of writing)
- Neuroskeptic
- Mindhacks
- Cognitive Lode
- Behavioural Insights Team Blog
- Roger Dooley's Neuroscience Marketing Blog
- Ideas42 Blog

25 Books I've Enjoyed and Found Useful

Marketing is about choice, and choice covers pretty much all of life, so the range of books that touch on relevant areas is huge—including behavioral sciences, evolutionary psychology, sociocultural anthropology, neuroscience, biology, urban planning, and books specifically about the practices of marketing and advertising. This range covers many books I have read over the years that have informed and inspired me, so the list below is a tight 25 that are the ones that relate most to the themes in this book, and have in most cases been a source of inspiration and reference to it:

- *Drunk Tank Pink: And Other Unexpected Forces that Shape How We Think, Feel, and Behave* by Adam Alter
- *Predictably Irrational: The Hidden Forces That Shape Our Decisions* by Dan Ariely
- *Thinking and Deciding* by Jonathan Baron
- *Contagious: Why Things Catch On* by Jonah Berger
- *The Invisible Gorilla: And Other Ways Our Intuitions Deceive Us* by Christopher Chabris and Daniel Simons
- *Influence: Science and Practice* by Robert B. Cialdini
- *Incognito: The Secret Lives of the Brain* by David Eagleman
- *Herd: How to Change Mass Behaviour by Harnessing Our True Nature* by Mark Earls

- *Delusions of Gender: How Our Minds, Society, and Neurosexism Create Difference* by Cordelia Fine
- *Gut Feelings: The Intelligence of the Unconscious* by Gerd Gigerenzer
- *The Rational Animal: How Evolution Made Us Smarter Than We Think* by Vladas Griskevicius and Douglas T. Kenrick
- *The Art of Choosing* by Sheena Iyengar
- *The Rough Guide to Psychology* by Christian Jarrett
- *Great Myths of the Brain* by Christian Jarrett
- *Thinking, Fast and Slow* by Daniel Kahneman
- *Spent: Sex, Evolution, and Consumer Behavior* by Geoffrey Miller
- *The Geography of Thought: How Asians and Westerners Think Differently...and Why* by Richard E. Nisbett
- *The Consuming Instinct: What Juicy Burgers, Ferraris, Pornography, and Gift Giving Reveal about Human Nature* by Gad Saad
- *The Paradox of Choice* by Barry Schwartz
- *How Brands Grow: What Marketers Don't Know* by Byron Sharp
- *Nudge: Improving Decisions About Health, Wealth, and Happiness* by Richard H. Thaler and Cass R. Sunstein
- *Unconscious Branding: How Neuroscience Can Empower (and Inspire) Marketing* by Douglas Van Praet
- *Traffic* by Tom Vanderbilt
- *Everything Is Obvious: *Once You Know the Answer* by Duncan J. Watts
- *Human Instinct* by Robert Winston

Index

commercials, "Hillside," 157-158

comparisons, 121-125

  anchoring

    associate coherence, 128

    reference points, 128-133

  cognitive pricing, Fair and Square Everyday Pricing, 123-124

confidence

  confirmation bias, 172-177

  self-efficacy, 97-99

    information overload, 99-101

confirmation bias, 172-177

consumers, xvii

The Consuming Instinct, 169

context effect, 147

contextual marketing, 135

  Good Samaritan experiment, 151-152

contextual targeting, 136-137

  context as trigger for evolutionary goals, 137-141

  gender stereotypes, 142-145

  matching content and context, 141

  names as labels, 146-149

Cowley, Elizabeth, 102

creativity, improving, 204-207

crowdsourcing, Mechanical Turk, 13

Cultural Dimensions Theory, 165

Culture quadrant (UIIA framework), 162-167

Customer Effort Score, 115

D

Darley, John, 152

De Neve, Dr. Jan-Emmanuel, 158

decision making, xvi, 2

  behavior of others as basis for, 53-58

  biases. *See biases*

  "brain out" approach, 8

  brands, 6-7

  changes through history, 23

  cognitive biases, 38-39

  comparisons, 121-125

    anchoring, 125-133

    associate coherence, 128

    reference points, 128-133

  confirmation bias, 172-177

  ecologically valid environments, 185-186

  heuristics, 34-38

  impact of age on, 169-170

  impact of environment on, 149-150

  impact of flattery on, 95-100

    implicit association, 96

    "Of the Bold and the Beautiful" study, 97

    self-efficacy, 97-99

  impact of previous contexts on, 150-152

  impact of technology on, 26-27

  intuition, 38

    role of, 11

  making choices easier, 208-209

  and marketing, 3-5

  non-conscious, xvi, 182-183

    influence on behavior, 16-17

hotel towel research study, 59-60
"Invisible Gorilla" experiment, 182
Levanthal's Tetanus Experiment, 112
nonreplicating, xiv
RCTs, 13-14
segmentation studies, 155-156
eye tracking measures, improving market research with, 189

F

facial expressions, 54-58
  emotional contagion, 56
  energy consumption study, 59
  as innate behavior, 56-57
  recognizing to improve market research, 188-189
  social norms, 59
Falk, Dean, 23, 122
"familiar with a twist," 46-47
familiarity, 41-51
  availability heuristic, 43
  cocktail party effect, 48-49
  dependence, 50
  effect on mood, 42
  "familiar with a twist," 46-47
  matching law, 49-50
  "Oreo Daily Twist" campaign, 51
  recognition heuristic, 43-44
  and variety, 50-51
Faro, David, 101
Fehr, Ernst, 64
FFA (fusiform face area), 56
Fine, Cordelia, 142

flattery
  effect on decision-making, 95-100
  implicit association, 96
  and lying, 102-103
  "Of the Bold and the Beautiful" study, 97
  self-efficacy, 97-99
    improving, 101-102
    information overload, 99-101
fMRI (functional magnetic resonance imaging) scanners, 13, 192-194
fomo (fear of missing out), 90
For God's Sake, 166
foreign policy decisions, impact of cognitive bias on, 197-198
FTR (future-time reference) languages, 164
function of the amygdala, xiii

G

gaze heuristic, 36-37
gender stereotype effect, 142-145
  schemas, 143
Genetic Makeup quadrant (UIIA framework), 160-162
Gerzema, John, 6
Gigerenzer, Gerd, 30, 34, 43
golden age of decision sciences, 10-14
  acceptance of intuition in decision making, 11
  availability of technology, 12-14
  popularity of behavioral research, 11-12

research studies. *See also*
  experiments; market research
    ecologically valid environments,
    185-186
Rink, David, 169
Robinson, Michael, 205
roles of marketing, 8
The Rough Guide to Psychology, xv

S

Saad, Gad, 50
Sands Research, 55
"Save More Tomorrow" program,
  76-77
scarcity principle, 30, 90-93.
  See also prospect theory
    and anticipation, 92-93
schemas, 143
Schwartz, Barry, 2
science
  experiments. *See also*
    experiments; market research
    nonreplicating, xiv
    RCTs, 13-14
  golden age of decision sciences,
    10-14
    *availability of technology,
    12-14*
    *intuition, role of in decision
    making, 11*
    *popularity of behavioral
    research, 11-12*
  and marketing, xii-xiii
  nonreplicating experiments, xiv
  p-hacking, xiv
  self-correcting nature of, xiv
Scientific Advertising, xvii
Segal, Heather, 137
segmentation studies, 155-156

Sela, Aner, 160
selection of luxury goods,
  recognition heuristic, 44
self-correcting nature of
  science, xiv
self-efficacy, 97-99
  improving, 101-102
  information overload, 99-101
self-protection as evolutionary
  drive, 139
semantic targeting, 136
serial position effect, 69-72
setting long-term objectives,
  201-202
Sey, Jen, 46
The Shallows, 100
shaming as form of persuasion, 63
Shapiro, Stewart, 47
Sharot, Tali, 72, 176
Shiv, Baba, 7, 175, 191
Simon, Dan, 182
Simonsen, Itamar, 160
Simonsohn, Uri, xiv
sleep, effect on problem
  solving, 204
*The Social Animal, The Hidden
  Sources of Love, Character, and
  Achievement*, 15
social norms, 59
  BIT randomized control test,
    65-67
  for private social behaviors, 61
social proof
  defaults, 108-109
  hotel towel study, 59-60
*Spent: Sex, Evolution, and
  Consumer Behavior*, 44
Spina, Alessandro, 20
spokespeople, xi